Jah Music

The Evolution of the Popular Jamaican Song

Steel Pulse, based in Handsworth, Birmingham, rose to be one of the most popular Reggae groups in England. (*Photo: D. Morris*)

Jah Music

The Evolution of the Popular Jamaican Song

Sebastian Clarke

Heinemann Educational Books Ltd
22 Bedford Square, London WC1B 3HH

LONDON EDINBURGH MELBOURNE AUCKLAND
HONG KONG SINGAPORE KUALA LUMPUR
NEW DELHI IBADAN NAIROBI JOHANNESBURG
EXETER (NH) KINGSTON PORT OF SPAIN

First published 1980
Reprinted 1981, 1983

British Library Cataloguing in Publication Data

Clarke, Sebastian
Jah music.
1. Music, Popular (Songs, etc.) – Jamaica
I. Title
780'.42'097292 ML3486.J3
ISBN 0-435-82140-7

Printed in Great Britain by
Biddles Ltd, Guildford, Surrey

This book is dedicated to
BASIL HANSON SMITH
and GARTH WHITE
two enthusiasts and critical
pioneers who introduced me
to a deeper understanding and
appreciation of the music.

Contents

Preface

This book was conceived a long time ago in the hope of promoting understanding of the historical origins of Jamaican music, from which the present Reggae music has evolved. Reggae owes its origins to the Afro-American R&B, but later expressed an identity that became associated with a specifically Jamaican musical language. The music has been in existence for less than twenty years, yet it has noticeably influenced current popular forms of music, as flavour or as an authentic influence to create new musical styles.

I have, in the main, been motivated by the social and political aspects of the music's evolution, but not, I hope, at the expense of the purely musical or cultural phenomenon. Since Jamaica gained its independence in 1962 (coincidentally, the same year that Ska manifested its presence), it has been ravaged by socio-political power struggles. The consequent terror and violence have had a direct influence on the music.

Jamaican music has grown to such an extent that it now provides employment for a significant number of Jamaicans, meaningfully contributing to a depressed Jamaican economy. There are four pressing plants in Jamaica which employ an average of 200 people in various capacities: factory hands, to salesmen, accountants, engineers, drivers, secretaries, etc. The record industry has, in turn, created an outlet for record shops, which also provide employment. Jamaica has banned all imports on records, and the major Jamaican companies have the franchise for distributing a number of American record catalogues, such as Warner Brothers, Atlantic Records, CBS Records, ABC Records, etc. Such accelerated export incentives have done much to help the Reggae industry. It is estimated that the Reggae industry alone brings in some 3 million Jamaican dollars per year, not including internal and invisible sales. Thus real figures of the actual sales power of Reggae would never be discovered completely.

The music not only benefits the Jamaican economy, it also projects abroad an image of a nation in motion, even though the statistics on crime have increased, and political violence still plays havoc with any real and meaningful progress. In 1964 the Jamaican government realized the music's potential as a tourist attraction when they exported certain musicians, dancers, and artists to the World Fair. The demand for national music festivals has grown proportionately, and they now exist without noticeable government participation, still being promoted by the private sector.

Jamaican music has evolved to be an important economic and political feature of Jamaican society, even though that society has only partially accepted its artists on a cultural level. When I was in Jamaica in late 1977, I visited the Institute of Jamaica and looked through 400 index cards in the music section. Only thirty of these dealt with Reggae, and they were all internationally famous artists. Yet a great deal of space was devoted to classical music, a dead European art that young Europeans have themselves rejected, and which exists solely by governmental subsidy. Thus language and culture are orientated towards the metropolitan centre's definition.

In researching this work I am grateful to Cecil Gutzmore and the Black People's Information Centre's Library and Resource Centre for their extended loan of books and for reading and suggesting ideas for parts of the book. In this regard I am also grateful to members of Brimstone and to John Kpiaye for technical information. This book sets out only to chronicle the historical origins of Reggae. It does not offer the minute and exhaustive details that would go into making a comprehensive study of the music. I have looked at the music's development solely through a particular perspective and orientation, and other books should be written on the subject to underline other aspects of the music's development and evolution.

Sebastian Clarke
March 1980

1 History and Roots

1

To get a clear perspective on the origins of popular Jamaican music it is necessary to look at how the island was 'founded' and where the inhabitants came from, who they were, and how they spent their lives. Christopher Columbus, accompanied by several black mariners[1] (who, after their initial conquest by Spain, were being chased out in the fourteenth and fifteenth centuries, and whose vast maritime knowledge was forcibly being placed at the disposal of the Spanish monarchy) seized Jamaica in 1494 to establish one of the cruellest reigns of terror history has ever known.

By 1509 the Spaniards had already installed the first shipment of West African slaves in Jamaica. The island's original inhabitants, the Indians of the Caribbean, were forcibly made to work the plantations for their new masters. The Indians, like the Africans who came after, worshipped their gods in a polytheistic fashion and had an organic relationship to the land that provided them with all their basic needs.

Colonization brought about a clash of cultures. The Spaniards rationalized their barbarous behaviour towards the Indians by characterizing the latter as 'heathens' or 'pagans'. With this convenient label their mass decimation was systematically pursued: poison, torture, and mass killings were the characteristic ritual. The Indians also committed mass suicide.[2]

The attack on Jamaica in 1655 by the British was one in a series sparked off by Oliver Cromwell in a systematic attempt to wrest 'all the vast territories held by Spain in the Caribbean'.[3] 'The island', states Robinson, 'was badly defended, poverty-stricken, underdeveloped and underpopulated; the Government officials corrupt or weak and ineffective.'[4] At the sight of the British fleet of thirty-eight ships and almost 8,000 men, the Spaniards surrendered the island without a fight.[5]

However, a small band of Spaniards under the leadership of Chritoval Arnaldo de Ysassi, Jamaican-born, took to the hills with some of their slaves and later persuaded the escaped and free Africans to join their fight against the British.

In the mountains of Clarendon a large number of Africans, under the leadership of Juan Lubolo (later to be canonized as Juan de Bolas), played an important role in keeping the Spaniards alive and in viciously attacking and killing the British who crossed their paths. These mountain Africans came to be known as the Maroons (consisting mainly of the war-like Coromantee of Ghana), the first band of former slaves successfully to outwit their masters and to establish some degree of autonomy. Lubolo and Ysassi teamed up to fight the British. They were so successful that Ysassi was bestowed with the token governorship of the island by the King of Spain.[6]

It is difficult to imagine what motivated the Africans to defend the Spaniards against the British when, ultimately, both represented the same interests. But with the final outcome undecided and the Africans at the mercy of either victor, the Spaniards' promise of total freedom and no reprisals proved highly motivating. The British, who were making the same observations as the Spaniards, attempted to outdo the Spaniards by offering the Africans instant freedom and land.[7] Once Lubolo placed himself at the disposal of the British in 1660, his task was never-ending. Having brought about the downfall of the Spaniards, he was himself ordered by the British to secure the surrender of those Africans who refused to accept the British offer of land and instant freedom. Lubolo and his men sought to locate the settlements of his brothers and destroy them, but he was defeated and killed by the Maroons.[8] Lubolo is now enshrined in Kingston, as a warrior of resistance by the Jamaica National Trust Commission.

After Lubolo's death there was peace for a time. The British almost totally gave up their pursuit of the Maroons, and set about the business of peopling and settling Jamaica. A variety of British criminals were sent there to work as indentured servants to the planter class. More slaves were brought from Africa: Ghana, Sierra Leone and the Windward Coast, Senegambia and Dahomey. The tribal groups that emerged from these areas were Mandingoes, Fulas, Waloffs, Jolas, Fantis, Coromantees, Mamprusi, Dagomba, Nankanse, Talense, Isala, Loba and many others, and they were systematically interwoven into a variety of tribal groups to ensure limited or no communication. However, the detribalization of the African eventually resulted in the fusion of 'the tribes, their customs and folklore'.[9] This also forced the Africans to recognize that 'they were one people and co-sufferers'.[10]

Simultaneous with the Spanish exodus from Jamaica was the founding of Port Royal. This had a magnetic attraction for pirates and buccaneers, resulting in another reign of terror. All types of people went to Port Royal, which became a breeding ground for lawlessness and licentiousness. The names of Henry Morgan, Roche Brasiliano and Mary Carleton (the German Princess) became synonymous with theft, cruelty, and death.[11]

To the slaves Port Royal had no relevance, but they heard about the existence of the Maroons and intended, with every opportunity, to do away with their masters and flee to the hills and freedom.

In 1673 the first important slave rebellion took place: 300 slaves slaughtered about thirteen European slave-owners in the parish of St Ann and fled to the interior, 'different sections of them settling in various parishes to the south-centre of the island. . . . These rebels formed the nucleus of what later became known as the leeward band of the Maroons.'[12] Between 1678 and 1685 several important slave insurrections took place; and deaths and wounds were inflicted on the slave-owners with little retaliation.[13] In 1690, however, the most important of slave rebellions took place on Sutton's estate in Clarendon, involving some 400 slaves. They seized arms and ammunition before some seventy of them were recaptured, their leaders executed, while the rest headed for 'open country'.[14] Theory has it that Cudjoe was among those who escaped.

From their vantage point these Africans made daring raids on the plantations; burnt, plundered, and looted; and kept in constant communication with friends who informed them of intended attacks by the militia. Added to all this turmoil, Jamaica experienced a series of natural disasters which almost destroyed the entire country: in 1692 there was a horrific earthquake which saw the almost total sinking of Port Royal and which affected surrounding areas;[15] in 1698 a fierce hurricane did tremendous damage to plants and buildings and an unknown 'plant disease wiped out almost all the cocoa plants on the island'.[16] In 1694 the French invaded the island and created havoc on the northern and eastern coasts, taking 1,300 Africans captive.[17]

In the seventeenth century the white planters never felt secure with so many Maroons at large, and increasing numbers of runaways who settled in the most mountainous and dangerous parts of the country formed themselves into bands and attacked the planters. The local militia were usually outwitted and sustained greater losses so that additional forces were brought in from Britain. The rains and the nature of the tropical climate also caused many deaths among the British. Two alternatives were open to the planters and the governor: 1. pursue, hunt and kill, or 2. subdue by pacification. The former was proving expensive, and perhaps to admit that the Maroons were limiting the extent to which the island could be settled was an acknowledgement of defeat. The longer the Maroons were at large the more they became entrenched in their African customs; and the more they utilized their traditional war tactics to destroy the enemy. For it was not only in Jamaica that rebellions were waged along what we now recognize as guerrilla lines, but in Haiti and other islands in the Caribbean. This meant that the Africans were familiar with war strategies and recognized what ideas to implement when modern ammunition and arms were at their disadvantage.

By 1730 a price of ten pounds was put on the head of every Maroon and three major expeditions against them were organized; in 1734 the planters had their first real taste of victory against the Maroons with the destruction of Nanny Town. The militia and King's soldiers were directed on a 'search and destroy' mission; they would locate small camps and attempt to destroy them, set up garrisons or forts in close proximity to the potential liberators, and create as many problems for the Maroons as they could. In addition, the planters brought in the Mosquito Indians from neighbouring Cuba to hunt and track down the Maroons. The African slaves were used by the planters and created a special force known as the 'Black Shot'. Their job was simple: locate Maroon settlements and provision grounds, then destroy them. The consequence for the Maroons was that men, women and children, with their grounds destroyed, were slowly starving. However, when the Maroons retaliated, they were merciless. They instilled the most terrifying fear into both the planters and the general white populace so that when final surrender came, it was a sad mistake that darkened the possibility of Jamaica's historical role as the first free state in the New World. As it was, half a century later, Haiti attained this position.

The Maroons were promised their freedom upon surrender; but they always mistrusted the slave-owners, so it was not until they were too tired and starving to go on that Cudjoe and his men surrendered. The first treaty was signed in 1739, and the hitherto fearless and freedom-loving Maroons were turned into snarling hunters who killed or brought back runaways, and persuaded other bands of Maroons to surrender. Not long after, Quao, another Maroon leader, pledged his allegiance to the treaty signed by Cudjoe. They were soon reduced to ridicule by the governor; they were given old muskets, old soldiers' uniforms, and medals on which their names were inscribed. Laws were enacted to ensure that the Maroons were confined to their lands; permission was needed in order to leave, and a dispersal strategy was instituted whereby Maroons could live anywhere on the island except in other Maroon towns. This was to encourage integration and to reduce the feeling of specialness.

The last confrontation between the Maroons and the colonial administration occurred in 1795 when the British set out to annex independent Maroon lands. The Maroons were also complaining about the insufficient lands originally agreed to in their treaty with the British, for their own community was rapidly expanding. The colonial administrator for the Maroon community was also abusing his powers of control; consequently, the Maroons ran him out of the community. In 1795 two Maroons stole two pigs in Montego Bay; they were caught and flogged by a slave. I have pointed out that the Maroons were used as slave-catchers, and the reversal of this role produced great humiliation among them.

Rebellion broke out and the Maroons were finally captured. They were subsequently shipped to Halifax, Nova Scotia, then finally to Sierra Leone where they were used to quell a rebellion by Black Americans for control of the country.[18]

The entire legal system was set up to protect the enormous profits made by the planters, as Phillippo so graphically states. The Africans had absolutely no legal rights:

> While however their oppressors, as caprice or passion dictated, could thus inflict upon their wretched vassals sufferings almost beyond endurance, a slave who raised his hand by nature's instinct for his own protection, or struck, or dared to strike, or used any violence towards, or compassed or imagined, the death of a master or mistress, was doomed to suffer death without benefit of clergy. On the other hand, the murder of a slave by a white man was a venial offence, and from the inadmissibility of slave evidence often escaped punishment altogether. The slave was therefore entirely unprotected from the tyranny of his master. . . . Should he be maimed by a free person, the damage would not be awarded to him, but to his master.[19]

The British monarchy and the Jamaican planters competed with each other over the profits to be reaped from its slave colony. The King exerted his powers to this end by taxation and custom duties and by maintaining a monopoly of trade and shipping with the colony. The planters, on the other hand, in order to maximize their profits, had no desire to comply with the King's wishes. But, as Hart points out, both the monarchy and the planters shared 'common interests. The British naval and military presence in the Caribbean was necessary to the aspirations of both.'[20] There followed turbulent confrontations between both sides. Since the establishment of civil government in Jamaica in 1661 (which was controlled by the Governor and his councillors, appointed by the King, and members of the assembly elected by the planters), the Jamaican house of assembly constantly reflected their economic interests by defending their rights first. This resulted in the King attempting to coerce the house of assembly under his jurisdiction.

The slaves had to toil up to sixteen hours a day and were expected to dig 100 cane holes per day; inability to do so resulted in whipping. They lived in hovels. 'The houses were . . . with few exceptions, wretched habitations. They consisted of posts put into the ground at the distance of about two feet asunder; the intermediate space being closed up with wattle, daubed over on the inside with mud.'[21] Many of the houses consisted of only one room for an entire family. They had no floors and varied in length between 15 and 20 feet long; the tops were covered with dried guinea grass, palmetto thatch, long-mountain thatch, or cane tops.[22] In spite of these conditions sustained or sporadic rebellion would continue to characterize the continuing struggle by the slave for total freedom.

2

The British conquest of Jamaica in the seventeenth century was justified in religious terms: '. . . promoting the glory of God, and enlarging the bounds of Christ's kingdom, which we do not doubt will appear to be the chief end of our late expedition in the West Indies'.[23] With seven clergymen accompanying the expedition to Jamaica, the destruction of the Spanish churches was the first symbolic expression of British Christian zeal. The churches built in their place were not used to teach Christianity to the slaves, but rather to symbolize the British conquest. 'The most we can say is that the church represented that religion of the white settlers and planters and officials; but it cannot claim to have been in any sense a missionary church to the black labourers.'[24] 'Their only associates', writes Lord Oliver, 'were planters and magistrates. . . . In private life they conformed to the current social morality: drinking, gambling and cohabiting openly with black and coloured women.'[25] The ministers themselves were observed to practise precisely what they were supposedly preaching against. It is, therefore, not surprising that the Africans turned to their own religious traditions for emotional sustenance. That they managed to sustain their beliefs throughout their enslavement and the fact that it has survived, in the form of syncretism, testifies to the total disregard the official church had for the slave.

Long was so outraged by the corruption and idleness of the clergy that he wrote: 'not all the exhortations of all the bishops in the world could possibly make the clergy of this island a respectable body of men'.[26] There is an incident told by Lord Oliver in which a Rev. D.W. Rose became annoyed with Mr Edward Gardiner and threatened the latter with physical violence because he refused to comply with his wish that for every slave baptized he must be paid a 'fee of a puncheon of rum'.[27] Another incident is recalled by Long of the burial of three seamen. The clergyman involved saw a short cut to a possibly long sermon by saying one prayer for all. The brother of one of the deceased objected and a fight followed in which the clergyman succeeded in 'hurling two or three of the combatants headlong into the very grave that had been prepared for their inanimate friends'.[28] Another, more interesting incident is related by Lady Nugent:

> Just before the service began, and when I thought the church doors were to be closed, in walked a strange gentleman and took his seat in our pew, and began making fine speeches about going to his house tomorrow. This invitation General Nugent very civilly declined, while I kept my eyes on my book and said nothing. General N. opened his, but the gentleman still talked on. The clergyman went to the Altar and everything appeared quite ready to begin the service. General N. then said: 'Pray, sir, do you stay for the communion?' 'Oh no,' was the answer. . . . When we went up to the Altar, the clergyman began his civilities – asking whether we would prefer having the bread and wine brought to the pew; then hoping that the heat was not too great; and in the midst of the service stopping to ask whether I would like a window opened that was over the Altar. . . . All this time the young ladies were talking and laughing, loud enough to be heard as they sat in the carriage at the church door. . . .[29]

How was it possible for the church to communicate to the African slaves when they spoke a totally different language? As indicated above, nothing was seriously attempted in the way of conversion. Just prior to emancipation in 1838 it was still possible for ministers of the established churches to 'assemble from fifty to one hundred slaves, ask them their names and then baptize them *en masse*, the rector receiving two shillings and sixpence for each slave'.[30]

In 1734 the Moravian missionaries landed in Jamaica after the conversion of two absentee plantation owners. Their activities seemed to have received some support from some of the other planters, but by 1763 they ran into problems with the assembly because they refused to join the militia. After half a century the Moravians had barely managed to convert 1,000 slaves. The Methodists and Baptists, however, who arrived in 1789 and 1784 respectively, were by far the most attractive to the slaves. The Baptist church in Jamaica was founded by George Liele (also referred to as Lisle and Sharp, the latter the name of his original slavemaster) in 1784. Liele went to Jamaica with his patron, a Colonel Kirkland, who secured Liele's release from gaol while in the United States. Liele had already been ordained a Baptist minister in Georgia and perhaps was already familiar with the concept of Ethiopianism (see Chapter 2), for he later named his church the Ethiopian Baptist church. With the experience of slavery in the States, Liele applied for permission from the slave-owners to preach to the slaves. He was accompanied by several other black preachers who helped to lay the foundation for the most fantastic religious activity Jamaica had seen since the introduction of Christianity. Liele and his cohorts, according to Lord Oliver, were largely

> 'uneducated; their religious exercises tended to degenerate into a mixture of hysterical revivalism. But as popular leaders they stood for the independence and liberty of their people . . . and it is not surprising that they were regarded with persistent hostility, and their faults and vices exaggerated by the dominant interests. And because they were pre-eminently and specially the native Baptist church, and the church of the black people, they specially became representatives of the black man's side in social antagonisms.[31]

The established church, with its orthodox method of preaching, its European mode of singing and its stiff ceremony, could never hope, even if it had tried, to capture the imagination and emotional proclivities that characterized African traditional religions. But native Baptists, under the leadership of former slaves, understood how to attract the Africans.

Although almost all the literature on slavery emphasized the 'savage' and 'heathen' aspects of the African mind with regard to religion, Phillippo testifies to the fact that the Africans did believe in a 'Supreme Being'. However, this may not have coincided with Phillippo's (himself a minister) or with other colonial Europeans' concepts of the complex and sophisticated theology that lay behind the seemingly 'confused and unbecoming'. Most African traditional societies had an explanation of God and the formation of the world. Basically, the variety of religious worship (yet coinciding, like the Baptists-Methodists, in Afro-Christian syncretisms) in Africa was a result of the rise of the European on the continent in the fifth century before the birth of the Christian era. Thus when ancient Egypt was destroyed and its scribes fled further into the interior, the indigenous religions were disseminated on the continent. So when the Africans reached the New World as slaves they took their religion with them. That religion was based on a Supreme Being and a pantheon of lesser gods (or saints in the Christian sense). The confrontation of African religion and European Christian religion in the Caribbean and in the Americas proposed a fusion, rather than an uncritical digestion, of the religion of the European slave-master. *It took black men, who had already fused the religions in themselves, in their sermons, body-movements and mode of singing, to succeed in persuading the slaves to acknowledge the Christian faith.*

It was not only the fact that the Baptist preachers were black that stirred and activated the slaves, but also the Old Testament story of the Jews' so-called enslavement in Egypt and their final liberation under Moses, and the story of Jesus Christ in the New Testament as the Messiah seeking to liberate all those who were in bondage and poverty. The African slaves were not to know that the symbols of liberation projected through the Bible were nothing more than ancient traditional myths retold in biblical form by Jewish scholars. This has led black people to identify with the Jews' condition, thus negating one of the most important segments of black history.

The Christian religion was analogous in symbolic representation to African religion. In Christianity there are churches, in traditional African religions there are sacred houses; Christianity has candles, paintings of Jesus Christ and the saints, an altar, incense, etc. – all these symbols were used in African religion in the sixteenth century. Even the prayers to God were similar. Two quotes, one from an African slave, Equiano, and the other from an African tribal group, illustrate these parallels: 1. 'He taught me . . . to read in the Bible, explaining many passages to me which I did not comprehend. I was wonderfully surprised to see the laws and rules of my country written almost exactly here, a circumstance which I believe tended *to impress our manners and customs more deeply on my memory.* I used to tell him of this resemblance, and many a time we have sat up the whole night together at this enjoyment.'[32] 2. 'Our father, it is Thy universe, it is Thy will, let us be at peace, let the souls of Thy people be cool; Thou art our father, remove all evil from our path.'[33] There are numerous other examples of the extent to which African religion flourished long before the coming of the first European to the continent. The reason for the rejection of Christianity as proposed by the European must be because its proponents were observed to be debased and corrupt.

Since in African religions God was invoked against suffering, there was no point in attempting to communicate with the God of the established church – an institution that served to oppress and keep them in their place. George Liele and the Ethiopian Baptist church managed to give the slaves faith and hope for deliverance. This is thought to have been the main influence in the rebellion of 1831, just before emancipation was declared. The report condemned the free churches for provoking the rebellion which involved attacks on the clergy and churches.[34]

The argument of African cultural retention in the Caribbean is too involved to go into here, but a reading of the literature of the period supplies abundant evidence as to the traditional African practices. Elaborate funerals are never held today, but the post-burial ceremony is still carried out in rural areas (and even in the cities).

Among other important practices were Obeah and Myalism. Obeah, which retains the same name in most English-speaking Caribbean countries, is a magical art that inflicts damage on an enemy, or protects against an enemy. Myalism, on the other hand, is the more passive magical art; its point of departure is to do good, not evil. Both supplied charms and amulets for or against death or destruction. In times of illness or serious problems, depending on the case, either the Obeah man or Myal man would be called in to handle the client. Many Africans distrusted European medicine. Alongside the belief and practice of Obeah and Myalism was the belief in spirits, ghosts, or the transformation of one's human body into another dimension.

The practice of healing was also very prevalent on the slave plantation. It was conducted with verve, and often proved effective. But the Europeans dubbed it 'superstition' and 'heathen practices', etc..

Whatever spare time the slaves had was spent in entertainment or the cultivation of their own small plots of land, given to them by the planters because of the latters' unwillingness to be responsible for feeding their slaves. Just after the British conquest, African slaves were observed selling their wares in the market. Eventually they were granted the right to have Sundays off; this was then used for making money (hence the idea that the blacks never observed the sabbath). The market also acted as a social centre where slaves who were separated from each other had the opportunity of conversing, trading information, and generally getting to know each other.

Sundays were also used for entertainment. This entertainment often involved enactments of scenes from their history: pageants and a variety of dances and skits were performed. The most celebrated occasion was the John Cunnu (Jonkunnu, John Canoe, Konny) festival which usually took place over the Christmas holiday. Lady Nugent was one of the earliest observers of this spectacle:

> Christmas Day! All night heard the music of Tom-Toms, etc. . . . After Church amuse myself very much with the strange processions, and figures called Johnny Canoes. All dance, and play a thousand anticks [sic]. Then there are groups of dancing men and women. They had a sort of leader or superior at their head, who sang a sort of recitative, and seemed to regulate all their proceedings; the rest joining at intervals in the air and the chorus. The instrument to accompany the song was a rude sort of drum, made of bark leaves, on this they beat with two sticks, while the singers do the same with their feet. Then there was a party of actors. Then a little child was introduced, supposed to be a king, who stabbed all the rest. They told me that some of the children who appeared were to represent Tippo Saib's children, and the man was Henry the 4th of France. . . . All were dressed very finely, and many of the blacks had really gold and silver fringe on their robes. After the tragedy, they all began dancing with the greatest glee. We dined in the Council Chamber, but went to bed early, but not to rest, for the noise of singing and dancing was incessant during the night.[35]

Lady Nugent then made entries through to 28 December noting that the festivities were still going on; she confessed she had a 'bad dinner' and that there were 'no servants to attend'. Phillippo talks about 'the wild festivals of Africa' and that the 'scenes were too disgusting to be looked upon'; his description made a few more distinctions:

> On such occasions each of the African tribes upon different estates formed itself into a distinct party, composed of men, women, and children. Each party had its King and Queen, who were distinguished by a mask of the most hideous appearance, and attired from head to foot in gaudy harlequin-like apparel. They paraded or gambolled in their respective neighbourhoods, dancing to the rude music, which was occasionally drowned by the most hideous yells from the whole party by way of chorus. . . . In the towns, such processions were preceded by a tall athletic man, attired in the same grotesque habiliments, in addition to which he wore a most hideous head-dress, surmounted by a pair of ox-horns, while from the lower part of the mask large boar-tusks protruded. This hero of the party was called John Connu, after the name of a celebrated African at Axim on the coast of Guinea, with whom the practice is supposed to have originated. He bore in his hand a large wooden sword which he occasionally brandished, accompanying its evolutions by a thousand fantastic freaks. Several companions were associated with him as musicians, beating banjas and tom-toms, blowing cow-horns, shaking a hard round bark seed, called Indian shot, in a calabash, and scraping the bones of animals together, which added to the vociferations of the crowd, filled with the air of the most discordant sounds. They were chiefly followed by children and disreputable women, the latter frequently supplying the performers with intoxicating drinks.[36]

Note the adjectives used to describe the African celebration: 'wild', 'hideous', 'gaudy', 'rude', 'grotesque', 'discordant', etc. This language illustrates the degree of contempt that Phillippo felt for black cultural expressions and celebrations that did not conform to European standards. Such descriptions have been inherited by white music and art critics in the New World wherever black people expressed themselves culturally or artistically. Where did this festival come from? Phillippo acknowledged that it came from Africa, but no corroborating evidence was offered. In so far as Jonkunnu is concerned, Judith Bettelheim has offered this explanation:

> John Konny lived and was reported to be around fifty years old in 1721. Konny worked for the Brandenberg African Company and their possessions at Pokoso were known as 'Connie's Castle'. Konny ruled over three Brandenberg trading forts. Pokoso, Tak-

> rama, and Akoda (on the coast of Ghana). Not only did Konny control much of the inland trade but . . . 'In and around Axim in particular the mere mention of Konny's name, let alone a suggestion of fighting him, made people quail.' It was not until 1724 that Konny's power waned and after the Dutch took over Great Fredricksburg castle, he went inland and took up residence at the court of Opoku Ware, the King of Asante. Undoubtedly the reputation of this black leader was so great that both slaves and traders arriving in Jamaica from ports on the Gold Coast brought with them tales of his exploits. . . . Konny's reputation as a leader, hero, and a black who stood up against European pressure became a symbol to the slaves in Jamaica.[37]

Bettelheim goes on to show that versions of Jonkunnu exist in several states outside Jamaica, in the Caribbean and South America. She also gives a description of a similar masked festival among the Manding of the Gambia (we have shown that a proportion of Africans who made up the slave population of Jamaica came from the Senegambia region):

> The *fara-kankurang* is a woven bark mask with tufts of straw on top and straw covering the lower parts of the body. It is this figure that has been called 'Mumbo Jumbo', or variations thereof, since it was first documented by Europeans in the nineteenth century. . . . (Among the Diola living south of the Gambia). . . . The *kankurang* often carries a sword or staff in each hand. Today, in the Gambia, the *kankurang* appears on Boxing Day.[38]

The picture of Jonkunnu is one of abandonment and joyous expression, which can be understood as a way out of the brutality of labour on the slave plantation. Other aspects of African culture found expression in Jamaica. These related to birth, death, protection from the living and the dead, healing and medicine, and an involvement in the black arts, among others. Phillippo observed the proceedings at a funeral and was duly shocked by what he saw:

> Their practices at funerals were unnatural and revolting in a high degree. No sooner did the spirit depart from the body of a relative or friend, than the most wild and frantic gesticulations were manifested, accompanied by the beating of drums and the singing of songs. When on the way with the corpse to interment, the bearers, who were often intoxicated, practised the most strange and ridiculous manoeuvres. They would sometimes make a sudden halt, put their ears in a listening attitude against the coffin, pretending that the corpse was endued with the gift of

> speech – that he was angry and required to be appeased, gave instructions for a different distribution of his property, objected to his mode of conveyance, or refused to proceed farther towards the place of burial until some debts due to him were discharged, some slanderous imputation on his character removed, some theft confessed . . . they would leave the corpse at the door or in the house of a debtor or neighbour indiscriminately, and resist every importunity for its removal, until his pretended demands were satisfied.[39]

Little did Phillippo recognize that the ritual to which he was a witness was a common practice among the ancient Egyptians before the Christian era. I am not suggesting here that the practice was solely Egyptian, but that the theory of dispensation after destruction and a subsequent unity in diversity of cultural practices was operational at the time of slavery.

> It is part of the trial of the soul before being admitted into the kingdom of Osiris, when the dead man recites all the sins which he has not committed during his time on earth. He denies that he has committed murder, adultery, robbery, false witness, or blasphemy against the gods or king. He has not defrauded the widow, oppressed the poor, plundered the orphan, nor slandered anyone.[40]

The burial rite observed by Phillippo shows a degree of transformation from that of the ancient Egyptian, but it certainly represents a similarity of purpose: that the dead man must be cleared of any guilt before he might 'depart victorious and mingle freely with the gods and the spirits of the dead, assigning to him a holding or homestead in his kingdom'.[41] The slave wanted all that was due to him and wanted to clear his name before he left to join his maker. Dancing seems to be a natural aspect of the ritual for, as Mbiti states: 'The procession . . . is accompanied with crying, singing, wailing and dancing. . . . On the way home, the party sings, jumps up, dances . . . and utters shrill cries.'[42]

Barrett gives graphic descriptions of healing in Jamaica today (which have been passed down from generation to generation) and in West Africa. The evidence is so complete that it is unnecessary to reproduce it in full. What I am suggesting here is that the almost entire cultural traditions of

Africa were re-expressed in the Jamaican environment. When that expression ran counter to colonial interests it was banned and sent underground; when, however, it did not necessarily affect their interests it was allowed to develop and grow. In this context one can understand the extent to which our contemporary lives have been informed by this persisting, sustaining *force* in our culture. In a later chapter details will be given as to how almost everything under discussion has been reflected in song.

Story-telling was another means of maintaining oral history. When this oral history achieves millennia of survival it is then craftily characterized by the European as myth. Thus a great deal of African history is kept from popular acceptance because it has been labelled 'mythical'. European literature spoke of the myth of Osiris until a piece of sculpture was discovered which restored him to life. One of the most enduring heroes of African story-telling is the figure of Anancy (Ananse in Ashanti). Anancy has appeared not only in Jamaica, but in other parts of the Caribbean, and it has fallen into common use to the extent that when one talks of a 'nancy story' it usually means you are telling a lie. In Ms Feldman's collected stories from a variety of African societies, she includes one told by the Ashanti; it is titled a 'Trickster Tale' and describes 'How Spider Read The Sky God Thoughts'.[43] The precise meaning applies in the Jamaican version, i.e. Anancy is always a spider and a trickster. He is often the underdog and usually emerges as the victor. Simply to apply its theme to the slave status would be wrong, for in the Ashanti tale it plays as precise a part as in the Jamaican situation.

3

Historical documentation of Jamaican Folk Music has been almost non-existent. Where charts exist they reflect the inability of the European to notate the music accurately, for as Astley Clerk says, 'Their preservers . . . knew little of music and would write the air in any key that came first to hand.'[44] What they did observe was the manner in which songs were sung, whether in low or high voices. There are several distinct categories and Edward Long says that their songs are usually 'impromptu, without the least particle of poetry, or poetic images, of which they seem to have no idea'.[45] Of course Long's observations about the poetic qualities of African songs were purely subjective and reflect an undercurrent of comparison (with the European song-poetry that he knew). But he admitted, unlike a lot of observers, that 'they have good ears for music'. The conditions of slavery imply several things: if the slave were to be a slave, whether accepting his condition as ephemeral or not, there had to be a degree of adjustment. That proposed that in order for the burden and weight of slavery to be borne the African had to vocalize his fears, memories, and all aspects of his inner world that caused him pain. There was very little that was comforting in his environment; all he had was the world that existed within him and other Africans whose fate he shared. He could probably wake up with song to give him courage to confront his task, work with song to make his tasks easier, and sing sadly of the loved ones who had been forcibly torn away from him. All the situations he confronted in his daily life proposed a multiplicity of song-situations. Most of these songs have been lost to us, because as the society went into the post-emancipation period there was little need to express what was now past. New songs emerged and new people, learning the method and style of the old, found new situations for their expressions.

The difference in meaning, function and appreciation of Western and African musics should be clarified. 'African musicians', says Francis Bebey, 'do not attempt to combine sounds in a manner pleasing to the ear. Their aim is simply to express life in all of its aspects through the medium of sound. . . . The African musician does not merely attempt to imitate nature by means of musical instruments; he reverses the procedure by taking natural sounds and incorporating them into his music.'[46] The inference can be drawn that the resulting musical expression can well be interpreted as 'grotesque' or 'cacophonous' from the standpoint of a culture that sees music as a combination of sounds that are pleasant to the ear. Thus Phillippo can say: 'Dancing, wrestling . . . met the eye in every direction, while the *horrid din of savage music fell distressingly upon the ear* [author's italics]'.[47] Phillippo, like the majority of Europeans before and since, were responding from their own mechanically ingrained training and concept of music. It has been commonly stated that music reflects language; more than that, language reflects place. Where did Phillippo and the other Europeans come from? Did their environment have lions, tigers, snakes, and a variety of other animal sounds as a daily expression? The answer is obvious. If the African, as Bebey claims, incorporated the sounds of his environment into his music, the resulting musical expression would obviously be different. Such a musical expression may well have hurt the ears of the European, and did.

There were very rare exceptions to the Phillippo stereotype (and this stereotype has by and large been inherited today by Phillippo's descendants; look at the historical responses of white music critics to each introduction of new black Afro-Western music beginning with Field Chants, Hollers, Spirituals, Blues, Jazz, right through to Reggae). So this perspective must always be in front of us as we read and respond to the documentation of the European in his (un) varying response to black musical expression. Added to his musical prejudices, one must always be aware that the relationship between the African and European on Jamaican soil was that of slave and slave-master and the latter's contempt and superiority was constantly in evidence.

There were a variety of ways in which the Africans' songs could have been expressed and preserved. The one below was obviously taken from the category of story-telling to children. The song is not isolated, but is intrinsically bound up with a story (thereby creating a context for its meaning and preservation).

MAN-CROW[48]

Good marnin to you, Man-crow
Good marnin to you, Man-crow

Good marnin to you, Man-crow
How are you this marnin

The above tune illustrates the 'call-and-refrain' mode that is one of mainly two types that dominated African music, not because it was limited in poetic qualities, but because it involved the whole community actively participating in the music. Traditionally in African societies there was no room for the 'professional' musician; everyone who belonged to the community made music. The only professional musician was the *griot* who consequently suffered because of it.

> The griot is essentially contemplative (hence static), individualistic, and preeminently self-interested. It is not orientated towards the future, but firmly entrenched in the past. It is not a collective art form; this is a distinct disadvantage in societies where art is regarded as a communal undertaking. When the *griot* speaks or sings, he expects immediate attention and he is ready with an insult if such attention is not forthcoming.[49]

Another song, in a much more matured development, went thus:

> Guinea Corn, I long to see you
> Guinea Corn, I long to plant you
> Guinea Corn, I long to mould you
> Guinea Corn, I long to weed you
> Guinea Corn, I long to hoe you
> Guinea Corn, I long to top you
> Guinea Corn, I long to cut you
> Guinea Corn, I long to dry you
> Guinea Corn, I long to beat you
> Guinea Corn, I long to trash you
> Guinea Corn, I long to parch you
> Guinea Corn, I long to grind you
> Guinea Corn, I long to turn you
> Guinea Corn, I long to eat you.[50]

By the standards of traditional African poetry this song embodies all the gifts of imagination; it uses 'Guinea Corn' as its object of desire and weaves a tapestry of possible emotional expression until, as Brathwaite says, it climaxes on the last line, 'eat you'. This style of writing is quite ancient and from time to time in contemporary black poetry, in varying degrees, the same form re-expresses itself.

Other songs were expressed in different situations. At night, after labouring in the fields, the slaves would sometimes get together under the moonlight to sing, dance and play their instruments. A great deal of the dances involved a ring being formed and two or three people dancing within. As a boy I remember that these games were enjoyed even by people over 20 years old. Many of the songs we sang were of the 'call-and-response' type.

> Their nightly dances or plays, which were frequent and general, were of a character the most licentious. They were usually accompanied by a band of the most rude and monotonous

> music, composed of instruments of African manufacture. The assemblage on such occasions consisted of both sexes, who ranged themselves in a circle round a male and female dancer, and performed to the music of their drums.
>
> The songs were sung by the other females of the party; one alternately singing, while her companions repeated in chorus; the singers and dancers observing the exactest precision as to time and measure. On some occasions the dance consisted of stamping the feet, accompanied by various contortions of the body, with strange and indecent attitudes: on others the head of each dancer was erect, or occasionally inclined forward; the hands nearly united in front; the elbows fixed, pointing from the sides; and the lower extremities being held firmly, the whole person was moved without raising the feet from the ground. Making the head and limbs fixed points, they writhed and turned the body on its own axis, slowly advancing towards each other, or retreating to the outer part of the circumference.[51]

Music-making in the African sense could never be complete unless it were linked to another art form, usually dance or story. Music itself in traditional African society was not only made by manufactured instruments, but by the very sound and noise of the human body. The entire human frame was involved in music-making when dance was involved. Many Africans decorate their bodies with a series of small percussion instruments hung about their arms, legs, thighs, neck, wrists, waists, etc. The stamping of feet was also highly contributory to music in its percussive aspect. And when one danced, as Phillippo witnessed, a drama of a relationship between the drums and the dancers propelled a variety of motions and movements. The drums spoke the language to the dancers who responded likewise in characteristic fashion. To the outsider it most certainly would have been 'obscene' or 'lewd' if their cultural programming dictated that for the body to achieve an articulateness of earthened expression was to be debased. It would seem that the European's concept of music as predetermined causality was also true for dance. In their musical context there is the conductor or composer, the piece is subsequently fixed within the set context; in dance a choreographer sets the context for movement. In both instances codification of expression was a prerequisite for art.[52] In the African context the musician is free within any given context, thus improvisation both in music and dance is a common feature in the African tradition.

Under the influence of European music, long before emancipation, the slaves would dress up, dance and imitate, thereby ridiculing the antics of the slave-master. In time European music was absorbed by the slave and transformed through conscious indigenization into their own traditional expression. So a Scottish, Welsh or English tune would be reworked and re-expressed with a different interpretation. In the post-emancipation situation two traditions developed alongside each other: the growing tradition of formulating or composing new songs within the context of the African tradition, and of formalizing European songs into a, let's say, *third stream* style. The two processes of growth and development continued right into the twentieth century with the former gaining new grounds and precedence. I can imagine that the 'Jamaican' personality was not seriously considered until after slavery was abolished. If, then, we imagine 1834-8 as the signal of the new era and transition, by then a continuum of formalizing the African song in the new environment had already taken final shape.

Most of these songs, however, used the same call-and-refrain or call-and-response patterns that characterized the African tradition. This pattern is still prevalent, not only in Jamaican Folk Music, but in contemporary Jamaican musical styles. The song-construction was sparse and the widest topic reduced to two or four lines. So conciseness must have been an essential art.

Work songs are characterized by the call-and-refrain pattern and what is known as *jamma* songs come directly from this tradition. This type of song was sung while digging the earth to plant, and the leader, called the *bomma*, has the role of stating the tune at the end of which the whole gang/group responds on the one-line chorus. The song, at a later date, seems to have been diversified, because other subject-matter was employed. Cassidy asserts that the word *bomma*, like *jamma*, 'is very like African, meaning either to shout, sing out, or join together', but does not state in what language.[53] The refrain is called the *bobbin*, Cassidy states, but is evidently English in origin: 'bob, the refrain or burden of a song'.[54] He gives a demonstration which is reproduced below. The song is divided into leader and chorus sections so as to give a clear identification to each.

(Bomma)	*(Bobbin)*
If me want for go in a Ebo,	Me can't go there!
Since them tief me from Guinea	Me can't go there!
If me want for go in a Congo,	Me can't go there!
Since dem tief me from my tatta,	Me can't go there!
If me want for go in a Kingston,	Me can't go there!
Since massa gone in a England,	Me can't go there!

The recognition of the limitation of the slave's movements and that he was a captive, forcibly held, is clear from the above. There were a number of dances that went with a lot of the songs. Phillippo states that the slaves' songs usually contained a 'ludicrous reference to the white people' and lists an example:

Sangaree kille de captain
O dear, he must die
New rum kill de sailor
O dear, he must die
Hard work kille de neger
O dear, he must die . . .[55]

The song is obviously more than a contemptuous reference to white people for it consciously projects the image of freedom that was not possible even in death: the white man could die how he liked, even with rum or sangaree (an alcoholic beverage), but the black man died from hard work. The slaves also recognized that despite their lowly status, they were still human beings like others:

One, two, tree
All de same
Black, white, brown
All de same
All de same . . .[56]

Many songs satirized their masters by means of a specially constructed language which the masters could not understand. A number of writers of the period testified to this ridiculing of the white masters by the slaves.

Let us take a look at melody and harmony in slave songs, and some of the songs that have survived from this period.

Ekwene demonstrates how Caribbean folk music has retained many of its original features. He uses a song that has achieved widespread popular appeal, the Jamaican *Banana Boat Song* or, as it is commonly called, 'Day-O'. He says that 'certain features of African melodies markedly appear in the music of black peoples of the new world. . . . A look at the shape of the melody shows that the highest point comes at the beginning, from where it gently works its way down to the lowest note which appears at the end. This is the general shape of most African melodies.'[57] Also, according to Ekwene, the 'slur, slide, or GLISSANDO common in spoken words is reflected in the music'. So that as well as leading in song, the *jamma* could also give directions in work, slipping from singing to speaking and back without missing time. I have seen this done a great deal, particularly in free church singing, such as the Baptists or Shango religion, and in Revivalist sects. Also, because African languages are tonal, 'melodic lines follow this natural linguistic feature of African words',[58] so the break into speech is facilitated.

Because African choral harmony has little in common with European harmony, the former has historically been described as without harmony. Ekwene shows that: 'Parallel harmony, guided by melodic scales, is the natural system of harmonising tunes. The larger intervals (5ths and 4ths) predominate in African areas, while 3rds (major and minor, sometimes neutral) dominate in others . . . . It is still largely the system of harmonisation employed in group singing amongst West Indians.'[59] Antiphony, like improvization, was also a common feature of African music and is abundant in Jamaican and other black New World vocal (and instrumental) expressions. Walton states that: 'Whenever a musical phrase, sung or played by a soloist, is afterwards repeated or answered by an instrumental or vocal chorus or group, antiphony takes place.'[60]

So that when the leader sings 'Day-O' and the chorus echoes him, you can be sure that antiphony is there. On a more popular level, when the live performer asks his audience in the act of singing: 'Do you feeeelll all right?' and the audience responds, there is something very old occurring. The vocal testimony is never isolated, it is bound up with the participation of the audience. In this way the black performer continues to express the depths of his tradition, unlike the common feature, in the European sense, of being silently intelligent!

Ring tunes or songs were also common features on the plantation and took the same form as above. The subject-matter was wide-ranging and conveyed commentary on personal and group relationships, etc. Jekyl is responsible for this one:

Whe me lover de?
See mya, see mya
Me lover gone a-sea?
See mya, see mya
Him gone a Colon bay
See mya, see mya
Go find you lover now
See mya, see mya
No make no 'tupid de
See mya, see mya
Fool dem let dem go
See mya, see mya
Me lover come back
See mya, see mya
Go take you lover now
See mya, see mya
Wheel him make me see
See mya, see mya
Throw a kiss to him
See mya, see mya
Wheel him let him go
See mya, see mya.[61]

Jekyl then offers an explanation of the song's meaning. (It is obvious that this song 'matured' in the late nineteenth or early twentieth century because of the reference to 'sea' and 'Colon' in Central America.) The song basically asks where the lover of the girl in the middle of the ring is. She no longer sees him, he has gone to sea, and to Colon Bay (presumably, to work). In the end she is happy at his return and they are reunited. Throughout the song the call-and-refrain pattern is constant.

As regards instrumentation, there is ample evidence that a great number of percussion and reed instruments were used. Flutes were made, usually of bamboo, and could be played conventionally with the mouth or with the nose (alternatively cited as Maroon and Coromantee, which shows that it was common among a variety of tribes). There was a variety of drums and percussion instruments (goombay, shakers, sticks, jenkoving, jawbone, cotta or cotter drums, bon or panya, grater, rhumba box), and there were guitars. All these instruments are quite similar in function and model to the original African ones.

The drums came in for the most condemnation because they could convey messages, and they were 'loud' and 'noisy'. Not only did they throw dancers into trances and make them catch the power, but they also literally spoke to the slaves in communicating ideas. One British observer testified to being awed by the power of the drums: 'After the first few deafening moments . . . the vibrations threatened to sever my spine, I found the rhythms of the drums stealing over my senses to such an extent that all the blare was forgotten in the supreme electric effect they engendered.'[62] He went on to say that the rhythms were so 'complicated' that it was 'quite impossible to take down in long-hand'.

It is important to recognize that music in the African sense, beyond the technical differences previously mentioned, was also functionally dissimilar to European music. The relationship between a man and his instrument was like that between two close friends. The instrument, therefore, expressed the actual language of the instrumentalist:

> He also 'teaches' the instrument the language it will 'speak', which is, of course, the musician's own mother tongue. . . . The Senegalese *Kora*, which talks *Wolof*, is not tuned in the same way as the Malinka *Kora*, which expresses itself in *Bambara*.[63]

> Music thus grows out of the intonations and rhythmic onomatopoeias of speech. . . . In the *Duala* language, which is typical of Bantu languages, any melodic contradiction between the way a word is spoken and the way it is sung is inconceivable. For example, the noun *moto* (which means 'man', as opposed to animal) is said in one note with identical stress on both syllables; this accentuation is adhered to in all *Duala* songs; if the two syllables were sung on different notes, the word would lose its meaning.[64]

Thus when the drum was beaten to entertain, communicate or for religious purposes, it threw the white slave-master into fear and apprehension. The drum was derided because it spoke the African's language. Consequently, the drum was banned and went underground for a while. The most emotional responses from the white overseer, slave-master or Christian missionary, were in relation to the drum. It perhaps provided the terrifying reminder that the African, through all brutalities, had not lost his native tongue and could still 'speak' and thus communicate.

The drum was banned not only in Jamaica, but throughout the whole Caribbean area and the Americas. It went underground, became a subculture, and was distanced from popular acceptance (even after emancipation). This was due to the European missionaries' influence on their new black converts. The black Christian, late of the slave world, thus emerged associating the drum with heathen or barbarian practices. In his duped state (emotional Christian, psychologically programmed with new values) the black convert did not recognize the European orientation of his new self. So a new type of Africanized expression came into being without the aid of drums. The Christian was only a Christian in so far as religious indoctrination, for he still expressed Africa culturally.

4

By the early nineteenth century there was a great deal of anti-slavery sentiment in England as well as the opposite view. A number of whites, using the Haitian Revolution as a basis for their objection to emancipation, felt that once the slaves were free, 'indiscriminate massacres of the whites' would ensue. The argument was settled in 1834 when the apprenticeship system was agreed upon: the slaves would still serve their master for a period of four years during which time they would work for wages. The wages were one shilling per day. Under slavery, the master provided clothes and food, but with payment for labour all this was taken away. Naturally, the slaves felt that they were working for nothing, and this resulted in large-scale abandonment of the plantation for the settling of their own homes. They were faced with two alternatives: pay rents or squat on 'government' property or on the land of the plantation owners. The coloured magistrates who were appointed to the bench were suspect, for they could 'not forget the injustice with which they were at one time treated'.[65]

The free churches played a useful role. They were given

money by a number of blacks for the bulk purchase of land, they paid for schools and churches to be built, and for teachers to be paid. In fact the enterprising spirit demonstrated by the black population, isolated by official society, was phenomenal. When emancipation was declared the planters were rewarded ('compensated'), while the freed men received absolutely no support or provision from the state. The concept of indolence was vocalized primarily by the same oppressors who refused to respond to the former slave's condition, thus perpetuating a myth that they themselves had created out of their own greed.

As early as 1839 Henry Taylor, a senior civil servant at the colonial office, issued a memorandum to the British Secretary of State. In it he disclosed that the house of assembly should be disbanded, because in time it would contain too many black people whose position would be 'recalcitrant'. By that he meant that blacks would be aiming for self-determination once they had control of the electorate. For the moment it was rejected by the British. The British felt confident, with the law stipulating that only people of property could vote, that there would be no need to remove the house.

By the 1850s Jamaica was in an uncertain position. The continued misuse of power by the magistrates was one of the main reasons behind the Morant Bay Rebellion of 1865. One of the most striking examples of the collaboration of the coloured (Euro-African mixture) and the blacks occurred during this period. The two most important people were George William Gordon (coloured) and Paul Bogle (black). Gordon's European father had abandoned him and he was almost completely self-taught. In 1844 he was elected to the house of assembly, but was removed because of his natural inclination for justice for the black poor. As a magistrate for St Thomas he had inspected a police station and discovered a sick man lying in a latrine, the reason for his being there was that he begged a Rev. Cooke for alms who promptly had him arrested. Because of Gordon's indignant letter to the Governor, and the collaboration of the German-born Council head for St Thomas with the planters, he was removed. In 1863, Gordon, aided by his enterprising campaign manager Paul Bogle (a man of property, who was ordained by Gordon himself as a Baptist deacon, and a leader of iron will), was re-elected to the assembly. In addition Gordon served as churchwarden for the same parish, but was expelled by the same German because of Gordon's religious denomination as Baptist.

The infamous 'Queen's Letter' dictating continued work for the planters for starvation wages was a cause for concern. A mass rally was called at Morant Bay on 12 August 1865. It was decided that Paul Bogle should lead a deputation to present their grievances to the Governor. Having walked 45 miles to Spanish Town, the contemptuous Governor refused to see them. Gordon, at heart a social reformer, advised that a deputation be sent to England to meet the Queen and to acquaint her first-hand with the conditions in the country. Bogle had already deduced that both the Governor (and house of assembly) and the British monarchy represented the same thing, and decided to demonstrate the people's will. He initiated drilling exercises for the men when news reached them that two of their men were being tried for assault and trespass. At the trial, one Alexander White was made to pay a fine with costs, whereupon one of Bogle's men shouted that the fine should not be paid. Court was disrupted and proceedings came to an end. The magistrates had the audacity to issue warrants for the arrest of twenty-eight men including Paul and Moses Bogle. In their attempt to arrest them, they themselves were made captive. The German returned from holiday and alerted the militia. The Court House was surrounded by policemen and Volunteers. Paul Bogle and 400 protesters, accompanied by horns, drums and conch shells, swarmed into town. It is said that Moses Bogle had a gun in his hand. The Volunteers shot down twenty men. Bogle's men responded, and armed with heavy sticks, cutlasses, spears, and muskets, killed six and wounded three. Paul Bogle gave orders for the Court House to be burned down; finally a school was set on fire and, assisted by strong winds, the Court House began to burn. The German, caught inside the burning building, made two attempts to escape and was finally slaughtered. Paul Bogle held a prayer meeting and gave thanks to God.

There followed a heavy-handed retaliatory measure by the Governor and his cohorts. Over 300 armed soldiers including Volunteers, the West India Regiment (similar to blacks in the Rhodesian/South African army) and the Sixth Royals, descended on the Morant Bay area killing, whipping, hanging and imprisoning people indiscriminately. The criminal Governor Eyre examined all possible ways of involving Gordon in the uprising. Finally Gordon gave himself up and was executed. He was taunted, clothes torn off him, but he walked bravely, handed his glasses to a sailor and faced death unblinking. It was not too ironic that the Maroons captured Paul Bogle and delivered him into the hands of official murderers, who hanged him on 24 October 1865.[66]

It is not surprising that the Morant Bay Rebellion happened in a period of Jamaican history when the free churches were on the upsurge, a period referred to as Revivalism. I have said that the free churches, especially since the coming of the Baptists under George Liele, a black man, had created for the black masses a socially mobile and expressive vehicle of their discontent and grievances. In the Baptist and Methodist churches the black masses experienced a degree of identification, with ritual and belief, that seemed impossible with the white church. When the preacher delivered a sermon it was expressive of the fiery oratory and incantative power akin to that of an African High Priest. When George Liele established his Ethiopian Baptist church, identification was total. Membership of the Baptist church exceeded that of every other denomination put together. It was a reflection of what the people thought and an expression of their needs and aspirations.

Prior to the upsurge in the spiritual reawakening of the black masses in the 1860s, the traditional African religion was practised, known as Pukumina (also as Kumina, Cumina and Pocomania), a word which seems to be a corruption of the Angolan Kumona: to see; possession.[67] Phillippo, writing in the mid-nineteenth century, made these observations about a cult he called 'Fetish', but which must have been Pukumina:

> The circumstances attending the Fetish oath, which was a pledge of inviolable secrecy, and usually administered previously to insurrections or individual murders, was terrible. Blood was drawn from each individual of the party present; this was mixed with grave-dirt and gunpowder in a bowl, and was partaken of by each individual in the secret ratification of his sincerity.[68]
>
> They adopted every possible means to increase their numbers,

> and proposed, as the advantages of membership, exemption from pain and premature death; from death, especially as designed by white men; or certain recovery from its influence when life was actually extinct.[69]

In the post-emancipation situation, aspects of Pukumina fused with the Baptist faith and both influenced the other. The Baptist meetings took on a more African flavour and Pukumina incorporated aspects of Christianity, especially in accepting the Bible as the magic book. Under these circumstances the Great Revival shook the foundations of the established church in the 1860s.[70] If these people were the same as those who followed Paul and Moses Bogle in 1865, then it is not surprising that they were so fearless. Before the advent of the European who saw material wealth as paramount, religion had been the most important influence on people's lives. Doubtless, with freedom and continued poverty, religious zeal brought people together. The Great Revival was active, procreative, and positive. It met confrontation with confrontation and did not succumb to political and military power.

Revivalists practised fowl-killing sacrifices, just as the old Christians of the Bible believed in offering 'burnt offerings'. Ground that was blessed with holy water and prayed upon became 'sealed' ground – sacred ground. Here ceremonies took place. The dancing around a pole accomplished a variety of things: 1. strengthened devotees in their faith and their contact with the spirit world, and 2. gradually leads to possession.[71] Drumming, singing, clapping and stamping of feet were common features. With the possible exception of the drum, the Baptists had similar prayer-meetings. Catching the power or possession were also part of Baptist ritual. Common among the leaders was the professed ability to 'foretell the future; to possess the gift of tongues; and to prophesy. They seldom delivered their instructions without a book, representing it as the Bible.'[72]

Without knowing it, Phillippo was describing an essentially African manner of worship. The Christian symbolism had taken over from the African, but the style of worship, of incorporating the African into the Euro-Christian, re-expressed the explosive qualities of the familiar and traditional.

After the violent upsurge of 1865, Governor Eyre persuaded the assembly to surrender the Constitution, and Britain took over the reins. The agony of Crown Colony government had begun. All vestiges of an electoral body were completely abandoned. There was little or no protest. Many people welcomed it in so far as power was removed from the hands of the planters. There were some improvements – mainly in education. As early as the last quarter of the previous century, Edward Long had made certain pertinent observations:

> Let me now ask, what are the mighty advantages which Britain, or the colony, has gained by the many hundreds who have received their education in the former? The answer may be, they have spent their fortunes in Britain, and learned to renounce their native place, their parents, and friends. Would it not have been better for both countries, that three-fourths of them had never crossed the Atlantic? Their industry, in general, for ever lost to the place where it might have been usefully exerted; and they waste their patrimony in a manner that rebounds not in the least to the national profit, having acquired a taste for pleasure and extravagance of every kind, far superior to the ability of their fortunes. . . . The education they usually receive in Great Britain does not qualify them for useful employment in Jamaica, unless they are bred to some of the learned professions; which nevertheless are not suitable to all, because those professions would soon be overstocked in the island, if every youth consigned from thence was to be trained to medicine*, divinity, or law. . . . They generally leave Britain at that critical age when the blood beats high. They regret their exit from the gay delights of London, from the connections of early friendship, and perhaps the softer attachments of love. . . . With this riveted prejudice against colony life, it is not to be wondered at, that they embrace the first convenient opportunity of returning to their favourite pursuits and intimacies. . . . Of the many students of law, natives of Jamaica, who after completing their terms in London have returned to assume the gown, I have not heard of one who gained £500 a year by his practice. . . . Many I have noted, who, arriving there after having (as it is called) *finished their education in England*, appeared unpardonably illiterate.[73]

*Long had 'physics' which I interpret to mean medicine.

Long was not writing as a man who was concerned with the general black population, but as a member of the planter class who had keenly observed the debilitating effect of education in Britain and of its irrelevance to the specific social conditions in Jamaica. However, exactly the same thing was still going on in the 1930s! The people who studied in Britain were usually white with a few coloured from the free and wealthy coloured middle stratum. Beyond the schools set up by the black population themselves, and the liberal efforts of the churches, no attempt was made to educate the black poor after emancipation, until the introduction of the Crown Colony system after 1865.

The Institute of Jamaica was founded in 1879.

> The institute was set up, as our letterhead states, 'For the encouragement of Literature, Science and Art.' One immediately asks – what kind of Literature, Science and Art? The answer is obvious – in general, British Literature, Science and Art and specifically (where this was possible) the Jamaican version or imitation . . . of British . . . Literature, Science and Art. . . . Cultural control was an essential part of colonial policy. It meant, among other things, that a 'cultured' Jamaican was one who spoke English with a certain accent, who thought that *music* was Bach and Beethoven (who could tell you the titles of the symphonies and – though this was rare – could hum some of the leading motifs), who *knew* that the *only* art had been created by Michelangelo, Leonardo da Vinci, Rembrandt etc.; who could quote long passages from Shakespeare, inappropriately; who, all told – our cultured Jamaican – was as near to being an Englishman as possible.[74]

This policy of imperial control of the island led to the development and entrenchment of the most visible and populous coloured and black middle class in the whole of the English-speaking Caribbean. Towards the last quarter of the nineteenth century Britain invaded West Africa (with the aid of the West Indian regiment of troops), not for slaves, but as part of its capitalist, expansionist drive. This sparked off a degree of protest on the island, led by Robert Love (a doctor), a black man, and publisher of *The Jamaica Advocate* and *The Jamaican.* By 1900 Love shared a platform with Sandy Cox who had founded in the same year Jamaica's first nationalist organization – the National Club. The NC's own newspaper was called *Our Own*. Both Love and Cox were members of the Legislative Council, but Cox lost his seat in 1912, and subsequently migrated to the United States. The club quickly waned away. Both Marcus Garvey and W.A. Domingo served the National Club as assistant secretaries. Domingo too migrated to the United States to become an opponent to Garvey when he in turn reached the country.[75]

Domingo, while in the United States, became a member of the Socialist Party and contributed to several black socialist periodicals, and was one of several Caribbeans, as well as Afro-Americans (including Du Bois), who vehemently opposed Marcus Garvey's political stance and orientation. This controversy is too complex to get into here, but the point made is that those early nationalists had their first experience of nationalism in Jamaica. The American controversy involved the integrationist ethic of both Caribbean and Afro-American intellectuals, and what also has been described as the Caribbean/Afro-American clash, one that was not simply confined to the intellectual sphere, but also involved the Caribbean working man's conflicts with the Afro-American over limited job opportunities.[76]

In 1936, after the Garvey–Domingo *et al.* débâcle had vanished, Domingo established, in conjunction with other Jamaicans, the Jamaican Progressive League which set about agitating for Jamaican self-rule. In 1937 Domingo and W. Adolphe Roberts (who had written a number of novels during the 1920s to 1940s) came to Jamaica to set up a local branch. The year previous to their arrival, a new nationalist magazine had been launched, called *Public Opinion.* The paper's publisher was a black man called O.T. Fairclough, previously a banker in Haiti. From the outset the movement had a number of British sympathizers and participants, including artists, intellectuals, and political thinkers. In 1937 Ken Hill formed a nationalist organization – the National Reform Association – out of which emerged the People's National Party. Fairclough persuaded Norman Manley to lead this party in 1938. That same year there were widespread protests, strikes, and violent upheavals in Jamaica and throughout the whole Caribbean area. Bustamante's trade union movement was soon formed. It is claimed that Bustamante was highly undemocratic in his practices by having his union's constitution amended to appoint himself president-for-life. Hart claims that as early as the 1940s, violent inter-party fratricide, led by Bustamante, was already common and had (and still has) tremendous and dangerous repercussions. Bustamante's release from gaol in 1942 was facilitated, Hart claims, by an active agreement with the Governor, Sir Arthur Richards, to create disorder and disruptions in P.N.P. meetings, which he proceeded to initiate upon his release. However, Sylvia Wynter holds the view that both Bustamante and Norman Manley were manipulated by Richards for the benefit of British interests. Thus the political alliances that Richards formed with either Bustamante or Manley were dictated primarily by British colonial interests.[77]

Marcus Garvey died in London in 1940, a poor man. Jamaica achieved its independence in 1962 after attaining full self-government in 1959. The three-year period of transition was likened by some people to the apprenticeship system of 1834, wherein the British remained in control. The population of Jamaica now stands at just over 2 million. In 1970 a census of population showed that 27 per cent of the total population was concentrated within the corporate area of Kingston and St Andrew, and in the same year a survey of employment in the island showed that in the age group 14 – 24, 35,339 were unemployed out of a total work-force (in the same age category) of 117,048; of a total work-force of 456,724, 62,021 were unemployed among males. Of a total work-force of 808,290, 181,777 (or 22.5 per cent) were out of work. Naturally, the greatest proportion of unemployed is concentrated within the Kingston/St Andrew area.[78] As there has been a yearly exodus from the rural parts of the country to the city, so also has there been an exodus from Jamaica to Britain, the United States and Canada. Kuper states that between the 1950s and 1960s, the years after the Second World War, nearly a quarter of a million Jamaicans migrated to Britain which he says 'has many features of a millenarian cult'.[79] This has not just been the flight of the country's poor, but that of the professionally trained and qualified as well.

Kuper remarks that: 'It may be that the immigration procedures are deliberately biased in order to skim off the skilled people.' Most of the unskilled workers are not involved in agricultural activity any more for 'agriculture, forestry and fishing contributed only 9 per cent of GDP' in 1972.[80] The distributive trades and manufacturing together account for 28 per cent of Jamaica's GDP, sectors that do not employ people

en masse, and those that are employed are in the professional, managerial, and clerical classes. This means that masses of people are unemployed and under-employed; added to these are young school-leavers who cannot be employed because there aren't sufficient opportunities. This leaves the country in a generally appalling state, where crime and murder become a living nightmare, where political corruption is rife, where a significant sector of the youth find themselves at the mercy of political tyrants.

2 Rastafari: The Concept of the Black Redeemer

Rastafari has played a key role in the development of Reggae. It has acted as a philosophical guiding force in the lives of the music's creators and as a reclaimer of those who otherwise would have been confused about their position in Jamaican society or who may have turned renegade. Rastafari has been in existence for nearly fifty years, but the seeds for its germination go back to the end of the eighteenth century, to the time when George Liele's Ethiopian Baptist church was established in 1784. Particularly important is the intense activity and response Ethiopianism elicited from the pronouncements of Marcus Garvey and the imminent rise of Ras Tafari to Emperor of Ethiopia in 1930.

As shown in Chapter 1, the free churches undermined the established church by encouraging the slaves to resist slavery. George Liele's church and the various off-shoots were particularly influential. The planters and the established churches were against teaching the Bible to the enslaved Afrikans (Ethiopians), and when the free churches did so, the sparse but significant (to the slaves) pronouncements it made to Afrika (Ethiopia) triggered off a feeling of tradition, of having participated in history. One of the most important citations was the controversial translation of Psalm 68: 31; 'Princes shall come out of Egypt; Ethiopia shall soon stretch out her hands unto God.' According to Geiss, however, 'A modern German translation directly from the Hebrew varies considerably from the translation of Luther or from the King James version.'[1] He then gives the translation as follows: 'Let bronze implements be brought from Egypt, May Kush raise its hands to Yahwe!' If Geiss is to be believed, the reference to Ethiopia (Kush) is the anticipation of the conversion of

Ethiopians to the Jewish faith. None the less, blacks interpreted these lines to mean that God was already accepted in Ethiopia and that a great civilization must have flourished at one time. The Bible was the only reading matter available to the slaves, thus any textual confirmation of any oral or spiritual transmission of their civilization came from that. It must also be understood that slaves were killed and flogged, churches burnt, and priests arrested only because slaves were taught to read and Christianity was projected as a healing religion.

The ancestral Ethiopia that the Bible referred to is certainly not the current Ethiopia of which the late Emperor Haile Selassie ruled, but Nubia (also referred to as Kush and Meroe) which was to the south of Egypt. Each conqueror, European or Arab, of Afrika renamed the territories. Present-day Sudan and all areas beyond Egypt were referred to by the Greeks as Ethiopia. This has led to widespread confusion as to the ancient high culture or civilization of Ethiopia. The first recorded nation in history to dominate the world stage was Ancient Egypt (called *Kemit* by the Egyptians themselves, from the root *Khem*, black, *Kemit*, land of the blacks[2]) and they themselves pointed to the south (Nubia/Kush) as their ancestral home, and in times of attack from Arabia or Europe, depended on the Kushites/Nubians for assistance.[3]

The Sudan, with Egypt, is the sole nation within Afrika which still has remnants of artefacts that have become associated with Ancient Egyptian civilization. These artefacts are characterized in the main by step pyramids and hieroglyphic writing. None of these exist in present-day Ethiopia whose ancient civilization is characterized in the main by the 'precedence' of its Christian conversion and its possession of early translations of the Bible as well as original ancient Christian texts. Its civilization is symbolized by its controversial association with King Solomon and the union of the Queen of Sheba, and the existence of a number of stelae, particularly in the city of Aksum. Ethiopia, however, clearly holds a place in ancient Afrikan civilization, but not preceding that of Kush/Sudan or Egypt. Nevertheless, it was the Ethiopia of the Bible whence Ethiopianism evolved as a cultural/political movement spearheaded by black churchmen.

The African Methodist Episcopal church was established in

the early part of the nineteenth century in Philadelphia and the African Methodist Episcopal Zion church followed soon after.[4] These churches were established by Afro-Americans and sent missionaries to Afrika to proselytize and work among Afrikans. They went first to Liberia, Sierra Leone and Ghana, but later they established churches in Azania (South Africa) and Nigeria.[5] Beyond its original identification with Afrika as the land of all blacks and scriptural associations, the Afrikan church created the climate first for Christian conversion, and second for the development of racial consciousness and nationalism. It was the church itself that invented the slogan: 'Africa for the Africans' in its protracted fight against the established churches and for decolonization.[6] The church, playing the role in Afrika that it had, included in its members a number of Caribbean churchmen from Jamaica, Trinidad, Barbados, and other islands. They travelled freely to Afrika and back, and in this way the concept of Afrika must have been communicated to those in the Caribbean in a real and dramatic way. Thus Ethiopianism was Pan-Afrikan by contact and communication, if not totally in practice.

By the 1920s there was already a considerable awareness of Ethiopia's ancient civilization. This had taken root through both the church movement and the more political pronouncements of Marcus Garvey. He had originally established his Universal Negro Improvement Association in Jamaica in August 1914 on the celebration of abolition of slavery which occurred on 1 August. Attempts were subsequently made by the authorities to place Garvey in gaol. The plot was to arrest Garvey under the Vagrancy Act on the grounds of his having no visible means of support.[7] Garvey's main contribution to the birth of Rastafari, however, was his prophecy to 'Look to Africa, when a black king shall be crowned, for the day of deliverance is near.'[8] To Garvey's followers this was prophetic, but Garvey – well travelled and an avid reader – was well aware of Ras Tafari's role as Regent for the young Ethiopian empress, Zauditu (daughter of the emperor Menelik),[9] and the possibility of his eventual ascension. The visual impact Garvey once created in the United States was recreated at Edelweiss Park, Jamaica, during a parade of his organization. 'Precisely at 8.10 p.m. the greatest Negro Leader of modern times . . . arrived wearing the uniform of the Provisional President of Africa. The band played the African Anthem, "Ethiopia the land of our fathers".'[10] But Garvey's status in relation to the Rastafarian movement was not earned simply because of his 'prophecies', but also because of his efforts to teach black and poor Jamaicans about their ancestry and the necessity for them to alter the course of their slave history.

As a result of Garvey's impact, there began a lively injection and regeneration of the Ethiopian theme. The African Methodist Episcopal church had also established a church in Kingston during the 1930s, and its minister was 'very active in the Garveyite movement and other Africa-oriented activities'.[11] It is not certain, however, what precise role this church played in the development of Ethiopianism or Rastafarianism. *Plain Talk*, a Jamaican periodical of the 1930s, carried an interesting letters page in which a L.F.C. Mantle (who prefixed his name with Doctor) was a regular contributor. Mantle's letter of August 1935 stated:

> The Romans or Italians are the same people that had barbarously and brutally crucified the Saviour 2,000 years ago, and Mussolini is now haunted to give the Italian nation as a ransom for the sacred blood of Jesus. . . . I am appealing to all men and women of the Negro race to leave off idolatry and come now and worship the true and living God of Israel. Be it understood that you are assisting the Romans to fight against yourselves even though we know they cannot win.[12]

Mantle was referring to the attack on Abyssinia/Ethiopia by the Italians and for which the Emperor Haile Selassie was seeking the support of blacks in the West. Mantle's letters to *Plain Talk* were focused primarily on Ethiopia as an ancient civilization – they did not preach the divinity of the Emperor.

The actual history of Ethiopia is punctuated with invasions from neighbouring territories and battles to retain its sovereignty. Jean Doresse claims that between 1000 and 400 years before the Christian Era, a tribe, few in number and of 'Semitic origin', migrated into Ethiopia from the Yemen (across the Red Sea) and were of Sabaean, Minaean origin.[13] When Doresse uses the word Semitic it is to express a European origin, i.e. white. But other writers have expressed totally different opinions about the peoples who inhabited Arabia at this point in antiquity. Ullendorff states that the

* Inserted by author.

'sons of Cush [Kush/Sudan*] all appear to be situated in Asia; no doubt . . . these Arabian peoples [were] either to be of African descent [or migration] or to be under African dominion'.[14] Cheik Anta Diop, quoting Lenormant, states that

> a Kushite Empire originally existed throughout Arabia. This was the epoch personified by the Adites of Ad, grandson of Ham, the Biblical ancestor of the blacks. Cheddade, a son of Ad and builder of the legendary 'Earthly Paradise' mentioned in the Koran, belongs to the epoch called that of the 'First Adites'. The empire was destroyed in the eighteenth century B.C. by an invasion of coarse, white Jectanide tribes, who apparently came to settle among the blacks. . . . Lenormant reports that after the Jectanide victory, some of the Adites crossed the Red Sea at Bab el Mandeo to settle in Ethiopia.[15]

He goes on to quote Lenormant verbatim: 'Long before the discovery of the Hymyaritic language and inscriptions, it had been noted that *Ghez* [also referred to as *Geez**], the Abyssinian language, is a living remnant of the ancient language of the Yemen.'[16] It is to be clearly understood, then, that Ethiopia received its cultural impetus, not from Arabs/Europeans from Arabia, but from blacks themselves who were fleeing attacks from white tribes. Doresse also states that: 'The oldest temples of Tigre [a province of Ethiopia*] still bear the names of sacred sites in Arabia dedicated to these gods.'[17] Before Ethiopia's conversion to Christianity 'inscriptions on stone were in Sabaean or Minaean dialects written in the elegant South Arabian form. . . . It will be remembered that this system of writing was closely related to the Phoenician.'[18] According to Anta Diop the Phoenicians themselves were black,[19] and Herodotus states that 'The Phoenicians . . . introduced into Greece . . . a number of accomplishments, of which the most important was writing, an art till then, I think, unknown to Greeks.'[20]

Ullendorff states that 'Old Testament influences and reflections had probably reached Ethiopia even before the introduction of Christianity in the fourth century and before the translation of the Bible.'[21] Christianity itself received its impetus from the model of the Ancient Egyptians' history of the birth of Heru (Horus) from the union of Ausar and Auset

* Inserted by author.

(Osiris and Isis). Thus early European Christianity had the Black Madonna and Child (Auset/Isis and Heru/Horus) as its most venerated symbol of ancient Christianity.[22] It is not surprising, therefore, that with the rise of Christianity, its acceptance was facilitated in the Afrikan territories simply because the concept of the One God was an already established fact of great antiquity in their societies. In addition it has also been stated that a Jewish element from South Arabia had settled in Ethiopia before the onslaught of Christianity.[23] It is said that Ethiopia officially became a Christian nation under King Ezana in the fourth century.[24] By 'official', the suggestion is that Ethiopia in antiquity was made up of a variety of small kingdoms, some provinces being annexed to it during periods of war. Thus these kingdoms had their own rulers, and the most powerful king was he who controlled the greatest number of kingdoms, though not necessarily all.

The capital of Ethiopia was changed from one city to another, depending on the success or failure of invaders; at one time it was Aksum, at another, Shoa, and still another, Kabar, in the year 872.[25] The wars with the Moslem world had dislocated the larger unity of the country, and subsequent attempts were made to reunite it. This was eventually accomplished by Yekuno-Amlak in collaboration with Takla-Haymanot who removed the usurped Zagwe dynasty, and re-instituted the Solomonic line.[26] This period of Ethiopian history is rather cloudy and one speculates as to the authenticity or credibility of the Solomonic line being restored from the inception of the King Solomon–Queen of Sheba myth. The union between these two resulted in the birth of Menelik I who lived with his mother. When he became of age, she sent him to visit his father, and on his return, stole the Ark of the Covenant. Ethiopia thus became the new Zion, and the Ark the living testimony to the existence of blood relations with Solomon. It is doubtful, however, throughout Ethiopia's history of external and internal wars, that that line could have remained unbroken. When contemporary observations are made in connection with the Solomonic line it is to be understood as authenticating the general historical connections between the Queen of Sheba and King Solomon.

The first recorded attempt at framing a Royal Charter was undertaken in the early fourteenth century under the rulership of 'Amda-Seyon, and this was later embodied in the

Serata Mangest.[27] It was during the fourteenth century that a great deal of Ethiopia's written literature appeared – primarily translations from the Arabic, Greek, and Hebrew. Ethiopia then experienced attacks from Portugal, Italy, and from the Arabs across the Red Sea. A succession of treaties, coupled with fierce fighting, preserved its sovereignty. In the nineteenth century, the power of the King began to wane, giving way to provincial kings. Kassa of Qwara defeated Ras Ali and had himself crowned *negus neghest* in 1855, and changed his name to Tewodros II (Theodore II). The *negus* of the Shoan province was Haile Malakot who fell fatally ill, and in a scrimmage with Tewodros II forces under Ras Engeda, Menelik, the son of Haile Malakot was given over as hostage. The young prince then lived in the palace of Tewodros and although a hostage, had special privileges granted to him. He also observed the progressive organizational abilities of the Emperor. When Menelik finally made his escape bid and ultimately became King of Shoa, he ruled this province for twenty-four years when he became *negus neghest* (King of Kings) in 1889. Tewodros committed suicide after the British under Lord Napier had sent an expeditionary force against him. In spite of Menelik's title as King of Shoa, he still had to contend with the Emperor Yohannes IV who was the crowned *negus neghest* and to whom Menelik gladly paid tribute. Both kings clashed on several occasions so Menelik proposed the signing of peace treaties. He also expanded his domain by conquests in different parts of Ethiopia and by having relations with Italy from whom he obtained arms. In 1889 Yohannes IV died from battle wounds and was succeeded by Menelik in that same year.[28]

Menelik introduced a variety of progressive changes into Ethiopia, attempting to bring the country into the Western sphere. In the battle of Adowa in 1896, he defeated the invading Italian army and so saved Ethiopia from European domination. He signed a peace treaty with the Italians in 1896 giving them the territory of Eritrea. Menelik died in 1913 and Ras Tafari ascended the throne in 1930 to become King of Kings, i.e. King of all the provinces of Ethiopia – a title that was revived sometime in the Middle Ages. Ras Tafari became known as Haile Selassie I and distinguished himself with the defeat of the Italians in the late 1930s. To the poor Jamaicans, particularly in Kingston, Ras Tafari's

Burning Spear whose music is dedicated to revitalizing the memory of Marcus Garvey. (*Photo: D. Morris.*)

Peter Tosh, one of the founding members of the original Wailers, is currently a well-known solo artist. (*Photo: D. Morris.*)

accession was the fulfilment of prophecy.

I have already stated that the movement of Ethiopianism was essentially a church movement, and that Marcus Garvey combined political objectives with religious expressions to create an impact, not only on the Jamaican masses, but on black peoples all over the world. In the face of their general lack of literacy and of education – a deliberate British colonial policy – these people did not have a coherent understanding of history. But they could understand a religious prophecy. So the masses awakened to the birth of the Black Redeemer, the same black king that Marcus Garvey spoke of. The general strikes and rebellion of the 1930s in Jamaica and the Caribbean resulted in the Moyne Report which stated that the wages of the poor in the 1930s had not risen since just after emancipation. In other words, one hundred years later the black man's material condition had barely improved. So the mass exodus thus began. Jamaicans migrated to Cuba, Central America, the United States, and other parts of the Caribbean.

The 1930s in Jamaica were characterized by Marcus Garvey and his role as organizer/agitator, the coronation of Haile Selassie I, the establishment of the African Methodist Episcopal church, the street-corner oratory of a number of religiously inspired black people, and all these things contributed to the formation of the Rastafarian movement. Texts from the Bible were consulted and affirmation of beliefs were sought. Certain passages in the Bible gave concrete proof to believers that Selassie I was indeed the reincarnated Christ, the returned, or embodiment of, the new messiah, the Black Redeemer come to release the children of Israel out of Egypt. These were not historical refcrences, but clearly biblical.

Revelation 5: 2-5: 'And I saw a strong angel proclaiming with a loud voice, Who is worthy to open the book, and to loose the seals thereof? And no man in heaven, nor in earth, neither under the earth, was able to open the book, neither to look thereon. And I wept much, because no man was found worthy to open and to read the book, neither to look thereon. And one of the elders saith unto me, Weep not: behold, the Lion of the tribe of Juda, the Root of David, hath prevailed to open the book, and to loose the seven seals thereof.' Jeremiah 13: 23, attests to the colour of the Ethiopians: 'Can the Ethiopian change his skin, or the leopard his spots?' When Ethiopia went to war against the Italian invasion, Revelation 19: 19: 'And I saw the beast, and the kings of the earth, and their armies, gathered together to make war against him that sat on the horse, and against his army.' These *signs* were understood literally as to invest the power of divinity in Selassie I. When he was crowned Emperor, he revived the titles of old, which stated, 'The Conquering Lion of the tribe of Juda, King of Kings, Lord of Lords, Elect of God. . .', etc.

The three main preachers of Rastafari during the 1930s were Leonard P. Howell, Joseph Nathaniel Hibbert, and H. Archibald Dunkley. Hibbert lived previously in Costa Rica and belonged to an Ethiopian Masonic Society; Dunkley was a former seaman who devoted over two years of his time studying the Bible to find Selassie's coronation confirmed in the holy scriptures. Howell projected himself as a mystic and laid claim to speaking an Afrikan language.[29] Dunkley established his King's Missionary Movement and preached exclusively in Kingston; in 1932 Howell permitted Hibbert to speak on his platform, and subsequently they worked together, but later broke up because Hibbert created a new order for their followers, the Ethiopian Coptic Faith.

In 1933 Howell sold 5,000 postcard-sized photographs of the Emperor at one shilling each, claiming that these were passports to Ethiopia. He was arrested at Trinityville, St Thomas, in December 1934.[30] Howell was sentenced to two years, and his deputy, Hinds, to one year. When he was released in 1940, he opened a bakery and established a new organization, the Ethiopian Salvation Society, registered as a friendly society and stated to be a local branch of an American organization.[31] He then established Pinnacle in Sligoville, an abandoned estate which he formed into a Rastafarian commune. In 1941 he was again arrested, this time for growing marijuana (ganja) and assaulting members of the community outside his organization. He was sentenced to two years. On release he returned to Pinnacle and conducted his affairs as before. Taxes were paid on the property, plots of land distributed to his followers, guard dogs used to protect his settlement, and dreadlocksed brethren, known as warriors (in the Afrikan tradition) protected the commune. It lasted until 1954 when he was again arrested, but appealed and won. He returned to Kingston, and claimed that he was divine, for which he was discredited by Rastafarians who firmly believed that only Selassie possessed such biblical qualities.[32] He was later confined to the Kingston Mental Hospital where, it is thought, he died.

In 1937, Haile Selassie I sent Dr Malaku E. Bayen to New York to establish the Ethiopian World Federation Inc., in order to solicit money and support for Ethiopia's war against the Italian invasion. The Emperor was aware of the affinity that black people of the West had to Afrika and to Ethiopia in particular. The EWF stated in its aims: 'We, the Black People of the World, in order to effect Unity, Solidarity, Liberty, Freedom and Self-Determination, to secure Justice and maintain the integrity of Ethiopia, which is our Divine heritage, also, the Brotherhood of Man and the Fatherhood of God, do hereby establish and ordain this Constitution for the Ethiopian World Federation, Inc.'[33] The first Local (branch) was established in Kingston in 1938, Local 17. It did not last long, and another was established in 1942, Local 31, 'but caused controversy within the Movement as this Local barred their Brethren who wore beards and were Rastafarians from joining. . . . Adverse propaganda was also launched against Rastafarians by members of Local 31, and as a result the group did not receive recognition or support from the Ethiopian World Federation Inc. headquarters in New York.'[34] Other groups were in operation, the Ethiopian Coptic church, the United Ethiopian Body, the United Afro-West Indian Brotherhood, the Ethiopian Youth Cosmic Faith, the African Cultural League, and the Brotherhood Solidarity of United Ethiopians.[35] In 1955, a Mrs Maymie Richardson visited Jamaica on behalf of the EWF of New York. Grievances were put to her regarding the exclusion of bearded Rastas from becoming members of Local 31. The grievances were settled and these brethren established their own Local 37 named after Emperor Haile Selassie I. Within two years the membership increased from fifty to 500 members.[36]

After the Second World War, migration to Britain was beginning to increase rapidly. Probably because of the general migration trend, many people believed that the government had intentions of returning them to Afrika. Thus a Mr Branford of Trench Town, Kingston, solicited clothes from City merchants with which to go to Ethiopia. 'He had dreamed that the Emperor told him to prepare and proceed to Palisadoes Airport, Kingston, where aircraft were awaiting him and his followers.'[37] In 1955 and 1956 several groups went to a number of Kingston piers having received similarly dream-inspired communications from the Emperor. It is not surprising that these expectations on the part of Rastafarians were so emphatically present, since the Emperor, through the EWF in New York, had personally granted 500 acres of his own land to blacks in the West who possessed skills or semi-professional skills and were prepared to work. He had also stated in his letter that upon satisfactory performance, additional lands would be granted. A statement attributed to Mrs Richardson also declared that the Emperor was engaged in organizing a merchant navy and that ships would, in the future, sail to United States ports, and perhaps Jamaica.[38]

After the last attack on Howell in 1954, police activity against Rastas increased tremendously. The number of Rastafarians also increased. The commissioner of police launched attacks against ganja cultivation and possession. Prison sentences were more harsh and more frequent. A group of eighteen Rastas were charged with contempt of court,rioting, and assembling with the intention of rioting. Three-quarters were sentenced to fifteen months each. That same year, thirty-two locksmen were arrested while marching in downtown Kingston, armed with a banner, Bibles, and demanding freedom. A group of Rastas attempted to capture Victoria Park, and when the police approached, one of them raised his hand and said: 'Touch not the Lord's anointed.' The police finally moved them away.[39] In 1959 a scrimmage broke out between a Rasta and a policeman. Other police assisted their colleague but were attacked by sympathetic citizens. A fire engine arrived on the scene and was also attacked and set alight. Finally, police reinforcements in large numbers arrived, overwhelmed the citizens, then proceeded to attack their impoverished dwelling places at Back-O-Wall, burned their homes, beat up the residents and forcibly shaved locksed brethren.[40]

The Rastas were always loyal to their religion and philosophy, and were never cowed by the system. Rather, they were quite vociferous and dramatic in demonstrating the extreme neglect to which the British colonial system had subjected poor blacks. Though at this time there was not any clear political objective except that of repatriation, they dramatized their social conditions effectively. They could not have been ignored. The colonial government had to recognize their existence, respond in a predictably violent manner, and treat the whole repatriation question as though it were the dreamed-up notion of madmen. If they were projected as madmen, then they could be treated like madmen. Jamaican society laughed, and could not envisage the prognosis for the future that the Rastas were indicating.

Prince Edward C. Edwards convened the first national Nyahbinghi (festive celebration) in March 1958. Reports state that 300 people appeared and the celebration took the form of drumming, dancing, reading psalms, and smoking the holy herb. After the Nyahbinghi, the camp of Prince Emmanuel, one of the convenors, was raided by police and razed to the ground.[41] He was arrested, tried, and released, and resumed living at Back-O-Wall (where his camp was) until 1966. In 1959, Claudius Henry ('Repairer of the Breach') formed an organization called the Afrikan Reformed church, and though he was a Christian preacher, he attracted a number of Rastas because of his emphasis on Afrika/Ethiopia. He later, like Howell in the 1930s, distributed thousands of cards announcing the imminent departure of followers for the land of Ethiopia. Either by coincidence or planned strategy, celebrations were held on 1 August, the day of emancipation. Hundreds of people bought these cards at a shilling each and gathered on 5 October, their belongings sold. Henry was later arrested and charged, and then fined £100.[42] Barrett also relates the story of a Bedward of the Native Baptist church who called his disciples together in December 1921, to ascend to heaven. As the hour approached for the ascension, it was put off for another day, until the Prophet was locked up.[43]

The Rastafarians believe in the divinity of Haile Selassie I, the late Emperor of Ethiopia, and whose death is regarded as 'Babylon propaganda', for it would be difficult to reconcile the Biblical 'wages of sin' with a holy man, a man who personified God himself for the Rastas. His divinity transcended that of Christ, because some followers, during baptism plans prior to entering into the Ethiopian Orthodox church, demanded that they be baptized in no other name than that of Ras Tafari. The visiting Ethiopian cleric, Archimandrate Mandetro, stated that neither the Emperor nor the church would sanction baptism in any other name than that of Christ.[44] The emphasis on Selassie's divinity in order to qualify as a Rasta has diminished over the years. Though there is by and large a strong emotional affinity to his divinity, the majority of young people who accept the cultural projection of Rastafarians, i.e. projecting the history and culture of Afrika, understanding the evil machinations of society, the relevance of dietary habits, etc., refuse to acknowledge that Selassie is God.

The meaning of Selassie's name before his coronation was quite appropriate for his supposed divinity. In Amharic (which, under Menelik, gradually replaced the varying dialects spoken around the country), *Ras* means *head*, and as a title it means *prince*; *Tafari* means *creator*. His crowned name, *Haile Selassie* means *Power of the Trinity*.[45] The Roman numeral I is pronounced like the letter I, thus seemingly securing personal attachment to God or to the Emperor. The use of the letter I is frequent in the Rastas' speech, so too is its combination 'I and I'. It is obvious this is an extension of its use after Selassie's name, thus by applying it to oneself, one is demonstrating a daily contact with Selassie. The combination *I and I* is used to denote plurality. The *you* or *we* is not used because it does not communicate a oneness of self. By combining the I and I, the plural is easily understood. Similarly, the singular and plural for a human being is *man*; *men* is never used except in reference to people who are either hostile to the concept of Rastafari or are unsympathetic. Thus the police are frequently characterized as *men* because of their hostility to Rastas. The use of *this man* and *that man* in the language of the Rastas stems directly from its frequent use in the Bible. To use biblical speech is to demonstrate a closer relationship to God. Also, the use of the word *beloved* stems from the Bible and is used mainly among brethren, but sympathizers are sometimes affectionately referred to as such.

The use of the holy herb is similar to the use of incense in the Christian church, it is also sanctioned by the Bible, Genesis 1: 29, 'And God said, Behold, I have given you every herb bearing seed, which is upon the face of the earth, and every tree, in which is the fruit of a tree yielding seed; to you it shall be for meat'; Revelation 22: 2, '. . . there the tree of life, which bare twelve manner of fruits, and yielded her fruit every month: and the leaves of the tree were for the healing of the nation'. To Rastas, smoking herb/ganja reduces tension and induces a feeling of relaxation and oneness with the world, particularly the inner world. Brethren state that it produces a sharpness of mind and induces sounder reasoning, i.e. more rational discussion. It is also claimed that it is used as a bodily curative. Peter Tosh in a recent song states that marijuana is used to cure glaucoma. Older, particularly country/rural folk, brew it as a tea for consumption. It is also claimed to cure colds and a variety of other illnesses. At formal or informal gatherings, when the chillum pipe is packed tight with *ital* (i.e. pure) ganja, brethren instinctively remove their tams or head coverings. This is in respect to God for partaking of the seed/herb of life. It is usually accompanied by recitations from the Bible, particularly the Psalms, or other prayers spontaneously created, but ending with 'Jah Rastafari'. Usually one brethren pronounces 'Jah' and the others respond with an ecstatic 'Rastafari!'

Ras Tafari applies to all manner of creation. If thunder rolls or lightning flashes, Rastas usually respond with a 'Rastafari!' Since Ras Tafari/Selassie I is God, he inhabits the entire universe. Thus rainfall, the rainbow, flood, earthquake, etc. are seen as manifestations of Ras Tafari/Selassie I. The Rastas have an aversion to war and would state that Jah (God, probably derived from the Jewish Yah or Yahweh) has his own methods of dealing with wicked men or overpopulation. A famine could wipe out thousands, so could floods or earthquakes, thus war is useless. Rastas are against any form of contraception, for similar reasons. Belief in Ras Tafari precludes belief in any traditional superstition, for example, in ghosts. The Rastas hold that the 'wages of sin is death, the gift of God is eternal life', thus he who dies is only rewarded with what he sowed in life. The fear of ghosts is therefore absent from their minds. Since God is the living man, Ras Tafari/Selassie I, there is an absence of belief in reaching heaven after death. This goes along with their belief that the body-structure of man is his temple, and the lack of emphasis on attending a church is no testimony to lack of faith. Since the incubatory period of Rastafarianism in the 1930s–1940s, there has been an absence of leaders. This lack of emphasis on leadership suggests a highly democratic process of interrelationships. Every Rasta can project his opinion without being ridiculed. Lack of cohesive organizational structure on a national scale is in the main responsible for the absence of the impetus to repatriate. Thus repatriation, though still attested to verbally and theoretically, has not been meaningfully undertaken.

In 1960 the University of the West Indies (previously called the University College of the West Indies, and referred to as UC as in *you see* for short, was popularly referred to by Rastas as *you blind* – the meaning is obvious) was approached by a number of Rasta brethren who requested them to undertake a study of their movement and submit it to the government. A team consisting of M.G. Smith, Rex Nettleford and Roy Augier, devoted two weeks to it and came up with a significant report. They made recommendations, and subsequently, a team of representative Rastas along with government officials undertook a feasibility tour of Afrika, particularly of Ethiopia and Nigeria. This was an unofficial visit and was followed two years later by an official governmental team.

The latter team discovered that the Afrikan countries with the exception of Ethiopia were primarily interested in skilled and professional people. Jamaica received its independence in 1962, the government changed, and the report's findings were shelved.[46] In 1965 three Rasta brethren made their own visit to Ethiopia and other parts of Afrika over a fifteen-month period. They returned to Jamaica, made recommendations to the government, were ignored, and so registered their organization, the Rasta Brethren Repatriation Association, which eventually accommodated itself to the social realities of Jamaica by entering a variety of self-help and co-operative ventures which were by and large successful.[47] This is also understood to be the current direction being pursued by Rastas: 'Liberation before Repatriation', which indicates a radical change in their material condition before repatriation can be seriously considered.

The Rastafarian concept of Israel as the homeland of blacks is primarily a traditional response to the condition of slavery. Emphasis was placed on the Bible as the only available source of reading, and the Rastas identified the so-called slavish condition of the Jews with their own real physical slavery. Thus Israel is transmitted through successive waves of religion, whether in the form of Baptists, Revivalists, Catholics, or Rastafarians. Most Rasta converts were already highly religious people, already identifying with biblical figures. The free churches have a number of songs where Pharoah is portrayed as a wicked, oppressive man, and Moses as the Saviour/Redeemer, come to liberate the oppressed Jews/blacks. However, there is no document to substantiate the Old Testament assertion that the Jews were slaves in Ancient Egypt. The Ancient Egyptians were fanatical in documenting their history in detail, yet there is not one reference to Jewish subjugation.

The majority of writers on this subject have agreed that the only document concerning a foreign people in Ancient Egypt was that pertaining to the Hycsos (or Hyksos), *hyc* meaning king and *sos*, shepherd. The Bible portrays the Jews as a race of shepherds. The Bible also relates the story of Joseph's abandonment by his brothers and his being taken to Egypt where he eventually enjoys the King's favours. Palestine underwent a famine and Joseph's people, the Jews, come into Egypt seeking assistance. The King gives Joseph permission for his people to come and partake of the food and shelter of the Egyptians. Joseph's father dies at the end of Genesis, and Exodus begins to rationalize the Jews' captivity by stating that a new king arose who did not know Joseph's people. Some scholars give the stay of the Hycsos in Egypt as 510 years, others 430 years. This corresponds with the so-called captivity of the Jews in Egypt. The Hycsos invaded Egypt and ruled the country for the same length of time that the Jews were supposed to be captured and worked as slaves there. Budge, who was a former Keeper of the Department of Egyptian and Assyrian antiquities in the British Museum, states that: 'The shepherd kings worshipped a god called *Sut* or *Sutech*, who was to the Egyptians a veritable abomination. . . . They adopted the manners and customs and writing of the Egyptians.'[48] Thus when they were expelled, they could worship a monotheistic God as they learnt to do in Egypt. Anta Diop states that the Egyptians referred to the Hycsos as 'accursed', 'pillagers', 'pestiferous' and 'thieves'.[49] When they finally left Egypt they settled in Jerusalem.[50] It is also claimed that the Jews and the Hycsos were separate peoples, and that it was during the reign of the Hycsos over

Egypt that the Jews were in captivity, and it was a Hycsos king who dreamed the dreams that Joseph deciphered.

At the inception of Rastafari in the late 1920s, there was already doctrinal credo, but no music. As previously mentioned, Rastafari evolved through the association with the Bible and the emphasis on Afrika, and its early members were themselves religious people. But if Afrika were being projected, it would have been contradictory to project the music of the (white) Christian church. When L. Howell began his early travelling across Jamaica he made his references to Rastafari, then proceeded to sing from the Sankey and Moody Hymnals.[51] But this did not express the Rastas' desire to project Afrika. The words to church songs were altered to project Rastafari and they were accompanied by handclaps. In the 1930s, the only form of Afrikan musical expression was that of the Burru people who came from Clarendon and settled in the slums of Kingston.[52] It is also said that 'Burru' denoted an Afrikan dance that was celebrated in Ghana around Christmas.[53] They also had a custom of welcoming discharged prisoners back to their communities by the beating of drums and festive dancing. Rastafari brethren would attend these meetings, and listen and learn from the Burru people.[54] The Burrus, on the other hand, had no theological Afrikan philosophy, and by the end of the 1930s, the two groups merged, each imparting an important learning to the other.

The Burru instruments consisted of the bass drum, the fundeh and the repeater, and a number of percussive instruments were also included – saxa or bottle saxes, bamboo scraper, shakkas and rhumba box. The principle of the saxa or bottle saxes, says Reckord, 'is reminiscent of the paper and comb. . . . Saran wrap or cellophane is stretched over the mouth of the bottle. The actual notes are produced with the voice. The bottle is held firmly with both hands, allowing the last three fingers of each hand to extend beyond the broken edge. These are then used to produce legato and vibrato.'[55] An additional influence was that of Kumina music, an off-shoot of the Afrikan tradition. Though Kumina people were avoided because of their belief in spirits and contact with the dead, they were nevertheless respected because they projected an Afrikan tradition. Kumina projected two drums as opposed to the Burrus' three. These were the

Kbandu and *Playing Cast* which were augmented by percussive instruments like grater, shakkas, and/or claves (sticks). An additional rhythm could also be set up by the beating of sticks against the open end of the drums; this was called *Katta*. Reckord goes on to state that 'Kumina drums are fairly large, deep single-headed drums which are played with hands and heel while the player sits astride the drums.'[56] Reckord also states that the function of the *Kbandu* is similar to the bass drum of the Burru and the fundeh of the Rasta. In early Burru music the bass drum plays the rhythm, the repeater plays the melody, and the fundeh syncopates.[57] In Rasta music, however, the fundeh plays the rhythm; the bass drum holds a similar pattern, but varies in pitch and tone; and the repeater leads or improvises.[58] The time signature of Rasta music is quite straightforward, with the notable exception of the repeater. The rhythm increases or decreases in pace, the metre remains consistent, but it is the improvisatory rhythms, speaking the ancestral language, through which the repeater manifests its difficulty.

The late Count Ossie was one of the early pioneers of Rasta music. He witnessed its birth through the intermingling of Rastas and Burru people, and was one of the early ones to observe closely the Burrus' ability to play drums. The Dungle was where the majority of the Burru lived, and a number of brethren would gather there to reason and make music. Later the sessions moved to Salt Lane with the master Burru drummer, Brother Job, whose main drum was the repeater. Ossie would attempt to play the fundeh, holding the rhythm line to Brother Job's highly stylish and improvised playing. According to Ossie he conducted rhythm experiments in his yard (place of abode) in relation to the patterns and rhythms learnt from Burru drummers. In its evolved state it received wider recognition among Rasta brethren who understood it as an expression of Afrikan culture. Ossie's main locale was on Slip Dock Road where he lived, but other Rasta camps were located at Back-O-Wall/Dungle, and Brother Issie Boat's camp was up Wareika Hills.[59] The rapid mobility of Rasta brethren, because of work and possible conflicts with the police, meant that this new contribution to Rasta development was diffused. Ossie was joined by Rico Rodriquez, Gaynair (saxophonist), Philmore Alvaranga, and the Rasta preacher – Brother Love – conducted the readings from the Bible.[60]

Count Ossie made recording history in the late 1950s by providing the rhythm section for the Folkes Brothers' big hit, 'Oh, Carolina'. Periodically, he was sought out by producers to provide the rhythm section for their productions. In 1951 Ossie's yard was torn apart by Hurricane Charlie, so he moved to Adasta Road until 1974, when, in collaboration with a variety of people, the Count Ossie Community and Cultural Centre was opened. It became the central focus for Rasta cultural activities and pursuits: music and dance were the primary subjects taught. A variety of people taught there, like Cedric Brooks (Im), Tommy McCook, and one of the pioneering members of the Rastafarian independent mission that surveyed Afrika, Samuel Clayton, who specializes in history and delivering the long characteristic reasonings on record and at live performances. In the late 1960s, the Mystic Revelation of Rastafari was formed, and later recorded their first album, *Grounation*, which consisted of a blend of Rasta/Reggae rhythms with Jazz overtones, augmented by Sam Clayton's vocal deliveries. It was not recorded as a commercial product but rather as a projection of the cultural modes of Rastafari. The Mystics constituted two groups, Count Ossie's several drummers and Cedric Brooks's musical ensemble which consisted of double bass, guitar, a number of brass instruments, and trap drums. The visual impact they created was effective and they became the central focus for the national projection of Rasta music. When Ossie died, Cedric Brooks continued his work.

Count Ossie's musical tradition has also been expanded by Ras Michael and the Sons of Negus who have produced two of the finest and most startling blends of Rasta music and modern Afro-American fusions. The first album, *Dada wa* (said to mean 'peace and love' in Amharic), was produced by Lloyd Charmers, a modernist producer who is best known for his hits with Ken Boothe. The album utilized the Jazz/Funk expressionism of a Miles Davis, for example, to blend Rasta rhythms and vocal ideas. This album also sparked off a great many imitations, both among the DJ/Dub movement and singers. Psalm 133, which begins with 'Behold, how good and how pleasant it is for brethren to dwell together in unity', was one of the themes, aided by improvisations. 'Seventy-two Nations' (the United Nations) created the most recorded spin-offs of the album, because it projected Jah Rastafari as the supreme God to whom the seventy-two nations pay tribute. The Psalms are used by a great number of popular artists to project a theme. Psalm 52 was used by Bob Marley to create 'Small Axe'. The Psalm opened with: 'Why boastest thou thyself in mischief, O mighty man? The goodness of God endureth continually.' Marley changed or scrambled the words around to say, 'Why boastest thy self, O evil man? The goodness of Jah endureth for Iver.' The song was also strenthened by the inclusion of bits of Ecclesiastes 10: 'He that diggeth a pit shall fall into it.' Marley's slightly changed lyrics say, 'And whosoever diggeth a pit shall fall in it.' On his 'Night Shift' he uses Psalm 121 as the opening line, 'The sun shall not smite thee by day, nor the moon by night.' Peter Tosh uses the whole of Psalm 23 in a slightly disguised form for his 'Jah Guide'. Psalm 137 was the basis for the Melodians' early hit, 'Rivers of Babylon' (which later sold 2 million copies in Britain alone for Boney M). Clearly the Bible is a source for all Rasta or Rasta-influenced recording artists. Life parallels can be drawn from it and contemporary experience issues directly from its sayings. The Bible is to the Rasta the Book of Life, and is regularly consulted for direction in personal life.

As I have already shown, Rastafari is not a reclining, submissive theology as many people think. The Rastas do believe in peace and love, but not to the detriment of man. They do not turn the other cheek. Most Rastas are or can be extremely aggressive and crude in their self-expression, not caring whether the truth hurts or not. In Jamaica it is not uncommon for a Rasta to remove his tam or head-covering if a passer-by continuously stares at him. This would be done with utmost aggression and drama, to demonstrate that he is proud to be a Rasta and is not afraid of anyone. This aggression has taken a multi-faceted form; but it has also led to revolutionary activity, employing the use of guns against the Jamaican government. Some Rastas may proclaim that it is not representative of their beliefs, but as already shown, the practice of a moral code within the biblical context can assume different forms. Thus an eye for an eye is not an alien philosophy to Rastas, just as peace and love is an intrinsic aspect of their credo. Jamaican Rastafari has contributed immensely to the personal salvation of the oppressed and not so oppressed nationals. It has transcended racial boundaries to include those who are committed to the establishment of truth. What is significant is that despite only partial acceptance and some middle-class following, it still retains its basic tenets and roots.

3 The Birth and Development of Jamaican Music

1

Stanley Motta, a Jamaican businessman, was one of the first people to record and produce records by local artists primarily for local consumption. The music was of the Mento/Calypso variety (the former a combination of Calypso fused with Latin-American musical influences that became identified with Jamaican music) which was sold on 78 r.p.m. For some time this music, though never achieving official recognition, was *the* music of Jamaica, i.e. a music that could be differentiated from Calypso and could therefore be termed Jamaican. The 1950s, then, saw a slight blossoming of Calypsonians and Mento people. However, there were two other musical outlets: 1. The religious expression of Rastafari accompanied by the lately adopted Burru drumming along with other musical instrumentation (this was confined to the slums).[1] And 2. the music that was broadcast via short-wave radio, including radio stations of the American South, primarily from the Florida belt. One of the most popular of these stations was WINZ which was broadcast direct from Miami. So, as well as the Afro-American rhythm and blues, Jamaicans were also listening to people like Frank Sinatra, Bing Crosby, Sammy Davis Jr, Dean Martin, and many others. These balladists, along with Nat King Cole, became the first models for Jamaican crooners.

In the late 1950s R&B took even greater hold of the Jamaican people, thanks to the influence of the balladists. The increasing popularity of R&B was reflected in the escalating importance of the sound system operators, the local DJs who had their own locally manufactured mobile discos and played at dances, socials and parties. The sound system seemed to have been introduced into Jamaica in the late 1940s, after the war, when migration from Jamaica to the U.S. (either for short spells or permanently) escalated. Some proportion of these migrants went on short contracts (from at least six months to a year or more) to work cane-cutting on the plantations of the American South. These were the people who would become the first to introduce R&B music into the country, thereby ultimately helping to create trade and liberation out of grinding poverty. Among the early cane-cutters was Clement Dodd, later to be known as Coxsone or Downbeat.[2] After Dodd's first trip he bought the equipment for his sound system. He returned on several other occasions bringing loads of records and materials to extend the range of his 'sound'.

Some of the popular 'sounds' of the early 1950s were Duke Reid, Nick's, Tom's (the Great Sebastian), Downbeat or Coxsone (Clement Dodd), Count P or Count Boysie, Count John, and others lesser known, who played primarily in the slums of western Kingston, in places like Carnival, Pioneer (in Jones Town), and Forrester's Hall (on North Street).[3] There were other clubs, but they catered for a different type of music. One method of purchasing records was from returning cane-cutters and American seamen were also constant suppliers. They would exchange records for money or rum.[4] 'Sounds' carried their individual following wherever they played and when rivals played at the same dances, fights would sometimes ensue. Rivalry was particularly connected with the playing of exclusive records which one's opponent could not obtain. When an exclusive record played, the 'sound' was assured not only of greater appreciation by fans, but by an increased number of followers. The slightest demonstration of partisan feelings could unleash violent eruptions. 'Sounds' guarded their records zealously by scratching off the title and artist on the records. Each 'sound' had a small group of employees who would go to rival dances and listen to what was played. If they thought the artist on a new record sounded familiar, they would inform their bosses and immediate attempts were made to obtain a copy. Prince Buster related an incident which highlights this occurrence:

> *Later For Gator* was quite an interesting record because that was what kept Coxsone in the top bracket for nine years, because

> people couldn't get the record. They used to call it 'Coxsone Hop'. And Duke Reid made about fifteen trips abroad to try to find the record and couldn't get it. . . . Well, I wouldn't tell you who told him the name, but they had the money to travel, so they went and bought the record. . . . Duke [Reid] told Coxsone he had got it (the record). Coxsone wouldn't believe him. In the morning Duke saw me and said, 'Later for Gator', I went and told Coxsone that Duke have the tune and him say, 'No!' Duke play out that night and we went to listen to him, and when Duke put on the tune, Coxsone pass out.[5]

Duke Reid was always respected because of his ruthlessness and toughness which, it is claimed, resulted from his years of contact with the black underworld in New York. Rivals would send their henchmen to disrupt another's dance, to create violence, and to spy on any development on the 'sound'. At a later date Coxsone developed a reputation for toughness, but that claim was dismissed by Prince Buster. Buster claims that a fight broke out at a dance where Coxsone was playing, Lee 'Scratch' Perry (who was employed by Coxsone) got knocked out, the violence became heavy, and Coxsone and his men ran off and left Perry. Buster claimed (and this was substantiated by others) that he fought off a number of people, picked Perry up and left.[6] Buster's story can be corroborated not only by other eye witnesses, but by the fact that he was a highly rated amateur boxer.

R&B's popularity in Jamaica heightened during the middle and late 1950s; there were performers like Fats Domino, Shirley and Lee, Bill Doggett (who played organ in Louis Jordan's band in 1950[7] and had a huge hit with 'Honky Tonk'), Rosco Gordon (another huge success in Jamaica, and who supplied the platform in America for a number of now successful Afro-American performers like B.B. King, Johnny Ace – also successful in Jamaica – and Bobby Bland, through his early group the Beale Streeters[8]), Chuck Berry, Ernie Freeman, and the greatest and most influential of all, Louis Jourdan. These performers set the standard, style, and musical models for the development, first of Jamaican R&B singers, and second of Ska.

R&B emerged out of traditional Blues (usually stated in the twelve-bar format), a music that emerged as a result of the drift from rural southern America to the urban North. The different urban conditions and new experiences were reflected in the music, giving rise to R&B, and later Soul and Disco. Perhaps the similar rural/urban conditions in Jamaica and America (leaving the plantations/farms to go and live in slums and continued poverty in the city) caused Jamaicans to identify with Afro-American music. Because once the R&B style was temporarily superseded by Rock and Roll, Jamaicans ceased to identify with it, and were forced to form their own version of R&B for local consumption.

For purposes of clarity, I am including a transcription of the bass and piano patterns of a popular R&B hit by Louis Jourdan:

Throughout the evolution of Jamaican music the boogie rhythm contained in the stabbing piano lines has been a constant. It has been stated by several people, including Prince Buster and Theophilius Beckford (a seminal piano player within the Jamaican music scene), that Ska originated through the musical ignorance of the slum dwellers, that because they were not proficient players they played more or less the piano lines delineated above on their guitars. Though this makes sense, it does not seem to be factual. *The limited ability of the slum dweller rendered the piano rhythm within easy reach of his expression.* It was conscious imitation and not left to chance. The added dimensions to this R&B rhythmic foundation came later.

During this R&B boom the local popular artists were people like Laurel Aitken, Owen Grey, Wilfred Jackie Edwards, Jimmy Tucker (he was defined by Alton Ellis as a 'classical singer' and was 'way, way out'), (Joe) Higgs and (Roy) Wilson, Lascal Perkins, Scully (Noel Simms) and Bunny, Alton (Ellis) and Eddy (Perkins), among others. Laurel Aitken specialized in boogie tunes made popular by Louis Jourdan, Wilfred Edwards became popular through his imitation of Nat King Cole, Owen Grey sang mainly ballads, etc. Most of the singers and musicians came through the mill of Vere John's *Opportunity Hour* shows which were held weekly at three main venues: the Ambassador, Palace and Majesty theatres. All three were located in downtown Kingston, within the slum area. Some local clubs where their music could be heard were Silver Slipper, Lins, Johnson's Drive-In, Glass Bucket, Club Parascene, and Magnal House. It was rare that the music was played over local radio, because of the predominance of foreign (American) music. The main outlet was, of course, the sound systems.

The local recording industry was primarily concerned with Calypso/Mento: Lord Tanamo (Joseph Gordon), Lord La Rue, Count Lasher, Lord Fly, and others,[9] while local R&B was primarily recorded for the 'sounds'. Exclusivity, as pointed out earlier, was the reason for this. The sound system operator was cutting records for his 'sound', to maintain his coveted position, and was not concerned about releasing records. An anecdote, which Alton Ellis told me, verifies this. Others told by Jackie Mittoo and Rico Rodriquez also substantiate this assertion. A man approached Coxsone about the potential sale of his acetates to the general public, but Coxsone laughed. The man asked Coxsone to give him an acetate and he would demonstrate what he meant. Coxsone obliged, the man pressed a few hundred and quickly sold them. Coxsone immediately went into the business of selling records. Other independent producers were Duke Reid (who later formed Treasure Isle Records and Studios), Prince Buster, King Edwards, Nation, Chris Blackwell (later to emerge in England as the majority shareholder of Island Records), and a few others.[10] With the exception of Chris Blackwell, all operated sound systems.

The sale of records was based on a unique Jamaican system. First an acetate was cut exclusively for the 'sound', then a nominal number were pressed for special distribution (say fifty to one hundred) and sold at the rate of five to ten pounds each; second it was released more generally on a blank label which would sell for £1; and third it would be released on a label with information. Sales deriving from the latter could reach up to 25,000 copies or more.[11] The famous duo Higgs and Wilson had their first massive hit with 'Manny O', produced and released by Edward Seaga in 1960. Theophilius Beckford received his nickname 'Easy Snappin'' from the title of his gigantic hit of the same name as early as 1959.[12] Prince Buster produced the Folkes Brothers with the Crusaders' tune 'Oh, Carolina' in 1959 to change the face of Jamaican music. Buster approached legendary Rasta percussionist Count Ossie to record for him, but Ossie's response was one of disbelief because of the association of the Rastafarian faith and music in the mind of middle Jamaica. Ossie agreed and Buster booked the one-track studio facilities at Jamaica Broadcasting Company (JBC). Buster stated that because rivalry and competition were so fierce, Duke Reid went in and booked the studio over his head, and he had to be accommodated in a much smaller room, which was made into a temporary studio. Owen Grey played piano, Ronnie Bop on bass drum, Buster on handclaps and imitating horn riffs, and Ossie and his four drummers. The song was cut in two takes with one mike. The engineer was Cecil Watts.[13]

The music was received with jubilation by most people, but there was little or no air play from the radio stations. Trevor Fearon states that:

> It is claimed that RJR's (Radio Jamaica Rediffusion, which went on the air in the 1950s as JBC) playing list could easily have been that of any major city in the North of the United States. In particular, when the Rock and Roll of Bill Haley, Elvis Presley, and others were making their bid for white Americans, RJR was out there in the forefront pushing such music, although locally, the rhythm and blues was still holding fort with the sound systems. . . . It is biased towards the somewhat antiseptic musical tastes of the middle classes.[14]

Graham Dowling, an Australian engineer who worked with the local radio station at the time, also supports Fearon's contention that local music was discriminated against.

> I was working at Federal (Records) at that time, and Ken [Khouri, proprietor of Federal Records] and I and you [Byron Lee] were there and we sat down in the office and called up Ken's friend, Bob Lightbourne, who got on to Wills O. Issacs, and Wills Issacs told the radio stations that if they didn't play at least *pro rata* of foreign music to local music, *pro rata* to sales, they would lose their licence.[15]

Of course, middle and upper Jamaica controlled the cultural fate of Jamaica, if only ephemerally. They defended their inferiority complexes by inundating radio with their American heroes, and looked contemptuously on the 'noise' that was being made by local Jamaicans. Since local (and poor ones at that) Jamaicans possessed no example of 'culture' or 'history' it would be an impossibility to accept that they had anything meaningful to say to them.

Middle Jamaica was ashamed of the new strivings for Jamaican cultural identity and viewed the musical expression with ridicule. Byron Lee, for example, despite his positive retrospective stance (after the music had achieved international acclaim and acceptance) had previously criticized the music as 'buff-buff', because of its drums and bass emphasis. However, Lee was not the only person who saw music, in its early manifestations, as primitive. But it was Lee who later reaped the greatest financial rewards from the music and is today a millionaire. He said: 'Nobody uptown didn't know what the music was about, they couldn't relate to it. It can be said that we [Byron Lee and the Dragonaires] were responsible for moving the music from West Kingston into the upper and middle classes who could afford to buy records and support the music. *Then radio picked up the music and it became the order of the day.*'[16] When Lee 'moved' the music from West Kingston (after spending a week or two playing with some of its creators) he *expressed his version and interpretation of the music.* Hence his inability then and now to reflect the living cultural ingredients of the music. In addition, it is important to understand that the Jamaican singers Lee promoted were always fairly conventional – forever outside the roots elements, no matter where the singer came from. The music, in spite of the poverty of the masses, had always been avidly supported. Radio then began picking up the music selectively. Beyond that, once it became the property of the money-men, it received wider support (but still only minimally).

The recording facilities were undoubtedly limited. RJR provided a great deal of activity, beyond its function as a radio station, for producers and musicians. As a one-track studio it had one mike, and a band consisting of eight pieces plus a singer would be recorded in one straight take. When the Jamaica Broadcasting Corporation came into being it contained two-track recording facilities. Recording was just as hazardous, but the sound was reproduced better because two microphones were used to pick up the variety of instruments. Outside the radio stations a lot of activity centred on Federal Records (an outgrowth of the Pioneer Company which was set up by Ken Khouri in September 1954, specializing in 78 r.p.m. records, and later, albums; its capital outlay was £3,000)[17] which also had two-track facilities. Graham Dowling states that: 'Federal was the key to the whole record industry, everything revolved around there.'[18] All the producers used to cut records at Ken Khouri's studios: Duke Reid, Nation, Chris Blackwell (the son of the wealthy Blackwell of Crosse & Blackwell fame; also, one time ADC to the Governor General of Jamaica), Clement Dodd, and even Edward Seaga, the present leader of Jamaica's opposition Labour Party. It is stated that Khouri used to wear a bib around his neck into which he placed all the money he collected from producers.

> 'Everybody used to have to go past his desk', stated Dowling. Producers and their associates would be at the studio from seven in the morning waiting for Dowling, the engineer, to arrive at eight. 'Duke Reid never had any money, so he used to send Cuttings down with four pounds, ten (shillings), which would give him enough for three demo discs . . . walk past Ken Khouri who would yell, "What you got there, Cuttings?" So Cuttings would come along – he's got five. "Five, that's seven pounds, ten." "Boy, sar, I only have four pound, ten." "Well, give me the four pounds, ten. I'll keep two."'[19] Cuttings would go away on his scooter, sell the acetates, and return for the rest.

The actual innovators of Jamaican music were the very people who came from the depressed sector of the population that middle Jamaica shunned. A great number of these early pioneers came through Alpha Boys' Catholic School (it still exists today), which seemed to run both as a sort of reform school and a school where parents could place wayward children. It is located in West Kingston, in the heart of the ghetto. Musicians who passed through Alpha were, to name only a few: Rico Rodriquez, Herman Marquiz, Tommy McCook, Leroy 'Horsemouth' Wallace, Eric 'Fish' Clarke, Bobby Ellis, Vincent Gordon, Don Drummond, Rupert Anderson, Joe Harriot. It can be said that 99 per cent of the horn men who came from Jamaica and became famous overseas or at home, served their apprenticeship at Alpha.

Most of these musicians went to Alpha quite young. Rico

Rodriquez, for example, went to Alpha before he was 10 years old. Before learning an instrument the boys had chores to perform around the school yard, like watering the garden, cleaning the toilets, scrubbing the floors, etc. There were two sections to the school band: one junior, the other senior. But before picking up an instrument, the students learnt theory. 'The first thing you learnt at Alpha', states Rico Rodriquez, 'was the rudiments of music, lines and spaces and scales. Theory was a must. You were asked questions on a blackboard and you gave your answers verbally. You didn't start to play like that, you had to know what you were doing.'[20] The penalty for not paying attention was a beating, a clout round the head, or a slap on the back. This strictness continued even when one became a member of the senior band.

Students were taught European classics and were discouraged from playing tunes they might have heard on the radio. Compositions like 'Happy Wanderer', 'Sleeping Beauty', 'Colonel Bogie', 'Life on the Ocean', were also taught to young students. There were prefects or monitors in addition to teachers who supervised what you learnt and how you conducted yourself. Members of the senior band, for example Don Drummond, would be persuaded to stay at school in order to teach the younger students. As Rico Rodriquez says: 'Drummond was a quiet person, but a very strict teacher. We were friends, but when it came to teaching, it was very serious. If Drummond didn't teach me so well, and the bandmaster came along to check on you, and you were not that good, that reflected on the teacher. So the standard had to be there at all times.'[21]

Members of the senior band played at garden parties and other functions, and the money they raised was ploughed back into the school. Some members of the senior band were also keenly involved with the challenge of playing jazz. Musicians like Joe Harriot (who later emigrated to England where he became one of the most outstanding jazz musicians in the country, and also significantly increased real interest in the music here by pioneering the Indo-Jazz fusions sessions with John Mayer), Little Jesus, Roy Harper, Don Drummond, and Wilton 'Bogey' Gaynair were some of the outstanding Jazz musicians in the early 1950s in Jamaica. The primary influences were people like Duke Ellington and Stan Kenton, the big band models. At that time, also, Radio

Jamaica had a one-hour Jazz show called *Jazz Hour* which featured the leading Afro-American musicians of the time: Miles Davis, Thelonius Monk, Art Blakey, Max Roach, etc. These people provided the stimulus for the young Jamaicans.

Because the Afro-Americans provided the models to build on, most of the local musicians converged on the metropolis to set the musical standard. Hardly any attention was paid to the rumblings within the slums towards a quest for religious affirmation and cultural identity. The music, as I have indicated earlier, was a fusion of Rasta drumming (borrowed from the Burru people who moved to the Kingston slums from the country), singing, recitation of poetry, reading of the Psalms, and the Bible. A different music that was popular mainly on the north coast (Montego Bay, Negril) was played at the big hotels and night clubs that catered almost totally for tourists. This was Latin music as exemplified by Pres Prado and the Trinidadian Edmundo Ross. On leaving Alpha a lot of the musicians joined these bands, but experienced enormous frustration playing this liquefied, supper-lounge type of music. For example, Rico Rodriquez recalls the nature of Don Drummond's frustration:

> Drummond wasn't doing any recording to feel frustration. He used to practise most of the time. He had a folio of about 300 selections that he and I used to work on together. Drummond was the best trombonist in Jamaica, and used to play in clubs with people like Eric Deans, Roy Coburne, and Bragonnaire. He used to play at the Glass Bucket, Silver Slipper, Union Hall and tear the place up. As far as I am concerned he was just creating, but he wasn't going into any studios. The frustration that he probably had was from playing in bands before.[22]

With the possible exception of Rico Rodriquez, most of the musicians were either working the clubs, out of the country, or simply rehearsing their music at home. This was before 1960. Rodriquez was already doing sessions for producers Clement Dodd and Duke Reid, as well as for Prince Buster. He provided the chorus solos on a number of tunes by artists like Laurel Aitken ('Judgement Day'), Derek Harriot and the Downbeats ('Over the River') and Theophilius Beckford (the seminal 'Easy Snappin" that Jackie Mittoo characterized as indicating the transition into Ska, away from Boogie Woogie/R&B). Sessions had no fixed price – a musician could get a ten-shilling piece for his work unless he complained. If he complained too loudly, the producer would drop him almost instantly. And when he was dropped he would resort to the religious/Rasta forms of musical expression and live a carefree life, catching fish from the sea to eat and 'grounding' among brethren. This was the sufferer's music, emitted from the soul which could not conform to official society. Because they were Rastafarians, or in close contact with Rastafarians, they were always kept under surveillance by the police. Count Ossie who moved to Rockforth, later moved to Wareika Hills around 1960. Rico Rodriquez and a few brethren also made Wareika Hills their base, but they were still molested by the police. Rodriquez says: 'Our music caters for the sufferers. Because is suffering you come from, more than the gay life, playing in hotels and all that, sentimental music. Because the music that come out of you is through suffering that it come out and what you feel you play. So the man who play our kind of music look upon it as a higher form of development.'[23]

The third component of the music was that which was termed 'rags' or *jamma* music. *Jamma* has already been defined as songs originating out of the Afrikan tradition and maintained through slavery. In the modern, twentieth-century sense, the connotation has remained unchanged: to sing *jamma* songs is to connect oneself with the lower classes, to recall contemporary pop songs that have no connection with 'culture'. The rags or *jamma* songs that some people know today are very similar in rhythm and tempo to the early Boogie Woogie tunes. An example is 'Rag Mop' in which words are spelt in rhythmic cadence. Similar to this is the counting of numbers in Rock and Roll music: '1, 2, 3, 4, 5, 6, 7, 8, 9, 10, 11, 12, we gonna rock, we gonna rock, we gonna rock around the clock tonight.' At the age of 13, Jackie Mittoo formed a band called: Jackie Mittoo's Ragtime Band, and they played rags/*jamma* as well as straight R&B.

Not only in Kingston, but also in other parts of Jamaica, young people were imitating and originating. Val Davidson who lived in Brown's Town in the country, was a Nat King Cole imitator. Jackie Mittoo, still a school-boy, living in York Castle, was already reproducing on the piano what he had heard on the radio. By the time he reached Kingston, at 13, he was able to support a number of well-established acts.

The Rivals was formed by Ansel Smart, a man who had money to buy an organ and bass guitar, but could not play either. Vivian Smith, who knew all the leading singers in Kingston, people like Jimmy Cliff, Derek Harriot, Wilfred Edwards, and Derek Morgan, was one of the singers along with Tony DaCosta who formerly sang with Jimmy Haughton as the Deccas. Dobbie Dobson, who later established himself as a balladist, and as producer of the Meditations, was one of the lead singers with the Sheiks, a group that Jackie Mittoo joined after the short-lived Rivals. Norma Frazer, Ken Lazarous (leader), and Lloyd Wates were also singing. Lester Stirling's brother Roy was playing sax, Hedley Bennett who later became one of Lee Perry's studio musicians, was also playing sax (tenor). Tony Blessed was the keyboard player (who left soon after for New York) and Bobby Gaynair was also in the band. Neither the Rivals nor the Sheiks became big-name groups. They were all playing light music, but most of the bands' members later established themselves as important musicians and singers. Norma Frazer became popular especially during the Rock Steady era on Clement Dodd's Coxsone and Studio One labels. These bands filled in time and gave their members an opportunity to work out their ideas and develop their talents.[24]

By 1962 Rico Rodriquez, frustrated by molestation from the police, left the country for England. He held two farewell dances, one of which was broken up by the police, the other a success. Laurel Aitken had already left, so had Wilfred Edwards, Joe Harriot, Broker Utta, a conga player, and a few others. The musicians who were recording after 1962 for a variety of producers were: Tommy McCook, Don Drummond, Jah Gerry (guitar), Arkland Parks (Drumbago, drums), Theophilius Beckford, Jackie Mittoo, Gladstone Anderson (piano), 'Dizzy' Johnny More (trumpet), Lester Stirling (alto sax), Roland Alphonso (tenor sax), Lloyd Knibbs (drums), 'Blues' (name not known) and Lloyd Brevette (basses), and Mr Campbell, a man who Jackie Mittoo says could play the Ska rhythm on his horn in any key and pattern imaginable; there were also Ernest Ranglin (guitar) and Cluett Johnson (bass). These musicians formed the nucleus of all the recording sessions for all the performing artists in Jamaica before and during the Ska era. All the sounds men who exhibited exclusivity for their scratched-out

Rico Rodriquez, a pioneer session musician in the Kingston context who played R&B, roots music and Ska when he came to London. Today, because of the current popularity of revamped Ska, he tours with the Specials and still records under his own name.
(*Photo: Vernon St. Hilaire.*)

Misty, based in Southall, Middlesex. (*Photo: Vernon St.Hilaire.*)

A group including Prince Buster (middle), Georgie Fame (second fro right), and Siggy Jackson (second from left). (*Photo: Thomas Watso*

records were using exactly the same musicians. All the wars that were fought, were fought over the same musicians playing for rival producers.[25]

As R&B became more difficult to obtain from the United States in the early 1960s because of the Rock and Roll phenomenon there, producers and musicians attempted to create their own version of R&B, and simultaneously to express the other aspects of their musical environment – Calypso/Mento, Jazz – either to forge new ground or establish Jamaican musical identity. Jamaica had 'received' its independence in 1962, and the Jamaican personality was undergoing radical changes: a battle was raging in the political arena for control of the country and to consolidate power. All this probably contributed to the rapid transformation of R&B into a peculiarly *Jamaican* music. The word Ska seems to have been derived from the rhythmic effect of the guitar. It has been said by some people that Ska was the root word, but other sources, particularly Jackie Mittoo, insist that the word Ska did not come from the slum dwellers or the musicians. The operative word was 'Staya Staya'. People would say they wanted to play 'some Staya Staya', which had the same guitar emphasis as Ska. But Jackie Mittoo, affecting the airs of middle Jamaica, insists that it was Byron Lee who introduced the word.

As demonstrated above, the stabbing piano rhythm was the basis of Boogie Woogie/R&B, and became the predominant distinguishing feature in Staya/Ska. Early Staya/Ska, like R&B and most popular music, had the accent placed on the first and third beats, but later versions of this indigenized music shifted the accents. But for now we should dwell a little on Ska. Below are the bass and piano patterns of a famous Prince Buster tune, 'Blackhead Chinee Man'.

In both the Louis Jourdan and Prince Buster illustrations the piano and bass patterns are similar, yet the Prince Buster version was already manifesting a specifically Ska proclivity.

What was changing in the music was the drumming accompaniment. Though both illustrations expressed the same 4/4 timing, the drumming emphasis was beginning to alter the character of the music. This subtle aberration in the music was responsible for the birth of Ska.

It was during 1963 that the Skatalites, Jamaica's most renowned instrumental band, was formed. As previously stated, the leading musicians in Jamaica were recording for a variety of producers, and recording was confined to solo artists (in the main) with a few groups. Lord Tanamo used to organize sessions for a couple of producers and he had certain musicians whom he worked with. Mr Tuari, the man who owned the Regal theatre, hired Lord Tanamo as the contract man for a session. The yet unnamed Skatalites would usually hang out in Rockforth, and they were assembled there talking when Tommy McCook asked: 'Why don't we get this band together?' Lord Tanamo suggested that the name of the group should be Satellite because of the Russian launching of a satellite into space. Tommy responded by saying; 'No, let's call it the Skatalites!' The name was obvious and appropriate.[26]

The Skatalites consisted of the cream of the nation's musicians; most of them had come through Alpha and had also gained tremendous reputations as serious Jazz musicians. When as individuals they played in a variety of leading bands, the audiences were primarily middle class because the population was emotionally involved with R&B. But when this set of musicians started playing together it sparked off a curiosity and an awareness among the middle classes. Why were these musicians, who were so gifted, playing this type of music? On Sundays the Skatalites were invited to play at Bournemouth Gardens, uptown Kingston, which was an official governmental spot for garden parties and music. At this location all the people in the middle- and upper-income bracket came out to hear their leading instrumentalists. The band consisted of Tommy McCook, Roland Alphonso (tenor saxes), Lester Stirling (alto sax), Don Drummond (trombone), 'Dizzy' Johnny Moore (trumpet), Jah Gerry (guitar), Lloyd Brevette (bass), Lloyd Knibbs (drums), Lord Tanamo and Tony DaCosta, formerly of the Sheiks (vocals). The audience was in the main receptive, even enthusiastic, and for the first time they were aware of the contradiction between the propaganda they had heard about ganja smokers and these musicians. The young ladies were now mixing with the very people their parents had warned them against. The Skatalites, on a purely musical level, were responsible for bringing together Jamaicans of disparate backgrounds, just as Bob Marley was responsible, years later, for creating a type of music that young middle- and upper-class youth could identify with.

The first place where the band played was the Hi-Hat, an old warehouse converted into a club. It was a totally acoustic band. While most other bands were picking up the organ, the Skatalites stuck to the piano and the acoustic bass. The financial situation of the Skatalites was reflected in their necessity to manufacture some of their equipment locally. A Mr Rogers made Lloyd Brevette's bass and Jah Gerry's amplifier. Byron Lee, who originally had his bass bin built by the local Bobby Arton, later imported his materials from the United States. The band's main source of work was through Clement Dodd (even though he did not pay well), but they also recorded for Duke Reid and Phillip Yap's Top Deck Records. When the band played out, they would play from music sheets and charts, or the various instrumentalists' parts would be written out. There was a feeling of comprehensiveness and order within the Skatalites, in spite of the personal jealousies and rivalries that went on. It was said that Tommy McCook and Roland Alphonso did not get on. This was put down to Clement Dodd's nepotism. He made a personal friend of Roland Alphonso and played him off against the group. The Skatalites disbanded after only two years, in late 1965.

The break-up of the Skatalites was caused not only by Dodd, but by financial difficulties and personal problems. Sometimes a member of the band would not turn up on the night of a gig. Brevette got into trouble on several occasions and did not turn up for a gig. Jackie Opel, the Trinidadian singer who became famous in Jamaica through singing R&B, replaced him on bass. Sometimes a horn man wouldn't show up, sometimes the drummer. Members never earned sufficient money to support both themselves and their families in a civilized manner. Don Drummond had a mental problem and would sometimes be admitted to the sanitorium where he would spend three to six weeks before returning. Each time he returned he would smile more and more. His problems could never be fully expressed verbally. In 1969 he stabbed and killed his girl-friend Margarita, with a knife he usually kept in his back pocket for peeling oranges or cutting cane stalk. He gave himself up to the police, and later committed suicide. Brevette also had a problem – heavy bouts of drinking.

Dodd felt the band was losing prestige and inveigled Roland Alphonso and Jackie Mittoo to leave. This caused the final collapse of the band. Soul Brothers, headed by Alphonso, came into existence almost immediately. Jackie Mittoo became the resident producer/arranger for all of Dodd's artists at his studio from the beginning of 1966 until he left the country in late 1968. From 1963 Bob Marley became special adviser to Clement Dodd. He had a room at the back of the studio stacked with imported records from which he would choose a particular tune for a singer. He would also recommend to Dodd those he felt were worthy of being recorded. Dodd always kept ahead of the trends because he surrounded himself with and gave responsibility to, the nation's best musical artists.

Thematically R&B was preoccupied with love. Sometimes themes would deal with gaol break-outs, bad treatment by society, etc. But the main thrust of the music was love. This theme was similarly reflected in the Jamaican versions. The emotional framework and reference – being foreign – would have made impossible the rendering of other types of personal or collective experiences with regard to Jamaican society. However, once the musicians had found the *forms* for their own expression, their world-view came into sharper conflict with the other society. Thus, form and language were prerequisites for the articulation of a particular world-view that could not have found compatibility in the 'straight English' of the R&B idiom.

I have already stated that middle Jamaica viewed the music with consternation. I should also add that this was precipitated by the thematic preoccupations of the singer/musician. For once the articulation of the oppressive world and environment of the masses came into focus, middle Jamaica felt threatened and apprehensive. The *status quo* was being vigorously questioned. Ska's formation unleashed an assertive and positive contribution to the society by the challenges it offered to the 'new' and independent Jamaica. Of course, the music was open to exploitation or development, depending on what mirror one is looking into or through what window the world opens on. From one perspective, it might be legitimizing and bringing respectability to the despised music. Certainly from the perspective of the urban poor, exploitation was their experience. And I have previously stated that legitimacy was given to a version of the music by advantageous elements. Though this version may have been legitimized and brought financial rewards for that class of imitators, the condition of the creators remained almost the same.

The singer, like the musician, was paid a one-off fee of between £10 and £20. The record could then be manufactured and distributed without a penny being paid to the singer. Whether the record made money or not, the artist was not presented with a statement. What facilitated this exploitation was the fact that most of the new breed of singers were teenagers and still at school, and were more concerned about the fame and sex-attraction than money.

Producers, of course, had an entirely different view of the matter:

1. That the artists themselves prefer an arrangement whereby they are paid up front as a one-off deal.[27]

2. That the first record was usually a hit (money was made and royalties paid out), and the follow-up a failure. In such a case, because the first record now ceases to sell and the second never did, no royalties are forthcoming, thus aggravation and the suspicion of foul play set in.[28]

3. That the artists get an advance, and in addition, make the weekly rounds to the office (before or after the record is released, but well before royalties are due) and issue a variety of complaints about their families' condition. When the statement does come, showing number of records sold, against various advances, depression and threats are expressed.[29]

It is more than probable that all these situations are factual, but it is doubtful whether they are consistently reflective of reality. Clement Dodd, who seems to be singled out as an example of the exploitative producer, is said to have slapped down Joe Higgs for making 'unreasonable' demands for money, and that a number of artists have been punched by him. Bob Marley has recently issued a writ against Dodd for the release of his double album, *The Birth of a Legend*, which included the works of the old Wailers. Two albums were licensed by Dodd to American companies, Buddah and United Artists, of Jackie Mittoo's early work without permission or advances and/or royalties being paid to Mittoo. It is also said that Dodd had a technique (and it is true of other producers) of paying his artists in small notes that cumulatively look like a lot of money, but on close inspection amount to peanuts.

By 1962 the music scene was warming up considerably. The youths responded to the music as the new doctrine which impelled them to respond to their oppressors. A number of records were also chronicling the violence that the youths felt towards society. The frustration of the youth, stemming primarily from the high unemployment rate, expressed itself in random destruction. They broke up dances, attacked poor people (and also the rich, but this was rare), and had frequent confrontations with the police. Alton Ellis's 'Dance Crashers' was typical in its response to the situation: 'Oh, dance crashers, please don't break it up/Don't make a fuss/Don't use a knife to take another's life/You will be sorry, cause there is a death sentence/You won't have a chance/And that will be your last dance.' Artists were also chronicling their distaste for the producers' exploitation of their talent. Toots and the Maytals cut their first record for Clement Dodd, 'Victory', with religious connotations, but when they finally left, they were singing 'Broadway Jungle', a song about escape from Dodd: 'We were caught in the jungle/By the hands of a man/We're out of the jungle/We're going to Broadway/When we reach out of the jungle/We're gonna jump and shout/Come on girl, come on boy/Jump in line/Everybody gonna be alright.' Towards the end of the 1960s, when Dodd's assistant, Lee Perry, left him, he too recorded a song about Dodd, 'People Funny, Boy'.

The earliest JBC record chart was that of August 1959. There was no local record represented in its Top Ten.[30] By the following month, Laurel Aitken's 'Boogie Rock' entered the chart at No. 18 and moved up to No. 1 two weeks later. By January 1960, Laurel Aitken had three records in the charts, 'Boogie in My Bones', 'Little Sheila'[31] (they were the A and B sides of the same record, but received widespread acclaim). Wilfred Edwards had two records in the charts by

April of that year: 'Your Eyes Are Dreaming' and 'We're Going to Love'. Owen Grey had his first chart success with 'Please Let Me Go'.[32] Prior to this all locally made records, though supported by the population, were not represented on radio. The fact that they finally were broadcast on radio was due to popular demand. *Teenage Dance Party*, however, was not created as a result of these demands, but in relation to the popular Afro-American R&B. Sonny Bradshaw, a jazz musician, was responsible for its production, and the programme, once entrenched, began to reflect what was happening musically in the country.[33] One can be sure that by the time Ska was being exposed on the radio, the music had already been in existence for some time. Garth White, the most astute observer of the music's development, said: 'You will hear offshoots of a particular style after the style done get acceptance.'[34]

In 1961 Byron Lee, in collaboration with Victor Sampson and Ronnie Nasralla, formed a production company called Lee Enterprises Limited. The principal reason for its formation was to promote live shows around the country. The shows would feature a variety of local popular talent, but all would be musically supported by Byron Lee and the Dragonaires. The tour could begin in Kingston or any one of the country towns, and move to outlying districts like Port Antonio, Port Maurice, Old Harbour, Lucea, Grange Hill, Highgate, Spanish Town, Mandeville, Santa Cruz, Montego Bay, Savannah la Mar, and other areas.[35] The time to start was normally just after the Christmas festivities, when things were slow. The halls would have a normal capacity of 1,000. A group consisting of three to four members would be paid anything between £60 and £80 per night; and a solo artist, regardless of his popularity, would be paid between £30 and £40 per night. However, on a bad night, he could receive as little as £25. Apart from Lee Enterprises Limited, there were two main promoters: Stephen Hill (who later moved on to manage Marvin Gaye), and Horace Forbes. But most artists preferred working for Lee Enterprises because of their financial reliability.[36] Tommy Cowan, who used to be a singer with the Rock Steady group, the Jamaicans, and later became one of the most successful entrepreneurs in the music business in Jamaica, remembers having to chase a promoter in his car and running him off the road. The promoter was attempting to escape without paying his artists. He paid up.

Lee Enterprises began to expand its operation to control a greater percentage of the promotion market. They brought over Sam Cooke, Chuck Berry, Jimmy Clanton, and others from the States for live appearances. 'We made sure that the artists were in the country a couple days before the show, [and we] presented them on radio and TV. . . . Shows were sometimes sold out two weeks in advance.'[37] In 1965 Lee Enterprises brought over the Drifters, Barbara Lynn, and as support had Carlos Malcolm and Lee's own band. Malcolm had a reputation as a serious musician and 'was largely responsible for the revival of public interest in mento music when he formed his Afro-Jamaica group' (in the middle 1960s).[38] For some time there was a protracted struggle between Malcolm and Lee to establish who possessed the most popular big band. According to Lee, 'The Carib was the show place of the nation', although the Regal ran a close second. The former had a seating capacity of 1,500, and for big shows it was booked by Lee Enterprises for three shows a day, four days a week (Friday, Saturday, Sunday, Monday).

In 1963, Clement Dodd, after years of recording in other people's studios, built his own – Jamaica Recording and Publishing Studio – which was a one-track. The studio was built by Hedley Jones and the electrics put in by Dodd's cousin, Sid Bucknor (who became, after a few months, the resident engineer there, the first being Dodd himself. Bucknor now works at Chalk Farm Studios, London). In 1964, George Benson (who is now the proprietor of one of the two biggest manufacturing and distribution companies in Jamaica, Record Specialists) and Clifford Ray were establishing West Indies Recording Studio on Bell Road (where Lee now has his offices, studios and manufacturing plant), which Byron Lee and his partner, Ronnie Nasralla, bought into. It was a three-track studio, then went to four, the mixing board built by a German, Luntz. It was later sold to King Tubby's studio. When Lee finally took the studio over he moved it to eight-track in 1969 and then to sixteen-track in the 1970s. His eight-track mixing board and other equipment were sold to the late Duke Reid's Treasure Isle Studios (which are now owned by Sonia Pottinger). In 1965 Dodd expanded his studio to a two-track and later converted it to an eight-track which it still is. Joe Gibbs, who originally formed Amalgamated Records in the middle 1960s, now has a sixteen-track studio under his own name. Harry Johnson, a fledgling producer, had his sixteen-track studio financed by Island Records in 1972. Aquarius Studios which is owned by Herman Chinloy is the only twenty-four-track studio in Jamaica. Lee Perry owns a well-equipped four-track studio and the Hookim brothers own a four-track, Channel One. Federal Recording Studio has sixteen-track facilities. If by 1964, Atlantic Records in the United States had eight-track recording facilities, Jamaica, by comparison, with its small industry and a population approaching 2 million, was making 'progress'.

Edward Seaga, a trained anthropologist, beyond being an occasional record producer (he produced Byron Lee's first record, 'Dumplings'), was also a politician. Perhaps motivated by the usefulness of the singer/musician to him in this capacity, he initiated an attempt to export the music via a team of musicians, singers and dancers, to the World Fair of 1964 (Millie Small had her million-selling international hit, 'My Boy Lollipop', on Island Records). There are many versions to the story, but the principal area of conflict and controversy was the use of Byron Lee and the Dragonaires as the support band for the artists. Many people claimed that 'government' (meaning Seaga) did not know who the musicians were, and consequently chose wrongly. This can be dismissed because Seaga, both as politician (his constituency was Western Kingston, in the area referred to as the now-bulldozed 'dungle') and as a record producer, was fully conscious of who was making music in Jamaica. The true details will probably never be known, but it was evident that nepotism was involved. Byron Lee was a businessman and Seaga a politician, so anyone can guess what the actual nature of the relationship could have been. Lee's version blows out the light totally on the assertion that it was the government who sponsored them: 'We were not', he stated unequivocably, 'let me get this clear, sent up or had tickets paid by the government.'[39] Ken Khouri stated: 'Mr Seaga wanted to take the bow . . . I wasn't even invited to be on the tour . . . although they came and did everything here (referring to the studio), rehearsed here. . . . The man who started it and had it here – used my record, my studios and everything – they never invited me.'[40] Clement Dodd's comments were, 'He [Seaga] just board the bandwagon . . . and right inside this studio we said, "You see the man them sending our people to represent the Ska business and they sending out people who don't know nothing 'bout it."'[41] Garth White unveiled the mask of innuendo and said: 'They chose wrongly. The first thing – they left out Skatalites and Bop and Persian (percussionists) in what seemed to be a class bias. There was absolutely no way you could compare Byron Lee of the period as a representative of Ska, with the Skatalites . . . which was the top and most authentic band of the time.'[42] Jackie Mittoo's comments parallel White's in a way: 'Them send Byron Lee because the Skatalites smoked ganja.'[43] Jimmy Cliff, Millie Small, and Prince Buster made the show. The show assisted in establishing Lee's credibility as a musician internationally, because Atlantic Records contracted him to record an album, and much later, when his business became even more successful, he acquired the franchise to distribute the Atlantic catalogue in the Caribbean.

In 1962, before the late Lesley Kong started his career as a producer, he was employed in a restaurant owned by another Chinese, Charlie Moo. Singer Derrick Morgan frequented the restaurant which was also engaged in 'pikka-pow' (illegal gambling) business. The reason for Morgan frequenting the place, according to Prince Buster, was that he ate there free, and he also brought his friends along for free meals. He was always accommodated by Kong, perhaps because he was a well-known entertainer and Kong himself wanted to become involved in the business. Subsequently, Kong did become one of the most successful producers on the island (he died in the 1970s, according to rumour, when his bank manager told him that he was a millionaire). The first song he financed was Derrick Morgan's 'Shake a Leg'. Buster was furious and when he met Morgan on Charles Street, downtown Kingston, he confronted him about working for Kong (because he was Chinese). The record was very successful and Kong later bought out the restaurant, as well as expanding into real estate. Buster asserted that black people should work with their own kind instead of allowing others to control their business. Buster led an exemplary life as a businessman: when he left Clement Dodd, he established a formidable reputation with his 'sound', Voice of the People, he bought his own record shop, and organized his own record label. To many black people Buster was a model. Morgan didn't seem to go along with racial partisan feelings. Buster subsequently recorded a song about Morgan, the mocking 'Black Head Chinee Man': 'You done stole my belongings/and give to your Chinee man/God in heaven knows/He knows that you are wrong/Are you a Chinee man, are you a black man/It don't need no eye-glass/to see you are a black man/Do you prefer your Chinee man/to your fellow black man.' Morgan in turn attacked Buster with 'Blazing Fire'. Buster's response was 'Creation'. Morgan again responded with 'Love Natty'. Buster finally responded with 'Praise Without Raise' which is self-explanatory. During the whole raging 'war', Buster had always maintained a warmth for and friendship with Morgan, and he encouraged Morgan to make a tour of England with him. There was a farewell show at the Palace theatre featuring the two singers.

When the Skatalites broke up in late 1965, Dodd quickly formed a new studio band, Soul Brothers, under Roland Alphonso's direction. With the disappearance of Lloyd Brevette from the scene, Lloyd Spence, the Sheiks' former bass player, stepped in. Brevette had revolutionized the concept of playing the bass, by playing his bass lines with long drawn-out spaces. Soul Brothers provided the musical support at the tail end of Ska, but worked right through Rock Steady under Jackie Mittoo's direction. Alphonso became responsible for all the horn arrangements, while Jackie wrote the music for all the singers who recorded with Studio One. Though Jackie was not credited with co-authorship at the time, he in fact played a seminal role in the music's development. He would give the bass player his lines, write out the chords for the guitarist, play keyboards himself, arrange and produce the records. Even today, when Jamaican singers enter the studio, all they have to do is sing, and the session leader puts the music to the singers' melodies. Later, this haphazard method caused tremendous controversy over the authorship of a number of records that became international hits. The Performing Right Society, when confronted with a plethora of composers/authors, usually freeze all payments.

The number of Dodd's artists for whom Mittoo produced and wrote music is large, but some important names are: Ken Boothe, Alton Ellis ('I'm Still in Love', co-composed by Ellis and Mittoo, found its way to the No. 1 spot on the

British Charts as 'Uptown Top Ranking' by Althea and Donna; the music was the same, but the lyrics different); the Heptones ('Fatty Fatty', Mittoo wrote the music and when the song was banned from Jamaican radio, Mittoo overdubbed the organ on top and released it as 'Ram Jam', the name of a club in England where Soul Brothers were due to play in 1967); Marcia Griffith ('Truly' and 'Feel Like Jumping'. Mittoo wrote the music for both, Bob Andy adding a verse lyric on 'Truly', but the latter claimed he wrote both songs which were re-released in 1978 on a Marcia Griffith album, *Naturally*); Delroy Wilson ('Conquer Me', which Jackie says was inspired by an older song, 'Cool Cool Collie'); Carlton and the Shoes, and many others.

Rock Steady came to the fore in 1966, but before it was popularly accepted as such, it was already being played by some musicians as early as the end of 1964. Jackie Mittoo and Theophilius Beckford both said that sometimes the musicians would get exhausted after playing to dancers for some time, and they would slow down the tempo which would alter the nature of the Ska rhythms. The delayed rhythmic drive was also dictated by mood. The Soul Brothers recorded songs like 'The Train Is Coming' and 'Dancing Mood' (Delroy Wilson sang the latter), which were markedly different from anything that Ska produced. But it was not from the Coxsone stable that the first record in the Rock Steady format was credited. That was credited to Hopeton Lewis. Jackie Mittoo points to 'Sound and Pressure' as being the first, while Byron Lee points to 'Take It Easy' by the same artist. The former tune was recorded for Merritone's (Winston Blake) sound system, while the latter was recorded for Federal. Soon after, Duke Reid produced Alton Ellis on 'Get Ready, Rock Steady', which was the definitive introduction to the heralded Rock Steady era. The piano rhythm in Ska was maintained in Rock Steady as Jamaica's own musical phenomenon, but slower; and horns were used much less because of their costliness. It was cheaper for young producers to produce a record without horns. This trend resulted from the introduction of Dub (which will be discussed in a later chapter).

During the height of the competition between Clement Dodd and Duke Reid, Alton Ellis scored a number of important hits for Duke Reid: 'Breaking Up', 'Girl, I've Got a

Date', 'Willow Tree' (a Chuck Jackson song), and a number of others. Ellis was paid £20 to £25 per record by Duke Reid, £5 to £10 better than Dodd, but Dodd succeeded in persuading Ellis to abandon Duke to tour England with the Soul Brothers (Jackie Mittoo changed the name of the band for this tour, to Soul Vendours, from a record called 'Peanut Vendor') which also featured Dodd's leading act at the time, Ken Boothe (who had hits with 'Puppet on a String' and 'Tomorrow'). Jackie Mittoo was subsequently set the task of re-recording all the hits that Ellis had with Duke Reid. On Ellis's return to Jamaica, Duke Reid persuaded him to break his contract with Dodd. The case was ready to go to court, and Duke took Ellis to New York for three months while the furore died away. In New York Ellis recorded two songs for Duke, one of which was 'Love Letter'. While he was in New York, Ellis's mother died and he returned immediately. Dodd held all royalties from an album Ellis had recorded for him, but Ellis went ahead and recorded 'Remember that Sunday' for Duke Reid. It was not an instant smash and was not released until nine months later, but it was instantly successful.[44]

Throughout the changes that the music made, dance was a primary element. Without dance there would be no music. The music was played almost exclusively for dancing from its inception via the sound systems to live performances. During Ska, because the rhythms were fast and pacy, the accent was placed on the feet, thus the shuffle and split were the qualitative ingredients of the music. Ska was a dance akin to the traditional expressionism of the free churches, the body could be expressed in whatever fashion, and it brought people together. When the rhythm slowed down, paradoxically the tension increased, and the body was now responding to an inner rhythmic drive. The tension of the external society was internalized by the dancer and expressed physically. Thus in Rock Steady, the dancer could remain on his spot of earth, shake his shoulders, make pounding motions with his arms and hands (at an invisible enemy, an anonymous force), without recourse to or consciousness of a partner. The internal tension was demonstratively and explosively expressed. Because the movement was stylized, its external appearance alone could be interpreted as tension-releasing, violence shimmering at the surface. Yet in Ska there was a happiness, a joy in the freedom of expression. This is not to say, however, that Rock Steady was not a joyous music but its slow tempo, its intensity and tension-building features separated it from Ska. The indigenization of the music had certainly occurred, and any connection with its Afro-American model was confined simply to the piano/guitar rhythmic chops.

The world the musician confronted was oppressive and instrumental music still contained the singer's abstracted expression of the real and menacing world. Thus the music was two-dimensional: a lyrical and instrumental expression of that world of terror.

During the Rock Steady era social consciousness and political and criminal violence escalated to new heights. I have already pointed out that political violence started during the 1930s with general strikes and confrontations with the colonial government. As a result of this, the two parties sought to consolidate power through the use of controlled political violence. The Jamaica Labour Party (JLP) secured political power in 1944 (after the British granted Jamaica adult suffrage) and won the elections again in 1949, but lost consecutively to the People's National Party (PNP) in 1955 and 1959. At the time of the next elections two principles were at stake: 1. Federating with the larger English-speaking Caribbean, and 2. Obtaining independence from Britain.[45] The JLP was pro-independence and won the election on this issue as well as on the issue of job victimization against their political and unionized supporters.[46] During the referendum of 1961 to settle the question of federation, political violence between parties erupted, resulting in the then PNP Minister of Home Affairs outlawing marches and motorcades in the Kingston/St Andrew Corporate area.[47]

Because the JLP was out of power for two consecutive terms, the 1962 general election was an important factor in the escalation of a new type of political violence. According to John Roberts,* Edward Seaga sought active membership of the PNP in the late 1950s, but this was conditional on him becoming a member of the Legislative Council. So he subsequently became a member of the JLP and was consigned to the Western Kingston constituency.

*A ficticious name for a leading member of one of the two political parties in Jamaica.

> You have to understand the constituency in which he was placed to understand why it was necessary for him to introduce the use of guns in Jamaican politics. Now Western Kingston, before Seaga started his reign of keeping the seat, has been famous for a candidate being unable to hold it for more than one term, and that included two former Prime Ministers. The first was Bustamante who left the seat after one term to go to Clarendon. The second was Hugh Shearer. Now, when Seaga moved into Western Kingston, it seemed that he was determined to make himself a political reputation, that he could do even what Bustamante could not, which was to hold Western Kingston. And he devised a whole new strategy for this sole purpose, and spent a lot of time there, learning how to deal with that particular problem. Now Western Kingston was at that time where the 'dungle' was, and it was in many ways a PNP stronghold. Seaga spent three whole years there prior to the elections of 1962. I think Seaga realized that political violence, not disorganized, sporadic violence, would hold the seat. In addition, he had tremendous organizing skills. The fact that a white Jamaican was prepared to live in Western Kingston also had a lot to do with him winning the seat. Seaga made a study of revivalist cults and made sure that all his political rallies had elements of these revival cults. For Jamaican politics it was a brand new era. . . . That sort of sophistication and organization was brand new.[48]

To compound the difficulties that Seaga confronted in Western Kingston, Dudley Thompson, with his rhetoric and 'his style of campaigning that everybody thought was foreign', made asinine remarks about Seaga especially concerning his colour.[49] All this contributed to Seaga's policy of introducing a hitherto unknown violence into Jamaica. During the reign of Bustamante he had made it known that he was hostile to the police whom, it was believed, were responsive to the PNP. Accordingly, Bustamante introduced 'budgetary attention . . . to the army rather than the police'.[50] Seaga then sought to rectify this situation when he entered Western Kingston.

> One of the first things that Seaga did was to infiltrate the police. He had gotten to the superintendant in charge of the Denham Town police station which was responsible for Western Kingston. He created a situation at a polling station through his followers . . . Michael Manley, because of his union background and his reputation as a tough guy, was given a certain responsibility within the area. He was to check the polling station there, so he rushed in without even thinking. . . . You must remember

> he was an important man, his father had been Premier. . . . So he went in expecting the police to do what he said. And this police inspector, under the Denham Town superintendant, rushed in and attacked Michael and beat him up. It inflamed the PNP supporters and in the scramble it gave the police an excuse to intervene with tear gas. At this polling station the PNP was expecting many votes and the JLP very few. Seaga insured that by the use of tear gas very few people turned up. The PNP lost the seat by that action and by a very small margin.[51]

Seaga, in contradistinction to the role assigned him by John Roberts, is also noted for his public stand against the police. In 1961, addressing the House of Representatives, he voiced his fears of the widening gap between the police and the masses and the police practice of framing people on ganja charges.[52] In November 1965, the JLP attempted to march through a PNP stronghold and clashes occurred between supporters of both parties. The police intervened with the use of tear gas, and subsequently Edward Seaga, with eleven others, was charged with assault and riot, causing an affray, and assault upon a police officer. The presiding magistrate characterized the police witnesses as 'unreliable' and threw the case out.[53] Clearly, the heroic stance by Seaga against the overwhelming support the PNP commanded from the police, while himself cultivating their patronage in his constituency, extended the range of his influence over the mass of the population, who themselves experienced vicarious satisfaction from Seaga's pronouncements against the police.

With the widespread use of guns for political ends, the police, knowing those responsible, were reluctant to make arrests. In 1966, the then Commissioner of Police, Gordon Langdon, stated that criminal acts 'may not be motivated by crime'.[54] In December 1966, the police raided the PNP headquarters, arresting between thirty and thirty-five people, fifteen of them having ninety-five previous convictions for 'assault, larceny, malicious wounding, shop-breaking and malicious destruction of property'.[55] Three of the arrested were bailed by Wills Issacs, a former Acting Prime Minister, at £200 each. In February 1967, a swoop was made on the JLP's Central Kingston headquarters, where they made twelve arrests and 'seized explosives, stolen goods, five loaded revolvers, two automatics and two hundred rounds of ammunition, along with molotov cocktails and two home-made bombs'.[56]

Hugh Shearer became Prime Minister of Jamaica in 1967 amidst speculation and intrigue:

> When Donald Sangster died there was a great deal of rumour that he was in fact killed. He was rushed off the island in a great deal of secrecy for an operation on his brain. But it was thought he was poisoned. Ken Jones, a member of the Cabinet, also died. It was said that he walked during his sleep and fell off a balcony, breaking his neck. People felt that he was thrown, punched or pushed from the balcony in a fight with the ruthless Clement Tavares. Bustamante personally intervened and made it clear that he did not want Clement Tavares to succeed as Prime Minister.[57]

Shearer, soon after inauguration, stepped up the JLP's programme of winning the support of the police. He stated quite clearly: 'When it comes to handling crime, in this country I do not expect any policeman, when he tackles a criminal, to recite any Beatitudes to him.'[58] But the question of political violence was never fully investigated nor tackled by Shearer or any other Prime Minister. In any police swoop, the minimum of damage and arrests and discoveries were made. This can only be so because of informed tip-offs, and the necessity of having only a handful arrested to demonstrate police zeal in stamping out political violence without preference to any party. John Roberts has stated that police, like the masses of people, hold partisan political affiliations and would volunteer their services for promotion, material reward, or simply because they belonged to a party. During Hugh Shearer's first year as the new Prime Minister the police were engaged in fifty-two shoot-outs, but none of them directed against the people who wielded political power. It was the poor people who were killed, maimed, or imprisoned. When Shearer did direct the police to use political violence, it was against 'fringe political groups intending . . . to overthrow Jamaican society'.[59]

The government-inspired attack against 'fringe political groups' resulted in the banning of Walter Rodney, a Guyanese lecturer at UWI, Kingston, who was responsible for increased political activity among the 'sufferers'. In response to his banning, university students and Black Power youths demonstrated and attacked symbols of big business in the city. Both the police and the Jamaica Defence Force (with deployment of armoured vehicles) attempted to quell the disturbances.[60] Yet the leaders of political violence were free to create havoc and destruction among the youth and the poor, consolidating and extending the range of their power.

In addition to the widespread use of political violence, there was also the question of the 'illegal' export of ganja. Second to bauxite, Jamaica's most profitable export is marijuana. It is said that twenty-two families own 80 per cent of land in Jamaica. The sufferers, among whom are Rastafarians, do not own the makeshift houses they sleep in, yet the unrelenting attacks upon them for ganja would suggest that they possessed agricultural lands to carry out their lucrative trade. These attacks are obviously motivated by the need to protect the major land barons and governmental (or political parties') involvement in the trade. The steady stream of headlines about Rasta arrests serves to deflect scrutiny from those people who are in the main responsible for 90 per cent of the ganja trade.

> After 1962 and the waning away of colonial restraint, it became much easier to get guns into Jamaica. Jamaica by air is less than ninety minutes away from Miami. Gun-running is common practice in Florida. Jamaica grows a lot of ganja, ganja is sold for a lot of money outside Jamaica. It is simple either to use cash or to exchange ganja for guns in Florida. As regards getting the guns into Jamaica, there are several methods. Initially, it was quite easy for light planes to land in country areas, roadways, etc. When they were blocked up by digging up the ground and putting stakes whereby the planes couldn't land, they started coming through customs. It was very simple, you spend some money in Florida, buy some guns, put them in fridges, furniture, any kind of hard material, and provided you know the right person(s) in the right place(s), they could come through quite easily. This practice was known to both parties and used by both parties. I have also been told by members of the JLP that Seaga used circuses to bring guns into the country. Because they had to unload a lot of things, nobody would bother to check.[61]

Because of the increased surveillance of the United States/Mexico border, the trade came to Jamaica. According to Terry Lacey: 'The Drug Enforcement Administration of the United States Department of Justice estimated in 1974 that about one ton of ganja (worth about $400,000) was exported from Jamaica to the United States every day.' Michael Manley has stated quite openly that the ganja trade is controlled by the Mafia. This, again, is like the Rasta = ganja bogey, an attempt to deflect accusations and investigations against the land barons and governmental officials.

To the hired hack from the ghetto, a man who is without an 'education', unemployed, and 'scrunting' for a meagre existence, the monetary reward for participating in political violence as a political gangster or even a hired gunman, is a temptation impossible to resist. So the ghetto then becomes a place not only infested with gunmen and gangsters, but a place where prestige and power are sought and settled with gun shots and deaths. So, in addition to the impoverished condition of the sufferers, for whom the politicians do nothing or very little, they compound their suffering by arming the young members of the ghetto who then further terrorize them.

What, then, is the role of the singer/musician under these circumstances? The artist sees his liberation from the ghetto by means of amassing money through his music, but simultaneously he remains physically, and perhaps even spiritually, a part of the ghetto. His music could by and large express the conditions that surround and engulf him. But he has to make his pact with his environment. This has led to some artists establishing a comradeship with notorious gunmen who could be used as a threatening force against producers who did not want to pay them or paid them too little. Some producers themselves became attached to either the police or members of the government. Bunny Lee, for example, a producer who has worked with numerous artists in Jamaica, stated: 'I have preacher friend, police friend, murderer friend, thief friend, government friend. Everybody is my friend and you don't know when you gon need one of them to do something for you.' According to Alton Ellis (and these tales were confirmed by other artists), Bunny Lee is an unusual man. He is known in the community where he lives and people frequently approach him about their personal problems. He would sometimes give as much as $200 to $300 to somebody in need. Singer Delroy Wilson's brother, according to Ellis, was charged for murder three times and three times Bunny Lee, through his various associates, had him freed. Ellis states that he himself was driving to the country when he was stopped for not having road tax, the police took away his car, and sent him back to Kingston by taxi. When he had bought the tax to reclaim the car, the police accused him of committing a robbery. He was put in gaol, but released soon after. While he was at home he saw Bunny Lee approaching in his car attached to Ellis's, and the police also dropped the charges against him. All artists speak in glowing terms about Lee, a thing that is unheard of in the Jamaican musical context.

In 1965, according to Garth White, there was a 'spontaneous rising against the Chinese community in downtown Kingston',[62] but in fact it was not that spontaneous. On 28 August of that year an employee of a Chinese-owned shop, Joyce Copeland, had an argument with her boss over a radio she was buying from the shop.

> She claimed that she was beaten up by three Chinese brothers in the presence of the clerks. She was subsequently questioned by police and found to have abrasions. An angry crowd then surrounded the store of her employers, the Lue brothers, and soon afterwards George Green, a labourer, was shot by a Chinese. In the following week of violence numerous Chinese business places were attacked by mobs, set on fire or looted, two policemen were shot (one accidentally shot dead), six civilians shot (wounded) and ninety people arrested.[63]

But this was only one incident that had roots in 1911 when the Chinese were accused of burning their property for insurance purposes. In fact the rage of the urban sufferers was expressed against the Chinese community in acts of destruction simply because the Chinese represented the nearest physical embodiment of their oppression.

> 'The Chinese', according to John Roberts, 'were no more oppressors of blacks than those who escaped their wrath. I think the reason for the attack on the Chinese is that they are located inside the communities, rather than outside, because you find that in both rural and urban areas the Chinese controlled the local shop and lived upstairs, on the same premises, unlike the Jews and Syrians who run businesses during the day and retreat at night. They also have a habit of accepting a tremendous amount of abuse if it meant their staying to make way. As with the ghettos, people who live there tend to get the worst of the anger that spills out from time to time. Whether it's directed against blacks themselves or another minority group.'[64]

It is this tendency of the suffering community to turn their anger inward, against themselves, that has made Jamaica one of the most frightening places to live in. The anger is expressed spontaneously and at random. There are numerous incidents of rape, murder, armed robbery, malicious wounding, etc., recorded directly inside the community. And these acts of terror, aided by the arming of the youths by political parties, have found expression in the music of the sufferers. At times the attitude of the artists is one of sympathy to the 'cause' of the 'rude' boy, but usually it is one of outrage and horror.

In 1967 Dandy Livingstone (who previously sang as the duo Sugar (Simone) and Dandy), recorded 'We Are Rude', a reply to Prince Buster's formidable attack on the rude boys, the ghetto youths who were armed to the teeth and wreaking havoc in the oppressed communities. Dandy's song was dedicated to the rude boy culture and glorified their new 'status' in the community: 'We are still rude/We are still tuff/We fear no one/Because we still have guns.' (As these lines are sung, a voice is spoken over the music.) 'He will have to give us 1,000 years, and even that can't stop us.' Here was the new-found emergent power of the rude boys glorified to the extent where violence is recognized as a strength and force. Prince Buster, in contradistinction to this attitude, attacked the reckless, undirected and delinquent behaviour of the youths who were not terrorizing their oppressors, but the poor members of their own community.

In that same year Junior Smith recorded the song 'Cool Down Your Temper', which was expressed within the Ska mould. 'Samson was a strong man/strong like a lion/Delilah cool him down/Goliath was a giant/strong like a lion/David cool him down/Young man look what you're doing/It ain't right/Cool down right now.' It would seem that producers were in part responsible for the type of songs that the artists recorded. The producer, since he himself was a sound man, could determine what type of songs would sell. They even went so far as to change the original titles of songs, so that they appealed more widely to the market they were catering for. Jackie Mittoo stated that: 'The producer could change the title if he felt like it. Sometimes it would be a very treacherous title, sometimes a very cool title. It depended on what he thought he could sell.' Another song that idolized the rude boy, but this time in a much more refined and sexual manner, was 'Rough and Tuff': the vocal refrain throughout the song was 'You rough, you tuff', and the singer would talk over the music, 'This is me, JD/The girls say I'm the most with the grooviest toast/I fear no one/So don't try to step on my toe/I'll never drink your soup/Because I'm not in your group/I'm exclusive though I'm not a fugitive . . ./These my words are like a bombshell/In your ears like a bell.' This was released on Clement Dodd's Coxsone label in 1967.

The sophistication is expressed in several places in the song. Clearly the singer attempts to distinguish himself from the 'ordinary' rude boys by referring to himself as 'JD'. If he were an ordinary hoodlum his name would have been totally different, say 'Duck' or 'Popeye' or something ridiculous like that. But he differentiates himself from the average group, and goes on to state that among women he is the 'grooviest toast', a word that would not be in fashion among rude boys. They would be 'tuff or rough', but never the 'grooviest toast'. Then this uptown rude boy states further that he is 'exclusive', that is, he hangs out in places where the normal rude boy does not. This at the same time exhibits contempt for the crude behaviour of rude boys. He also says that he is no 'fugitive', i.e. someone running from the law. In short the song expresses a fearlessness to any challenge, whether that challenge comes from the rude boys themselves or the police. But it certainly does contain elements of contempt for the crudity of the rude boys' behaviour, while being influenced by their fashion and vogue.

A much more characteristic rude boy attitude is contained in 'Rudies in Court' which came out on Lesley Kong's record company, Beverley's, in 1967. It follows the pattern of most of the rude songs with the chorus being sung by several singers, and the verse being provided by the DJ. The chorus commences, 'Your honour, rudies don't fear/rudies don't fear/Rougher than rough/Tougher than tough/Strong like iron/We are iron.' Then the voice gives the toast, which is an impersonation of the Judge: 'You're brought here for gun-shooting/Rachet-using and bomb-throwing/Now tell me rude boys/What have you got to say for yourselves?' The reply is the chorus being sung, contemptuously and unrepentingly in the Judge's face. These songs were developments of earlier rude songs that come out as early as 1962 in both instrumental and vocal forms. The Wailers had recorded 'Put It

On' (supported by the Skatalites) as early as 1965, the title being sung to suggest a zealous desire to destroy the system, and it has an audacious line stating: 'I'll rule my destiny'.

Justin Hinds and the Dominoes were more precise, religious, and political in their lyrics. Their formidable hit, 'Carry Go Bring Come' of 1967, had stated their need to look away from Jamaica for contentment: 'It's better to seek a home in Mount Zion . . .' and also asks rhetorically: 'How long will the wicked reign over my people?' Increasingly it would be this type of lyrics that would dominate the music scene and impart awareness to the youths. But the declaimer to rudeness and rude boys found its apotheosis in Prince Buster. Buster, by naming his sound Voice of the People, was expressing the political motivations that were already at work on him in the late 1950s. Buster's pioneering and seminal song 'Judge Dread' certainly created widespread response to the line he took on the rude boys, a line that did not look sympathetically on their cause, and which reflected Buster's ability to express the fears and disenchantment with the community without fear of reprisals. 'Judge Dread' was Buster's response to the havoc that the rude boys were creating in the community. Political violence had evolved into random and senseless violence, and when it was directed against poor blacks in the poor community, very little court action was taken to stamp it out, Buster stated. On the other hand, if one's voice were raised uptown, the police would make an arrest for disturbing the peace. There was, in short, no redress for the poor. The government's attitude was classic, the rude boys' action did not interfere with the rich, therefore no action was necessary. Buster, then, expressed the fears and horrors of poor black people in their attempt to seek justice for their terrorized condition.

'Judge Dread' is not an intellectual record where the artist works out the condition of the rude boys themselves and the criminal uses they were put to by the government and the rich. It was merely a statement of indignation. The lines 'You rough, you tough' are sung as the introduction to the atmosphere of the court room, with the rude boys appearing before this notorious black Judge. The Judge shouts: 'Order!/While my court is in session/Will you please stand/Now allow me to introduce myself/My name is Judge 100 Years/Some people call me Judge Dread/Now I am from Ethiopia/To try all you rude boys for shooting black people . . .' The reference to Ethiopia is a classic of authority, because the Rastas claimed Ethiopia as their ancestral home. So a judge from Ethiopia is invested with the powers of justice, especially to judge the black world. He then warns his court that: 'I'm the only rude boy here today.' His authority is final and no one should dare contest his right to judge. He calls out the names of the charged rude boys and reads the nature of the charges against them, then one by one he calls them out and asks them to plead guilty or no. The first one is sentenced to 100 years, rude boy Emmanuel Zachariah Zakipong is charged with fifteen counts of shooting with intent, fifteen murder charges, and the Judge says: 'I heard you was the one who told the Judge down there in Sutton Street, "Well, rude boys don't care." Well, this is King Street and I'm Judge 100 Years and I don't care, take 400 years.' When the defendant argues, the Judge rebukes him: 'Hush up! Take 400 more years!' Adolphous James is charged with robbing school-children, burning people's homes and 'shooting black people'. The rude boy interjects and the judge shouts: 'Hush up! Contempt! 100 years for that.' Then he sentences him to 400 years with 500 lashes and threatens: 'I'm going to set an example. . .'

Throughout Prince Buster's song, or to be more accurate, song-play, there is perpetual reference to 'black people' and it is taken as a crime even to contemplate committing crimes against blacks. If Jamaica is a so-called black society, why then is it necessary for Buster to differentiate between black people and any other? Buster understood that though 90 per cent of the population of Jamaica were Afrikan descendants, there was an uneven distribution of wealth in the nation. The whites, Syrians, and Jews, controlled the primary resources of the country, the Chinese were in the middle with the light-skinned blacks, and there were just blacks at the bottom of the social and economic ladder. Thus to commit a crime against black people, especially those from the poorest of environments, was to commit a crime against oneself. Buster's song epitomizes the consciousness of racial stratification in a so-called black society, and illustrates the disequilibrium embedded in the courts, the police force (even though themselves black) and the vapid minds of the society itself. 'Judge Dread' thus received widespread popularity and opened the way to many songs either glorifying the lives of the rude boys or warning them of their eventual destruction. Even Dandy Livingstone eventually changed his tune and sang of 'Rudy, a Message to You', which implored the youths to change their ways.

After 'Judge Dread' was released in 1966 to controversial response, Prince Buster followed it up with 'The Appeal' which sentenced the 'dreadlocks' defending barrister himself. The jargon at the time was that those criminals who paraded themselves as Rasta brethren were 'knotty head' or 'dreadlocks' and not righteous Rasta brethren. Buster led a highly politically active life. In 1968 after the banning of Walter Rodney, Buster is reputed to have grabbed the mike from the RJR announcer and spoken to the nation over the radio. He was subsequently molested both by the police and the military and his record shop was broken into by them. Also, in 1968 he led a demonstration on the question of the illegal and immoral régime in Rhodesia. He was subsequently charged and tried for obstructing traffic. In the middle 1960s he became a Muslim (on the Afro-American model) and the publications of the now deceased Elijah Mohammad sect were seized by the police. He was charged with being in possession of prohibited literature, and when the case came to court, in order that the government should not lose too much face, an order of *sine die* was granted, a virtual declaration of victory for Buster.

On the other hand, Buster also had a reputation as an exploiter among musicians. Big Youth, the DJ/toaster, was produced by Buster on two rhythm tracks, 'Chi Chi Run' and 'Leave Your Skeng', which, in addition to being issued as singles, were also used on an album and released in England without his knowledge. 'I walked into his record shop,' said Big Youth, 'and a gun was pointed at my head by one of his runarounds. Every time I go ask for money, so he send his police friends to pull guns on me.'[65] Producer Lloyd Charmers also had some bad tales to tell. In the 1960s he was recording with Roy Willis as the Charmers and had their biggest hit, 'Time After Time', under Prince Buster's producership.

> We used to have to live at Buster's place to pick up the money. . . . Like he comes and sees us and says, 'I'll be back in another five or ten minutes,' and we wait for hours. Once he told us to

> meet him nine o'clock one morning and we waited and waited. He showed up at eleven o'clock in the night and then tells us he's sorry he can't see us. . . . Ask him for some taxi fare he give us something like two shillings. He was nice in the studio, but after the studio work was finished he's a different person. Buster still owes us royalties until today. . . . As a matter of fact we never got any statement from him. Delroy Wilson got something like £7 for 'Dancing Mood' which sell . . . like over sixty odd thousand in JA.[66]

Buster's inconsistencies are typical of someone attempting to elevate himself out of the ghetto and simultaneously to attack the political structure. On the one hand there is the starkly real economic world, and on the other the ideal of seeking a moral equilibrium. The conflict of business and politics became an enormous problem to resolve, not only for Buster, but for others.

Political commentary in the music of the sufferer, according to one writer, can be characterized as mere 'reportage', and he suggests that: 'We need some way to distinguish . . . between what is essentially "political protest" and "social reportage" . . . protest goes beyond reporting and suggests some form of resolution – or even some suggestion of alternatives.'[67] If one can accept the plea for the distribution of wealth as a resolution or alternative, then the Jamaican singer has posed alternatives. If, however, a greater depth of vision and clarity is sought, then the music can be dismissed. If the sufferer, in his attempt merely to get his hands on the larger Jamaican pie, and in succeeding ceases to protest or fight, then the lack of principle behind his motivation for self-improvement is exposed. Thus, the stage of protest is fraught with contradictions.

'Quite often,' says Fearon, 'the artists are not necessarily protesting against a *system* as such. Quite often they are protesting against their place in such a system, and quite often it seems clear that were roles reversed, they would be satisfied.'[68] This, then, is the dilemma that confronts the singer/sufferer in his attempt to reflect the conditions of his life and of his community. In the case of the Rastafari there is ample evidence of a written programme as to the alternatives they seek. But in the main the singer/sufferer is himself not a Rasta, and has only an emotional affinity to the goals and principles of Rastafari, and finally, does not himself belong to any Rastafarian organization. Further, the singer/sufferer understands the needs of the commercial world, and locks his hair and makes references to Rastafari, but does not give to the cause, either financially or otherwise. According to Cedric Brooks, the highly rated saxophonist and Rasta:

> People are band-wagonning; they use Rasta music as an expression of suffering, but they stop at the level of protest as if there were no deeper philosophy. . . . Let us take the conditioning of Bob Marley. . . . Marley was not an active Rasta man up to a couple of years when he committed himself to Rastafari. . . . It is unlikely that he could yet be secure enough psychologically and financially to go back and bring development to the area from which he came.[69]

The expression of political protestations in song are not clearly indicative of the level of commitment on the part of the artists, but these expressions have been used from time to time by politicians. The year 1972 was the climax of the uses to which the political expressions of the singer/sufferer were put. Delroy Wilson's 1971 song, 'Better Must Come', was used as the official theme song for Michael Manley's PNP party. The PNP went so far as to recruit an artist/promoter, Clancy Eccles, to recruit new talent for the dissemination of PNP politics. However, both the PNP and JLP have been instrumental in banning songs that they considered antithetical to their political strategies. 'As the JLP thought it prudent to ban songs interpreted as being antagonistic to the party, so has the PNP recently banned songs that it has felt may have had "disruptive" effects on the society.'[70]

Political protest, then, has been used by both the politician and the businessman to serve their own ends. And the artist himself has suffered from a depth of vision in his response to his deprivation and social condition. This has led, quite clearly, to the easiness with which he has perennially been used by the politician and big businessman. His own relationship with members of his community can itself be exploitative once he has begun to liberate himself from the confines of the ghetto. Therefore, political protest, without the concomitant philosophical or political organizational structure, has not led to any specific improvement in the condition of the sufferers. Political action, however, on the part of the mass of sufferers has precipitated changes within the context of their lives.

In its formation, Rock Steady began to express the specifically Jamaican experience as diversely as possible. Political protest was on the increase, but songs speaking of other themes were also part and parcel of the music scene. By 1968 Rock Steady was evidently being overtaken by another type of rhythmic invention, Reggae, which was faster and a synthesis of both Rock Steady and Ska. Like both former types of music, no one tune can be pin-pointed as the originator of this new period, but certainly Toots and the Maytals with their 'Do the Reggay' were the first to use the word in recordings. The word Reggae has its beginnings in sex-talk language, akin to the Afro-American funky, which was originally a definition of a state of sexiness, later applied to hard Soul. Similarly, Reggae evolved from nonsense words used in sex-talk. The music was then tagged with this nomenclature which has since been used to define all areas of Jamaican popular musical expression.

The two dominant labels during this period were Clement Dodd's Studio One and Lesley Kong's Beverley's. Kong had acquired Toots and the Maytals and Jimmy Cliff, as well as Desmond Dekker, among others. And this new input into the music was beginning to create an atmosphere where a single label could not dominate. New producers were also entering the business, and new musicians were being discovered. The original musicians who created the music were confronting new personal problems and were moving away from the scene, thus new musicians came to the fore. All of them, like their predecessors, from the ghettos of Western Kingston and similar areas had rehearsed on crude instruments that they made themselves. But unlike their predecessors, they were not trained in an orthodox way, and learnt by trial and error. But the emotional input that they communicated into the music made up for any technical deficiencies.

What, then, was to be the future of the music, given the amount of manipulation to which the artists were subjected? In the late 1960s there was a movement by the artists to form collectives and own their own labels and undertake their own distribution. But this also created problems, for in order for the record to sell it needed exposure. Radio, it would seem, was controlled by the larger independent companies who carried more influence. And by and large artists' co-operatives proved to be a failure. The artist then reverted to his previous relationship with the producer, except now he was not dealing with Dodd, Reid or Kong, but perhaps a musician or singer who had become disenchanted with being exploited and was making a real effort to launch himself as an independent producer and label-owner. Most of these people had worked for producers themselves and understood the mechanics involved in running a label, and also the frustrations. It is these new producers who contributed most to the further evolution of the music and the introduction of rhythmic innovation, as well as improving production techniques to precipitate the music into the international arena.

4 Bob Marley, Peter Tosh, Bunny Wailer - Three Modernists

Through a combination of fate and talent the Wailers, both as a group and as individuals, have contributed significantly to the development and international status of Reggae. As a group they held and still hold a social significance that is historically unparalleled in Jamaica. As individuals they have participated in social issues and problems that have been sensitive and controversial. Their perception of the world and of Jamaica in particular has been coloured and influenced by the position of black people in Jamaica and in the world. This vision of the world has brought them into conflict with society, for which they still suffer abuse. It is important, then, to understand some of their backgrounds and why they have been consistent in their reflection of reality.

Bob Marley was born in the village of Rhoden Hall in the parish of St Ann, the same parish that political visionary Marcus Garvey came from, and Burning Spear (Winston Rodney), a man whose very life is dedicated to keeping alive the memory and philosophy of Marcus Garvey. For whatever reason it is highly significant that these three important people, in varying degrees, should be dedicated to the freedom of the black man. Marley's mother was called Cedella Booker and the family farmed coffee, bananas, and yams.[1] Marley's father is said to have been a captain in the English army, but no clear biographical data is available. Marley himself has confessed that he has never met his father, yet in one conversation he said he was taken to the woods in England and he was shown this bearded white man and told he was his father. There was no conversation between them.[2] Whether or not this is true, Bob Marley does not speak of his father. When he was 9 years old his mother moved the family: Bob, two brothers and a sister, to Waltham Park in Kingston, a then slum area, and later they moved to Trench Town where he spent most of his teenage and adult life.[3] Marley remained at high school until he was 16 and then did an apprenticeship as a welder where he met Desmond Dekker in 1961. Dekker encouraged Marley to play a bit of guitar and to sing.[4] In that same year he recorded a single, 'Judge Not', and later recorded a couple of other tunes for Beverly's Records under the late Lesley Kong's production, one of which was 'One Cup of Coffee' by Brook Benton.[5] The introduction to Kong was facilitated by Jimmy Cliff who was already a popular recording artist.

Peter Tosh (Winston Hubert McIntosh) was born in Westmoreland in 1944. Though he is the eldest of the Wailers, he has always had that youthful look. Since he was a baby he was brought up by his aunt because, as he says, 'my mother was out slaving'. He has said that though he was influenced by church music, he was not influenced by the church itself. At the age of 15 he moved to Kingston where he stayed with a great aunt until she died, then he lived with an uncle. McIntosh has no brothers or sisters. When he came to Kingston he lived at Denham Town and later moved to Trench Town. Neville O'Riley Livingstone (Bunny Wailer), on the other hand, was born in Kingston and there are no biographical details about him except that he is the youngest of the three Wailers.

They were all living in Trench Town where the majority of the early Jamaican artists came from, singing on the sidewalk or in somebody's back yard. Marley was making little progress as a professional singer and was intending to form a band along the lines of the Impressions. Both Peter Tosh and Bunny Wailer joined forces with Marley along with Junior Brathwaite and Beverley Kelso (also called Cherry). Under the direction of singer Joe Higgs they were taught phrasing, pitch, voice control, intonation, etc. Higgs was a partner in the then famous singing duo, Higgs and Wilson. In 1964 the Wailers went to audition for the Coxsone/Studio One label on a Sunday. According to Tosh, they were taken there by Francisco Willie Pep, a percussionist. Clement Dodd and his cousin, Sid Bucknor, conducted auditions every Sunday and they asked the Wailers to sing some of their compositions.

They sang three tunes and were told to return in three months. As they were about to leave, Peter Tosh stated that they had another tune, 'Simmer Down', but the band objected because the composition was not complete. Dodd asked them to sing the tune and, having heard it, asked them to return to the studio the following Thursday for recording.[6] The song was instantly successful.

Both Marley and Wailer claimed they were hardly paid any royalties at all, but Peter Tosh states that Dodd paid them fifteen to twenty pounds each for every song they recorded, bought them stage suits and pointed-tip shoes, and paid them each three pounds per week, all of which was deducted from any forthcoming royalties. According to all three, Dodd never supplied them with any statements. Wailer has said that he has never signed any legal agreement with any company, but in 1972 he did sign a contract with Island Records as a member of the Wailers. The band worked seasonally, i.e. primarily during the summer vacation for North Americans and Europeans.

From the start of the Wailers' career they had always strongly identified with the rebelliousness and arrogance of Jamaica's youth. Oppression was/is not a sociological category, but a real experience for all three. Poverty was their experience and their environment. Violence was aggravated by the politicians, as stated in Chapter 3, and all these experiences were reflected in their songs. The Wailers commanded a particular response from their audience. Because they identified with and reflected in song the conditions of the urban slums, they were greeted with heroic responses. Songs like 'One Love', 'Love and Affection', 'Jailhouse Keeps Empty' and 'Rude Boy Ska' all reflected both the appalling conditions and the desire for some degree of change. Bunny Wailer sums up the reason for the contents of their songs:

> You've been taught a whole pack of bullrush and you come to realize a certain amount of truth, and you start to establish these truths – your teachers, your family, everyone gon disagree with you because them already drink up the old wine, so now the new wine is being poured out there is no space. You can't put new wine in old bottles. The struggle had to go on. . . . It was just youth consciousness. . . . Every youth had to get conscious of the things around him, knowing what's true, and as soon as him find out the things you tell him was false, he must rebel against it.[7]

By the time the Wailers were together as a band, Marley and Wailer were firm friends and later shared a room together. Marley had the zeal and enthusiasm of a man who had already seen his future. This zeal had been nurtured and encouraged by Clement Dodd who gave Marley the privilege of a room at the back of his studio where Marley would listen to records and choose songs for certain singers to sing. Wailer has said that: 'Bob was bursting with ideas, almost too much for one man. . .'[8] But by 1966 Marley had left Jamaica for Wilmington, Delaware, where he worked in a Chrysler car factory on the assembly line.[9] After he lost his job he applied for welfare, but was turned down – probably on the grounds that he was not yet a permanent resident. He was then sent a draft card for service in the American army and quickly returned to Jamaica.[10] On his return his compositions had begun to mellow out, or at least to diversify. He began writing love lyrics like 'Stir It Up', 'Bend Down Low', etc. The band came together once more and again recorded for the Coxsone/Studio One labels. By the end of 1967 the Wailers had left Dodd for good, but prior to that, Wailer states that at one time: 'Bob was going on a Coxsone trip. . . . He started acting like he wasn't emotionally stable.'[11] It seemed that Dodd had a habit of paying particular interest in his artists at a particular period, encouraging them, egging them on to the acceptance of a successful future, but they could never reconcile Dodd's words with the way he treated them. Consequently, the artists would unleash their anger, frustration, and disappointment against Dodd verbally, either to him personally or to friends.

Tosh, for example, recalls that Dodd used to give his artists mint balls (a sweet) and a bus fare if they demanded money. He was also violent in his response to verbal or threatened violence. In 1967, Tosh states, he was asked by Jimmy Rodway who worked for Dodd to play somebody's tune on an organ. Tosh refused and went with Wailer to sit in the studio. When Dodd returned, he asked them to leave, but Tosh stated that it was his blood, sweat and tears that had built the studio. An argument ensued in which Tosh and Wailer abused him and they goaded him to go for his gun (which he was always known to carry around with him. The late Duke Reid was also reputed to have walked with a revolver as well as a rifle.). Dodd called in the police. The

Wailers finally left Dodd's label in late 1967, and formed their own Wailin' Soul label in 1968 with Rita Marley (Marley and Rita met during their stay with Dodd). The label did not last very long because of financial difficulties and lack of promotion and plays on radio. During this same year Wailer was arrested on a ganja charge and sentenced to prison. His response to his prison sentence was a song: 'Battering Down Sentence' (later reissued as 'Fighting Against Convictions' on his *Black Heart Man* album) in which he sums up the classic situation of an urban sufferer (himself): poverty and hardship, a large family and pregnant wife dependent upon him, the injustice of judge and jury, final imprisonment and solitude, but all endured with faith, hope, and resolve intact.

Their next attempt at forming a label produced Tuff Gong which seems to have a special meaning for Marley. According to Tosh, to be called 'gong' was to be tough, the boss, and the Big Bad One, and Marley used to be (and still is) called Gong by close friends and associates. The combination of the two words spell out the attitude of Marley and the Wailers. In that same year Johnny Nash and his business partner, Danny Simms, came to Jamaica to discover new talents among composers and songwriters. Nash had previously suffered a setback in his career, but received an injection in that same year with 'Cupid' and 'Hold Me Tight'. The Wailers were on everybody's lips as talented artists. The Nash/Simms company was called JAD (Johnny And Danny) and they proceeded to sign the Wailers as songwriters. They also recorded two albums of backing tracks for Nash which were never released. JAD paid the Wailers fifty dollars a week each, but this only lasted for three months, according to Tosh.[12] The Wailers did not give up their label to work for Nash/Simms exclusively, but felt they were being used and were powerless to correct it.

In 1968 Tosh was arrested and charged with obstruction after demonstrating with Prince Buster and others against the régime in Rhodesia. Tosh's overtly political stance would forever place him under the scrutiny of the law and the government and exert tremendous pressures on him. Marley had also served a short prison sentence for possession of marijuana, which he later dismissed as a traffic offence. Tuff Gong Records were not making a lot of money, but at times they were able to sell as many as 15,000 copies of a single.

Bunny Wailer, a founding member of the original Wailers, well respected for his individuality and personal vision. (*Photo: D. Morris.*)

Lee Perry at his studios, The Black Ark, Kingston. (*Photo: D. Morris.*)

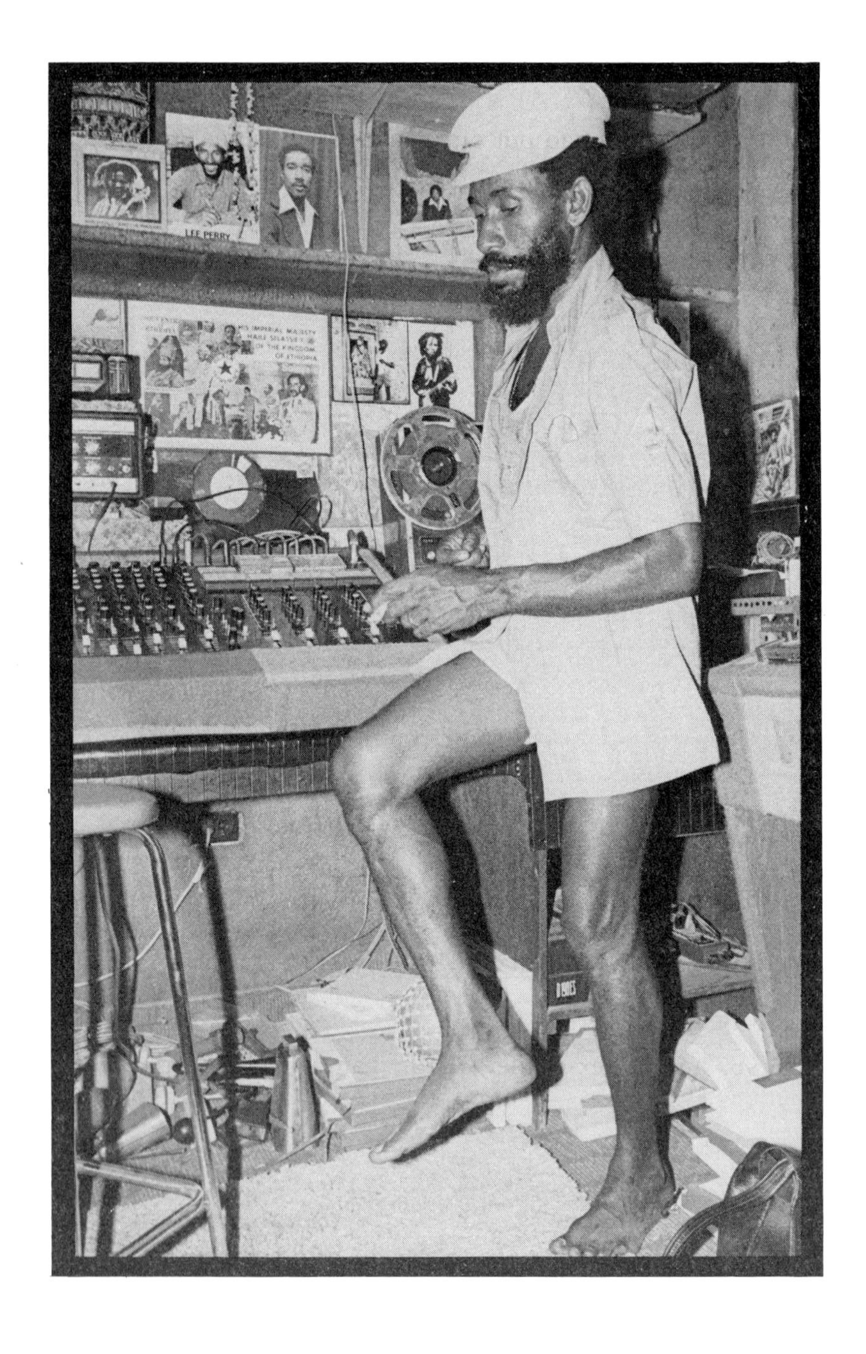

The Wailers had no real impact abroad. Names like Alton Ellis and Desmond Dekker were far better known. The reason was the controversial status the band had as rebels, and very few deals were secured for them abroad. As early as 1965 they had released a single, 'Put It On', on Island Records in the United Kingdom through Clement Dodd. However, though Island had put out a number of Jamaican records during their early history, they later clamped down on the music to specialize in Rock.

The relationship with JAD was an uneasy one. Nash was an international recording star and the Wailers were unknown internationally. When Nash offered them a recording and publishing deal they were naïve enough to believe that JAD was really serious. JAD's concerns were centred around Nash, and the least consideration was paid to the Wailers. In 1969 the Wailers were encouraged by Lee Perry (who had previously worked with Clement Dodd) to join his new set-up, Upsetter Records. Perry's set-up was recognized as the Upsetter, most probably named after Roland Alphonso and the Upsetters, a band that existed in the early 1960s. They decided to give Perry a try and some of their best songwriting was done while with Perry. There are conflicting stories as to the real writer of 'Small Axe', a tune that both Perry and Marley claim to have written, but Tosh has stated that he was the main songwriter. He said that when Perry approached the Wailers to join his stable he told them that the 'Big Three' – represented by Dynamic, Federal, and Jamaica Recording Studios – were out to destroy him. Tosh said that his response was that if they were the 'Big Three', then the Wailers were the small axe, and started there and then to write the song.[13] It is also true to say that Perry has been credited by several artists as being a fine lyricist, but had no conception of executing the musical side. The song, therefore, could have been a collaboration involving all three.

In 1967 another ex-welder, Aston 'Family Man' Barrett and his younger brother, Carlton Barrett, had formed a band called the Hippy Boys and also worked under a variety of names – Rhythm Force and Soul Mates. They were soon spotted by Lee Perry and used as his studio musicians. It was through Perry's set-up that the Wailers and the Barretts formally met. Perry had had a hit with the Upsetters with 'Return of Django' in the British charts and the Barretts toured Europe as part of the band. From the time of the meeting of the Wailers and the Barretts there was a mutual respect for each other's ability and talent. Aston Barrett almost immediately undertook the task of bandmaster and arranger for the Wailers even though Barrett himself does not like to say so. The collaboration, however, was one of the most creative and productive of their recording life. Instead of being preoccupied with one theme, they expanded to include a variety of ideas, though still maintaining their fundamental reputations as rebels.

It was their *Soul Rebel* album (which was released in the United Kingdom as *Rasta Revolution*) which contained some excellent compositions, including the title tune, Tosh's '400 Years' and Marley's response to gaol, 'Duppy Conqueror'. Marley has said of that tune, 'It's just that man utter dark sayings and who can pick it up, pick it up. . . . We conquer duppy now. It's life we a-deal with. We not deal with death again. It's life. He that see the light and know the light will live.'[14] 'Duppy Conqueror' has lines that speak of being wrongly accused and challenges the society to a fight: 'Don't show off/Or I will cut you off/I will cut your rass off.' The later Island version on *Burnin'* does not contain the last lines. It seems to have been recorded without them because they might be offensive. If this were any indication of things to come, it was worth looking at. Although they had a reasonably productive relationship with Perry, it did not seem to have paid off financially. Marley in particular had an on-and-off relationship with Perry which continued into the 1970s.

In 1972 the Wailers, along with the Barretts, came to England to join Marley who had arrived in advance with Nash/Simms to write the score for a film Nash was starring in in Sweden. The film was never released. Nash/Simms came to London where they negotiated a contract with CBS for Nash. The Wailers had intended to do a tour of England, but instead they were used for recording purposes. The backing tracks for Nash's *I Can See Clearly Now* album were laid down by the Wailers. The band members were annoyed at the manner in which they were handled and were disgusted with the treatment they received. In that same year Marley released a solo single through CBS Records called 'Reggae on

Broadway'. CBS showed no interest in the record and it was through the efforts of Nash's promotion manager, Brent Clarke, that the single eventually sold 3,000 copies. The Wailers were rehearsing, during this period, in the basement at Condor Music in Surrey, and were staying in an hotel in Bayswater in which they had no proper facilities to cook or conduct themselves in the manner in which they preferred.

Brent Clarke, a young Trinidadian promoter, who had previously been involved with the music business through promoting dances and putting on bands, first met Nash/Simms/Marley at Mr Bees Club (now known as the Bouncing Ball) in Peckham, South London. Simms introduced himself and they struck up a conversation. According to Clarke, Marley was quite happy to meet a Caribbean to whom he could talk, for at this particular time he had not met up with his Jamaican friends who were living in London. After a long conversation, Clarke accepted Simms's invitation to be Nash's promotion manager. After Nash had his biggest hit with 'I Can See Clearly Now', and a great deal of abuse from the Wailers through the mouth-piece of Bunny Wailer, Simms suggested to Clarke that he devote all his time and energy to the Wailers. The first thing that Clarke did was to move the Wailers out of their hotel and into a small three-bedroomed, semi-detached house in Neasden. This was a morale-booster for the Wailers for they began to attract the young black musicians in London, and also met up with a number of their friends. When Nash's album came out it contained a number of Marley's compositions. This was the first real break for Marley as an individual.

The relationship between JAD and the Wailers had deteriorated so badly that the Wailers' passports were with the Home Office pending permits to work in the country. Nash/Simms left the country for the United States to pursue their own business, and abandoned the Wailers to themselves. On their departure, Clarke sought a job as promotion manager with Island and was assigned to work on Greyhound's 'Dream Lover' and Lorna Bennett's 'Breakfast in Bed'. He later approached Chris Blackwell, Island's Jamaican-born proprietor, and showed him the songs that Marley had written for Nash. Blackwell was impressed and divulged that he had wanted to sign the Wailers for several years, but did not approach them directly because of their reputation as rebels and non-signatories. At the same time, Island's biggest Reggae artist, Jimmy Cliff, had completed his first feature film, *The Harder They Come,* and had also released the single of the film's title on which Clarke also worked. But Cliff did not want to remain with Island because he felt that he was not being paid the advances that he wanted, and Island had suppressed certain songs he wanted to record – songs such as 'Let Your Yeah Be Yeah' which became a chart hit for the Pioneers, and 'You Can Get It' which also became a chart hit for Desmond Dekker. Cliff was reputed to have received £14,000 for his contract with Island and asked Island for £20,000 in order to re-sign. They did not want to pay that kind of advance at the time (though later they were paying out six-figure sums to Reggae acts).

It was under these circumstances that Clarke's approach to Island was made, and Blackwell was enthusiastic about the offer. Clarke negotiated the contract on their behalf and got £8,000 advance for them per album. He also stipulated that the Wailers should retain the rights to release the record in the Caribbean. The reason for this was that the band was based in Jamaica, and though they were guaranteed £8,000, there was no certainty about how well their records would sell internationally, and they would, therefore, not have to depend on overseas royalties for sustenance. The terms were agreed to and contracts signed. A cheque for £1,000 was paid over to Clarke by way of commission, the remaining £7,000 to be paid into Byron Lee's bank account in Jamaica which the Wailers would receive upon return. Clarke loaned the Wailers £750 towards their return tickets to Jamaica. When the contracts were signed the Wailers seemed to become suspicious of Clarke's good intentions and refused to sign a management contract. It is true to say that Bunny Wailer was the most obsessively distrustful of all the members of the group.

The Wailers then returned to Jamaica to record the rhythm tracks for their first international album, *Catch a Fire,* at Dynamic Studios. Though the album credits the Wailers as the only instrumentalists, a great number of session musicians also played on it. In Jamaica, Robbie Shakespeare played bass on 'Concrete Jungle', Tyrone Downey played organ on 'Concrete Jungle' and 'Stir It Up', Winston Wright also played organ, Francisco Willie Pep played congas and bongoes, and when Marley brought the tapes back to Island in the winter of 1972, a number of white session musicians also played on the album. Wayne Perkins played the lead guitar on 'Stir It Up' and other tracks, Chris Karen played tablas on 'Concrete Jungle' and John 'Rabbit' Bundrick played clavinet, electric piano, and moog synthesizer on most of the tracks. Bundrick was a member of Johnny Nash's road band before he joined the rock band, Free, on Island. Clarke believes that Marley's use of Bundrick on his first album was not only due to his musical talent, but to superstition on Marley's part: he was said to believe that since Bundrick played with Nash and Nash was successful, then if Bundrick played with him, he too would be successful. Blackwell played an important role in supervising, editing, and helping to choose the musicians for the remix.

It was during Marley's return to England that CBS sent their legal man, Bob White, over to Island to confirm that Marley was signed to CBS through Danny Simms. The contract was half a type-written page. Blackwell wanted to avoid court cases which would consume time, but Clarke's thinking was that they had a case of mismanagement. Blackwell then suggested to Marley that he should fly to New York, explain the situation to Simms, and ask him what he wanted. Simms wanted £5,000 for Marley's release, and Blackwell paid it. Marley then refused to have any further dealings with Clarke and never repaid the £750 that was loaned to the band. Blackwell had taken a special interest in Marley as opposed to the band and this led to eventual conflict between band members which caused the ultimate split.

The Wailers toured the United States and Europe in 1973. They appeared at Max's Kansas City in New York working three half-hour sets a night for seven days. The winter tour of England was abandoned when Tosh and Wailer refused to tour because of the cold. That was one reasonable explanation, the other was lack of comprehension on the part of Tosh and Wailer of the emphasis on Marley as leader. Blackwell was looking for an angle to sell the group in order to create immediate controversy and interest. The image that Island projected was one of rebels and dreaded Rasta brethren. Marley was not 'locksed' in 1972–3, neither was Tosh. The only person who wore locks and was a confirmed and committed Rasta man was Wailer. In London, while

Marley and Tosh enjoyed the company of female companionship, Wailer was withdrawn and meditative. According to Clarke, he 'read the Bible and thought about his woman in Jamaica. He was . . . more conscious of food and hygiene and the right way of living'.[15] Although Marley was not locksed, he spoke constantly of Rasta. Then, late in 1973, Marley began the process of locksing his hair and visually projecting his public image. Then in 1974 the Wailers broke up.

According to Wailer, Blackwell had a conversation with the members of the band during that same year, and said to Wailer that because he was nobody and the world did not know who he was, he should tour in order to awaken interest in the band. Wailer considered what he said, and thought that a 'body' was a dead person, and that he was not dead. (To Rastas a 'body' is a dead person). And that if he was nothing, he would remain nothing by not touring.[16] Tosh's arguments were primarily business ones. 'After waiting several months to get some funds we were confronted wid a whole pile of papers so high' (he indicated a great height), 'telling us that we owe Island Records £42,000 as tour expenses. . . . And before we made the tour there was an agreement that Island Records would cover all the expenses of the tour.'[17] On a subsequent visit to Jamaica, Blackwell had talks with Tosh who became infuriated, left and returned with a machete to confront Blackwell who left immediately.

Just before the Wailers' final split, Tosh had already begun recording his first solo album, although the band had issued singles individually on their Tuff Gong label. Tosh ran out of money and approached Marley for $2,000 J (about £1,000 at the time). Marley said he had no money.[18] Lee Jaffe, a white American who had worked as the Wailers' roadie during their 1973 tour of America, on behalf of Tosh, contacted Carl Radle, an ex-Eric Clapton bass-player, who financed the recording. The album was sold to Colombia in the United States, and later Tosh severed his relationship with Radle over a reputed debt to Colombia of $20,000. Tosh also claims that most of the advance was taken by Radle, ostensibly to offset recording costs.[19] Tosh's first solo album was his paean to marijuana legalization, 'Legalise It', which was a markedly uneven work. The Wailers continued to appear live in Jamaica until 1976. Marley, by 1975, was already an international recording star.

Tosh and Wailer were committed friends and helped each other out on their respective solo albums. This was probably a result of Marley's continuing withdrawal from any real contact with them. Yet Tosh and Wailer exhibited a kind of sophistication in manners that can only be explained by the guilding philosophy of Rastafari. Rasta philosophy does not permit absolute responses, but accepts the possibility of an open-ended situation. If the politician, for example, oppresses the people, Rasta philosophy would permit the good points of the politician's policies to be seen, at the same time as condemning his oppression. It is as though everything and everyone is open to change. It was this type of guiding philosophy that allowed them to continue relating to Marley, in spite of their bitterness and criticism. And this relationship continues today.

The three individuals who made up the original Wailers have completely separate personalities and approaches, but are ultimately unified in their commitment to two things: music and the freedom of the black man in the modern world. Of the three, Tosh is the most materialistic in accepting the material world and approaching its problems in realistic terms. He believes, for example, in revolutionary war for the liberation of Afrikans around the world. Wailer's world is highly influenced by a spiritual mysticism which permeates his recordings and sayings. Marley, on the other hand, is less easy to categorize. He is political only in his belief that the black man should ultimately be free. But, simultaneously, his outlook is clouded by his feeling that the individual should propose the solution. And he very rarely speaks out what he actually believes because of the fear of death.

It would be ignorant to dismiss Marley as being politically naïve, as some British music journalists have done. He completely understands the consequences of an important public figure, such as himself, making political statements. He is therefore unlikely to make any statements about the Jamaican political parties. 'Pure politics can hurt certain people, so you 'ave to get hard, get soft, 'cos guns don't argue, an' if you talk too much an' get too strong, they'll kill ya because Babylon set up [their] own system an' it no want nobody to change it. . . . So is not everything you can talk 'bout 'cos them kill ya.'[20] Marley, of course, is thinking of the death of Malcolm X and Martin Luther King in the United States, and the political deaths of Jamaicans who ran counter to the policies and aims of the two political parties. 'Me no gonna go back to Jamaica to set myself up as a target again, for the Government, the Opposition, or anyone else.'[21]

In December 1976, Marley, for whatever reason, had agreed to do a concert for 'the people', and as a consequence an assassination attempt was made on him. Marley himself said that he went to the government to organize the concert because they had the organizational skills and the facility to do so. On the other hand, it seems highly likely that Marley agreed to do the concert at the request of the leader of the People's National Party (PNP), Michael Manley, to lend credibility and support to his election campaign. The Rastafarians have accepted the image of Michael Manley as a man committed to change the social conditions of poor blacks and promote Rastafari as an important cultural contributor to the development of Jamaican society. Manley had also projected himself to the masses of poor people as a modern-day Joshua. This has been expressed in song by both Max Romeo and Junior Murvin. The latter's song states that Moses gave Joshua the right to lead the people, while Haile Selassie I gave Manley the rod to lead the people. It was the populist approach of Manley, who used the religious beliefs of the Rastafarians to enhance his credibility and reputation, that surely persuaded Marley to appear in the concert.

It has been suggested by a number of political observers that Edward Seaga's JLP party was responsible for the shooting. Marley himself has consistently attempted to conceal his knowledge of precisely whom was responsible. He has said it could have been the government, the opposition, or business people. But he has then contradicted this by saying that his willingness to do the 1976 concert could have been interpreted as support for the PNP, and that 'The other party didn't like it.'[22] It is obvious, then, that Marley does know who shot at him, but refuses to divulge his knowledge. Subsequent developments substantiate this. In April 1978 the henchmen of the leaders of the two parties – the late Claudie Massop of the JLP and Bucky Marshall of the PNP – came together and decided that they would no longer unleash violence on the supporters (primarily poor and without political punch) of the parties they represented. Both Massop and Marshall came to London earlier that same year and approached Marley about doing the concert. Marley, himself from the Kingston ghetto and having therefore experienced violent political warfare, made them both guarantee that no assassination attempt would be made on him. They agreed. It is theoretically sound to imagine that under the circumstances of the truce, they would both reveal to Marley the machinations of their past operations, and precisely who was responsible for shooting at him. Marley's manager, Don Taylor, who threw himself in front of Marley when he was shot at and was severely injured, has stated 'Claudie and Bucky and them . . . I went to school with them, and they're the *cause* of the trouble there's been in the past, so if they say no trouble there won't be any. Anyone trying anything would just . . . disappear. . .'[23]

The heralded Peace Concert of April 1978 featured a plethora of talents from the island, Big Youth, Dillinger, the Meditations, Althea and Donna, the Mighty Diamonds, Culture, Peter Tosh, and Bob Marley and the Wailers. The concert was attended by the Prime Minister, Michael Manley, and the Opposition leader, Edward Seaga. All the participants expressed their desire to believe in the peace truce, except Peter Tosh who saw the whole operation as futile. On the political level, true peace could only be obtained by improving the material condition of the urban poor. To speak of peace when the same social conditions existed was hypocritical. And it was this that Tosh saw through.

> Stand here at what dem seh call Peace Concert. It was a Peace Concert and I man never love come in it. . . . Our left-wing people realize what the word Peace means. You see, most intellectual people in the society think the word Peace means coming together. *Peace is the diploma you get in the cemetery,* seen? *On top of your grave – here lies the body of John Stokes, rest in peace.* . . . White man teach I&I seh I&I a go dead a go a-heaven. Why? That them can tek away the sun and inherit the bloodclaat earth and we gone away to the land of milk and honey. . . . Learn this, man, this is some little game that Columbus and Henry Morgan and Sir Francis Drake thought to scatter us when they come with their cross round their neck to

come check black people and say, well, bwoy, right now black people is Israel, so we wanna hold them, only thing we can hold them with is tell them seh, see the cross here? That Jesus huh? Him soon come back. *Look how bloodclaat long we wait pon Jesus! All the war in the earth and Jesus can't do anything 'bout it. . .*

Equal Rights – everyone is crying out for peace, no one is crying out for justice – I don't want no peace, we all need equal rights and justice – *right here in Jamaica*. . . . This colonial shitstem a rule the underprivileged. I am one of them who happen to be in the underprivileged sector. . . . Right now, Mr Manley, me wan talk to you personal cos me and you is friends, so you seh. . . . Right now as a man of power and a ruler of this little country here, not you alone, Mr Seaga too, we would like the Members of Parliament must come together to deal with the poor people and the suffering class and the police to know that they brutalize poor people, and fe what? A little draw of herb [marijuana]. . . . Me go through the lowest degradation, humiliation and discrimination and brutality, and yet me no bend my mind and say, bwoy, let me try and lick off a man in a shop and hold sum'p. I no seh that my brother is a criminal. Cos when Columbus, Henry Morgan and Francis Drake come up, dey call dem pirate and put dem in a reading book and give us observation that we must look up and live the life of and the principle of pirates. So the youth dem know fe fire dem guns like Henry Morgan same way. . . . Is just a shitstem lay down to belittle the poor. Poor people go to jail every time. Is pure poor poor people me see in there. . .[24]

Tosh's speech was electrically received by the 20,000 capacity audience and it was reported that a near rebellion could have emerged if he did not arrange his musical programme a certain way. In October of the same year, Tosh was arrested by the police for smoking a joint of ganja, and taken to the police station where he was vigorously beaten. His arm was broken and he had to have multiple stitches in his head. This kind of torture is still carried out by the Jamaican police or army to stamp out political dissent. Since the Peace Treaty was declared there has been a resurgence of violence. Marley's fear for his life may be understood in the light of organized political violence.

The musical paths taken by Marley, Tosh and Wailer are diverse but unified thematically. Of the three, Marley retains more of the cultural and paradigmatic qualities of the Afrikan vocal tradition, in spite of his music's technical transformation. As shown in Chapter 1, the Afrikan vocal tradition is characterized by a variety of cultural traits: the slur, slide or glissando common in spoken words, and melodic structure in which the highest point commences at the beginning of a song. On Marley's *Natty Dread* album, he uses a variety of these traits. In the song 'Revolution' he employs his harmony group, the I-Threes, to sing out the first lines with him: 'Revolution, reveals thy truth,' then the I-Threes sing the word 'Revolution' four times in succession, after which Marley enters the body of the tune. The opening lines of the song are heavily emphasized and are in fact the highest point of the tune, which gently works down as Marley enters the verse passages. On his latest album, *Kaya*, he employs an unusual vocal practice, that of singing in an almost talking voice. This technique is successfully employed in 'Running Away' on the same album. This particular song reflects Marley's nagging doubts about the righteousness and quality of his life. It is self-searching in that he questions why he was shot at, why his toe had to be operated on, why he had to be living abroad away from possible assassinations for two years, when he is in fact a Jamaican. The vocal delivery oscillates between singing and almost talking. 'Running Away' does not resolve itself thematically, but answers his questions petulantly. After the song has consistently questioned his running away ('You must have done something, you don't want nobody to know about. . . . You must have done something wrong'), he answers it in the last verse: 'No, no, no, I'm not running away/don't say that/. . . I've got to protect my life/and I don't want to live with no strife/It is better to live on the house top/than to live in a house full of confusion/so I made my decision, and I left you/now you coming to tell me that I'm running away/but it's not true, I am not running away.'

Why does Marley employ a talking voice to say these lines? Because the accusation, though real, was posed by his conscience. He was talking to convince both his listeners and to appease his conscience. This is the only song in which Marley employs the talk-sing characteristic totally. In an older song, 'Soul Rebel', Marley employed the talk-sing characteristic to great effect. After stating that he was a rebel, he speaks to the next door neighbour ('Do you hear them, Lizzie?'), then goes back to state that he was a rebel.

Being a rebel was Marley's real angst, a personal angst, as opposed to a collective response to oppression in Jamaica. According to Brent Clarke: 'Bob was seeing himself more as a rebel than a Rasta. He saw himself as a rebel against society.'[25] Rebels, if they do not take stock and identify themselves with political struggle, usually end up in the other camp or alone. Marley was converted to Rastafarianism, and his faith in Rastafari, he has said, is not shaken because of events over the last two years. His album *Kaya* was widely criticized by British journalists because of his uncharacteristic lack of preoccupation with political/religious themes. Given Marley's fear of death if he speaks out, it is no surprise that he has rationalized his approach to include a wider selection of love songs (although he has always written love songs) after the attempt on his life. It is quite probable that Marley's preoccupation will continue, but that he will become more philosophical about his situation in Jamaica (the Rastas have rationalized the exodus question with the statement that JA - MA(KE)-YA: Jah make here equals Jamaica). Marley is also abandoning his own vocal characteristics in favour of the blander, international approach, straightforward vocal delivery without the frills of tradition (see *Kaya*).

On the other hand, though Peter Tosh has publicly declaimed Calypso, his music and vocal delivery, unlike those of the other two, are heavily influenced by Calypso rhythms. This is probably unconscious, and can be traced back to his style when playing with the original Wailers. His vocal delivery in songs like '400 Years' and 'One Foundation' are most certainly within the Reggae mould, yet when he cut his first solo album, *Legalise It*, his vocal approach was entirely different. Tosh sings with a slow, clear, almost monotonous drone, but within the calypsonic vocal patterns. His vision of the world is a mixture of Rasta religion with political insights. His songs have always been preoccupied with contemporary social issues. The question of slavery, marijuana, sex, love, apartheid, religion, etc., are all contained in his songs.

In his song 'Apartheid', Tosh states that Palestinians are fighting for their homeland, Israel, and that the Europeans who live in that country have stolen it from its native inhabitants. In a sense, this is a material approach to reality, as Israel, according to Rasta philosophy, is the black man's rightful land. But because Tosh's world-view is historical and material, he seems at times to be in conflict with Rasta doctrines. He has also stated that Ancient Egypt (and the Pharaohs) was the black man's civilization centre. This runs counter to the Rasta's belief that the children of Israel were persecuted by the Pharaohs. In this overtly political stand, Tosh makes himself a target for political adversaries. Also, his recent business alliance with Mick Jagger of the Rolling Stones (and their singing together on '(You Gotta Walk) Don't Look Back' and on his albums *Bush Doctor* and *Mystic Man*) poses some serious questions about his integrity. Tosh seems to follow any route that promises not so much international stardom, as financial security. And it is this, perhaps, that has motivated him to sign with the Stones' record company. If the relationship inhibits Tosh's political freedom, then the entire history of the Wailers since they signed with Island Records might as well be wiped out.

Bunny Wailer is the most pop-orientated of all the Wailers. His music is both highly personalized and invested with a heavy artistic style. This is particularly evident on his first solo album, *Black Heart Man,* which reflects the changes in his life. The album can be defined as autobiographical. While Tosh speaks to collective experience, and Marley combines personal vision with collective wishes, Wailer defines his world within the Rastafarian schema. His songs are laden with the personal suffering he has experienced – and by extension all Rasta brethren have endured – and he projects this theme with an immensity of conviction and emotion. Wailer's belief in Rastafari has carried him through the years with the Wailers. He rarely smiles and has an awesome reputation among musicians. Though *Black Heart Man* was a great achievement artistically, it was not an instant seller, but his follow-up, *Protest,* was ill-conceived, ill-defined and badly executed. It sold badly both in Jamaica and the rest of the world. With the exception of three tracks, the musical approach was not as well planned as on his previous album.

Wailer tries desperately to avoid live appearances. He is extremely wary of being ripped-off and exploited. He claims he has not signed a contract with Island Records, but this is doubtful. In Jamaica he supervises the design and pressing of his record sleeves, produces his recordings himself, and when taking the lacquer for manufacture, he removes the stamper after the required number of records are pressed. He is not really concerned about the international impact of his music. He seems to emphasize that he is a Jamaican and Jamaica is where he belongs. However, if he succeeds in creating an international hit, it is unlikely that he would refuse to tour.

Though Wailer is the most mystic/spiritual of the three, he is the least traditional in his approach to music. He is international in his musical perspective and can relate to Bob Dylan, for example, so his musical creations usually have been stated within these cultural terms. His production ability can be efficacious and his use of subtlety in his music is a great asset. His most important song, 'Dreamland', has had coverage in Jamaica and abroad. The song projects the other-worldliness of Wailer's vision – he sees a Garden of Eden and a state of serenity and peace, without war, suffering and death. This song embodies the Rasta credo.

Without doubt, the original Wailers have been the most important vocal group Jamaica has ever seen. Not only because of their vocal abilities, but because of the position they occupied in society and the collective experiences they expressed in song. Their experiences of the Jamaica of the poor and oppressed black man, and their steadfastness as rebels who were against selling out. The reason for the disintegration of the Wailers can be summed up as follows: signing to an international record company that has made an investment and anticipates commercial returns. Marley made his decision to travel the route of success regardless of the hassles. Additionally, his decision to sell the band implied an angle: rebels and Rastafari. It is difficult to accept the commercial projection of a man's basic religious beliefs. But Marley understood and accommodated this imposition. Yet one cannot say that because he accommodated Island Records, he sold himself out. Marley is the only artist I know who has been accepted as a commercial proposition by the international market while severely criticizing the system that he operates in. But with *Kaya*, for reasons observed earlier, there is a noticeable shift in emphasis. This shift in emphasis is also clearly perceived on Tosh's album *Bush Doctor*. Unless an artist wants to remain obscure, it would seem, he has to accommodate the reality of commercial demands. The reality of the modern world imposes on all our lives, but our artist-heroes who make public decisions are expected not to be mere mortals. The political reality of our world imposes, in spite of this, a need for public heroes to transcend the demands of the white commercial world. But death faces mortals as a definite, certain and irremovable reality, and our artist-heroes are glaringly aware of this. Decisions, then, are formed around this acceptation of death as a solution to speaking out.

5 The Power of the Spoken Word

The phenomenon of the toaster or DJ in Reggae music has created a large audience, one which acknowledges it as a new form of Roots music. The DJ in Reggae dates back to the period of R&B where, while the records were being played, the sound man's assistant would scat, in other words, utter nonsensical sounds or words into the microphone. This would be executed in an effort to urge the dancer on to greater emotional frenzy and also to inject more feeling into the music. Over the years this style has developed into a specific genre in Reggae and a number of artists now earn a living exclusively from this. Because the DJ was part and parcel of the sound system set-up, he cannot be separated from the latter's own development. It was the sound system itself that created the opportunity for the DJ as artist to emerge. Sounds were identified, not only by the exclusivity of records, and the weight and power of their amplification, but by the type of DJ they had. This identification led to a greater emphasis on the sound system as a cultural progenitor.

One of the earliest sounds that gained popularity through its widely acclaimed DJ was Coxsone/Downbeat. One of the first DJs he worked with was King Sporty (he later emigrated to Miami, Florida, and became distinguished as a vocalist/producer) who had as his second the great King Stitt. Before these two emerged on the scene, Coxsone's dominant DJ was Count Machuki. He transmitted his knowledge to King Stitt who remained with Coxsone from 1957 to 1969. Stitt was a tall man with enormously long front teeth which, in some people's minds, illustrated his genius. Stitt's scatting and word-play created an enormous following for

Coxsone, but in spite of recording for Coxsone his recordings were never released. It was not until 1969 that he recorded *Fire Corner* for Clancy Eccles and a number of other titles for other producers. Stitt's DJing was not a new phenomenon to the listeners, because they had already grown accustomed to it through Jazz and R&B. But with the demise of Afro-American music in Jamaica, new artists emerged, and the importance of DJs increased because of the proliferation of locally manufactured records.

The first popular artist to emerge in this genre was U-Roy, born Ewart Beckford. U-Roy started his DJ career with Dickie's Dynamic (the proprietor being Dickie Wong), and later moved to Sir George (Clarke) Atomic in the early 1960s.[1] In 1968 King Tubby (Osborne Ruddock) built a professional sound system and had U-Roy as his first DJ. U-Roy himself was influenced by the great Count Machuki.[2] Ruddock had a custom-made record of the Techniques' song 'You Don't Care', which was supplied to him by Duke Reid.[3] This was then DJed over by U-Roy and thus became the signature tune for Tubby's sound. Ruddock played an important part in urging U-Roy to take up the art more seriously, and subsequently took him to Duke Reid to cut a record, 'Wake the Town', which the Duke released on his own label.[4] It soared to the top of the charts almost immediately. U-Roy has since emerged as the cultural paradigm on whom younger artists modelled their work.

Though Ruddock has said that he was the first to have U-Roy recorded, Keith Hudson has stated that he was the first to produce U-Roy on a version of Ken Boothe's 'Old Fashion Way', retitled 'Dynamic Fashion Way'. U-Roy's themes have been diverse, matching the original song or transcending it by projecting ideas of his own. Since the inception of the form, the DJ has not been an originator, but one whose role was to add colour to the original. As a result there could be the singer's original version on the market and, simultaneously, the DJ could do a version of the song using the original tapes, or record a version with a different singer and voice his ideas over the track. This has led to great bitterness on the part of singers who feel that the DJ is not an originator, but an imitator.[5] Also, if the DJ's version is on the market at the same time as the original, there is added competition. This sometimes results in the DJ's version slowing up the potential sales of the singer's original.

The importance of the DJ as a cultural force can be understood if one considers the constant changes that the music has undergone over the years. It can also be understood if one considers that the spoken word projects greater power than the sung word. The spoken word, in this context, seems to transmit as close a relationship between the DJ and his audience as a conversation between two friends. And the DJ is telling his audience something, whether it is about the state of the nation or the state of a woman's mind. This interaction through speech is perhaps more fundamental than interaction through song, and also perhaps the DJ gains a following *first* with a sound, and then ventures into recording. Upon popular acceptance, the DJ usually retains his popularity by continuing to DJ with a sound. 'Whether my tune is big or not, I never stop working a sound. Or even if I'm doing a whole heap of recording, I still must play a sound. 'Cause sound-system to me is a very big thing. I start there, so I couldn't ignore it like that.'[6]

The general construction of the tune over which the DJ talks runs something like the following: the tune is either opened by the DJ himself or by the singer. On 'Runaway Girl', for example (which is sung by the Ken Boothe imitator Barrington Spence, and DJed by U-Roy), the tune begins with the singer humming the melody line, then U-Roy enters the tune speaking these lines: 'Just another girl you are/And a little girl you remain, you know/Don't stop your running wild and change your style 'cause you're gonna get spoil, you know.' The theme of the song is the attempt by the protagonist to maintain his superiority over his beloved girlfriend. He attempts this by enforcing into the girl's consciousness that she is 'just another girl', therefore she should be grateful for his affections and attention. When U-Roy completes the above statement, the singer comes in on a verse: 'Just another girl, that's what you are/Maybe nice, but you're not that smart/I love you and remember that you're just another girl.' The chorus of the song, which repeats itself often, is: 'I know and you know it's true/That this love is really really true.' The role of U-Roy in this particular song is to emphasize the intentions of the singer who is insecure in his relationship with his beloved. So the double emphasis, when it reaches the audience, is a dynamic one. The audience identifies with U-Roy's rhythmic concatenation of word-sense, as well as his rhythmic connection to the body-rhythms of the music. The totality of the tune propels the imaginary audience to dance, rather than to think and analyse. This is not to say, however, that the audience is not sharply critical of DJs who 'chat fockery' (the local slang for talking irrelevant nonsense).

The language the DJ uses in his talk-over is that of the urban poor. His art was formulated through dance and he was encouraged by his particular audience, so his language is orientated towards the people who were responsible for his popularity. Middle Jamaica, which has now partly overcome its horror of popular Jamaican music, has absorbed certain aspects of the music as their own. Artists like Bob Andy, John Holt and Ken Boothe, are now *understood* by middle Jamaica, and with their new discoveries they have erected barriers against the incursion of the poor man's music into their minds. The DJ, therefore, is seen as a cultural reflector of this urban poor man's music, and is usually dismissed as incomprehensible. However, the children of the middle class have begun to accept this music as a new cultural tool or armour.

With the success of U-Roy's recordings, the way was opened for similar acts. One of the earliest acts following in U-Roy's wake was Big Youth (born Manley Buchannan). The Youth started his career attempting to inculcate the phrasings and tonalities of his predecessor, but slowly emerged as an identifiable and distinguished DJ. He was once a DJ for the Tippertone sound and having developed popularity and response there, he was encouraged to record. Gregory Issacs, a gifted singer-cum-producer, provided the facilities for his first recording, a version of Errol Dunkley's 'Movie Star'.[7] Issacs and Dunkley had teamed up to form their own label, Afrikan Museum, after their frustrations in not receiving just financial rewards for their various recordings. And it was on this label that Youth first appeared. However, it was only with Keith Hudson's production on 'S.90 Skank' (a popular motor bike) that Big Youth achieved his first big hit.

As a result of U-Roy's immense popularity, Roy Reid, a former government employed accountant, turned I-Roy and made his debut in 1970 with 'Musical Pleasure' for producer Harry Moodie. I-Roy loved controversy and recorded a controversial sex single, 'Welding', in 1975. The record opened with the snores of a sleeping person who suddenly wakes up and asks angrily: 'Ah who come knock down me door when I man just start to catch me puss nap?' A voice answers sheepishly, 'Is me. I come to get my welding.' The male's voice, now aroused, answers, 'Well, step forward yah!' Then I-Roy begins his genital paean: 'According to the feels, well, sister love, you got to wait until I have my meals, yeah. Welding is what the young girl want, welding . . .' This sparked off a response by Big Youth who said on record, 'Natty Dread She Want', 'Natty dread is what the young girl want . . ./She don't want no soldering.' In the background there is a female singing: 'Soldering is what the young girl want, soldering.' This serves as the contrast for Big Youth's commentary. The feud over the state of the female's desires symbolizes a social battle between two elements: one that enjoys the pleasures of life, and the other that projects a philosophy beyond reality and the empirical. I-Roy characterizes the former movement and has consistently come into conflict with the nation's top DJs. At one time he conflicted with U-Roy who dismissed him as an 'imitator' and said that even Roy Reid's name, I-Roy, was first used by him;[8] at another time he conflicted with Prince Jazzbo who said of him: 'I-Roy, you is a boy, to imitate the great U-Roy' ('Straight To I-Roy Head'), and I-Roy responded with 'Jazzbo, why do you hate I or do you want to fly me down to the sky? . . . Jazzbo, if you were a juke-box I wouldn't put a dime into you.' By and large these public attitudes help to sell records and promote the artists, but in private I-Roy seems to be regarded with some resentment.

Of all the contemporary DJs, I-Roy is the only one who, in spite of incorporating the roots vocal approach to his DJ style, uses almost totally correct grammar in his speech. This is almost contrary to the essence of the DJ himself, but I-Roy, a secular man and a modernist, adapts a variety of positions without contradiction. His themes are not limited to a particular philosophical approach or context, but span the spectrum of life.

Instead of restricting his themes to a particular audience, he speaks to the world. It is, therefore, not surprising that I-Roy can speak of sex on the one hand, and on the other, condemn the exploitation inherent in a capitalist society. In

1974, he made 'Sufferer's Psalm', in which he uses a popular theme for the majority of poor people. The 23rd Psalm is used as its model, but adapted: 'If the capitalist is our shepherd, we will always want/They maketh us to lie down on the sidewalk/They anointeth our income with taxation and victimization/Yea though we walk through the fields and factories of our labour/not even a favour/Because of their ruthless political behaviour/But Jah is our Saviour . . .' The record sold 27,000, mainly in Jamaica and in selected areas of the Caribbean. The record could have been influenced by the political rhetoric of the PNP in their effort to mobilize the people behind them. I-Roy himself has stated his predilection for socialist political and economic institutions. So this song was an important contribution to the impact that the party made on the people. It was not just the singer who identified and proselytized on behalf of political parties, but also the DJ.

By contrast U-Roy, Big Youth, and other Roots DJs dissociated themselves from specific political commentary and concerned themselves only with the issues of the urban sufferer and the position of the black man in the world, and Rastafari. This last became such an issue in the country that Winston Blake (of Merritone sound) published an article in the *Jamaican Daily News*, stating:

> What concerns me is whether songs praising 'JAH' should not be termed religious and programmed like other religious songs praising God and Jesus Christ. Radio stations should therefore create guide-lines defining clearly what is religious music and what is popular music. Religious bodies should therefore demand equal play for all categories of religious music, and such music must be projected in the time allocated for it. . . . There can be no justification for the continuous barrage of commercial, repetitive, monotonous religious Reggae music.[9]

The difference, of course, between Blake's definition of religious and that of DJs, for example, is that DJs interpret and express Rastafari as a cultural and political force – not as a purely religious one. The attitude is that Rastafari is the tool for the liberation of the black man, and not simply the acceptance of God.

The DJ genre can also be explained through tradition and history. It derives from the story-teller: first in the Afrikan tradition, and second in the Caribbean. Thus the orality of the DJ appeals to a ready and available audience in that the form, the rap, is a familiar pattern of black life. The issues that are brought up in natural conversation are publicly expressed by the DJ. What is spoken in private is now expressed for the whole of society to hear and react to. The DJ thus plays a singularly important role, both in his function as 'toaster' with the sound man/dance scene, and within the community. The DJ's voice does not have to be cultivated in the same manner as the singer's. In contrast, a rough voice and crude approach are assets. However, if the DJ does not possess a unique style in phrasing, rhyming, expression and wit, he will never achieve true renown.

There have been many DJs who have either their own particular approach or are imitators. U-Roy has been the most consistent since the DJ movement began, as well as Big Youth and I-Roy, both of whom have slipped in popularity in recent years. In 1974 Prince Jazzbo created enormous impact with a single, 'Step Forward Youth'. His vocal style was totally different from anything recorded in the past: his voice possessed a bass sound and he spoke lazily. But the content of his material stirred minds and inspired a film and a record company in London to be named after his record. The actual content of Jazzbo's material was not particularly political, but the power of the spoken word supported by a virulent and hypnotic dubonic rhythm made a great impact on the dancer/listener. Also, it spoke directly to the youth. Jazzbo commenced his tune with the following lines: 'For now is the time that black people should look into themselves and see that their backs are against the wall/that is what the man Marcus Garvey ah prophesise, you know.' After this general statement about the realization of the condition of blacks, Jazzbo deals with what he thinks could resolve this condition: 'Step forward, youth, and let I tell you the truth/Step forward, youth, for the Babylon ah brute/Ah say they take a oath upon they mother/And they take a gun to use upon they son/Say it dread ina Jamdown [Jamaica].' Then Jazzbo wails painfully, 'I feel it, I feel it, black people, I tell you I feel it, etc. . . . Run, capitalist, I and I want socialist.' Usually, in speaking for his community, the DJ does not himself analyse the situation that he reports. Thus Jazzbo, for example, can talk about the death of capitalism and equate that with the rise of socialism. Since the PNP's propaganda machine has been disseminating its clichés and rhetoric to the poor communities, and directing its members' energies towards the death of the invisible capitalist, its true limitation and ineffectiveness in alleviating the social ills of the society are disguised. So Jazzbo's records would reach the people and reinforce the PNP's propaganda, and gather more supporters. Perhaps even unknown to Jazzbo himself!

This enormous influence that the DJ has on Roots audiences (who are mainly of the youth) can and does create problems. But it also solidifies the resolve of the youth against the evils of society. Jazzbo talks about the Pope eating pork, which can be interpreted literally or symbolically. The eating of pork by the Pope symbolizes the dirt and stench of official society. He also points out that the 'Babylon ah brute', that the oppressor is devilish and what Jazzbo has to tell the youth is the 'truth'. The youth, whether in Jamaica, London, or New York empirically comprehends what Jazzbo is talking about and identifies with it. Their daily confrontations with 'Babylon' reinforce their resolve to withstand it and perhaps to attempt in their own way to defeat it. The DJ, then, is the rebel *par excellence* in Roots culture. He speaks their language, adopts a justified hardened attitude to society, and more meaningfully, projects the need to combat its tyranny. The DJ's audience is understandably small in comparison to that of the singer, but his audience is a resolute and solid one.

Concomitant with the rise of Dub music, DJs have become more popular and more numerous. In 1965 Dennis Alcapone (born Dennis Smith) founded his own sound with a friend. They called it El Paso. He served his apprenticeship period with El Paso until 1970 when he went into recording. During the early 1970s Alcapone had enough important records to carve his name into the history of DJs, such tunes as 'Alcapone Guns Don't Argue' and 'It Must Come' (a version of Delroy Wilson's mesmeric PNP anthem, 'Better Must Come'). These early recordings demonstrate that DJing had not developed into a fully formed art, because he was still confined to his role with the sound, colouring the singer's lyrics, investing more energy and feeling into the dancers' ears. Another DJ who emerged to dominate the scene briefly was Dillinger (born Lester Bullocks). Dillinger was originally influenced by his predecessors U-Roy and Dennis Alcapone, and recorded several tunes that were soon forgotten. After abandoning the recording scene for two years, he returned in 1975, after being persuaded by Channel One's proprietor, Jo Jo Hookim, and recorded two of his most important hits: 'Plantation Heights' and 'CB 200',[10] the latter attaining international release on Island Records. Dillinger attained the unique status of reaching the No. 1 position on the Dutch charts with 'Marijuana in My Brain'. Since leaving Hookim, Dillinger has had less success and has been unable to reproduce the same degree of production efficacy as while working with Hookim. The route to success taken by any recording artist is usually through recordings that propel him into the public's mind, but Tapper Zukie did not follow this success route. Unlike most of the popular DJs, he lived in England where he recorded for various producers without success. He then left the country and through the interest of Scotty Bennett (born Peter Simon, alias Penny Reel), a white journalist with esoteric preoccupations in Reggae, expressed an interest in Zukie to producer Bunny Lee, who on his return trip to London brought Zukie with him. Zukie was then treated to a full-page interview in *Black Echoes*, a white-owned paper specializing in black music. Bennett, who also worked for Klick Records, now bankrupt, expressed his enthusiasm to the company's executives who released Zukie's 'MPLA' single. The record created enormous impact and an album of the same name was subsequently released. Zukie then became one of the two biggest names among contemporary DJs. Zukie's early recordings with producer Clement Bushay were remarkable for the absence of a singer and for his child-like vocalizations. Zukie, like all good DJs, diversified his material, from the revolutionary paean and the MPLA's victory in Angola to the cynical sex parody of 'She Want a Phensic'. This record differs from earlier sex themes in that it satirizes a middle-class girl. Zukie's voice, now matured, idiosyncratic, stylish, opens with: 'Ride on, girl, go find somewhere you can roam,' then goes into the body of the tune, 'Wha do de chick? She must be sick/She must be want a Phensic/She jump out of me big strong bed/She go on like she nearly dead . . ./When me get her in meh garage/Me give her little massage/She run left her blue drawers . . . /That little girl is a mickey mouse . . ./Put her in me bed/And she go on like she dead/Put her on the floor/And she want some more . . ./Girl, I say yuh little/But yuh big underneath/Girl, I say yuh little/But yuh pum pum sweet . . ./The gal just a go on like a 'ristocrat/The gal just a go on like a acrobat/The gal just a go on like a idiot.' Zukie's toast ridicules and belittles the trend in some Kingston circles to gravitate toward the 'ghetto' and its now famous artists. It is at once suggesting that the nameless middle-class girl finds the 'ghetto' man both attractive and repulsive. The attraction is primarily primitive sex as conceptualized by her, and Zukie does not spare her the embarrassment and the ridicule of his tongue.

It is obvious that the DJ phenomenon will continue, but it seems likely that the style and method will change. The DJ usually approaches his subject-matter spontaneously. His response to his environment, its problems and issues, is immediate and long-felt, but not sufficiently thought out in the manner that the singer/lyricist, for example, approaches his art – writing and rewriting his lyrics, until they finally evolve into the correct shape and form. The Jamaican poet Linton Johnson (who lives in London) received inspiration from the traditional textual source, but, discovering that the models were not suitable for his cultural expression, sought the DJ as his model, and in particular I-Roy and Big Youth. He has since developed his poetry from the oral tradition (which is found in all black cultures) and has made two albums using Reggae rhythms as the musical backdrop. They have been mainly successful. Prince Far I is the only Jamaican-based artist who seems now to be approaching the form with more seriousness and projecting conscious poetic images. Like Louise Bennet, the famous oral poet, the DJ will have to change to survive the 1980s.

6 The Dub Masters

Towards the end of 1965, when Rock Steady was in evidence, a number of records were being released by the Coxsone/Studio One labels without horn solos. This was due to the non-appearance of the horn player to overdub his solo. Because of time factors, the records were released without the solo and this became known as 'ridim solo', because where the solo should have been, there was only the rhythm track. This became popular with sound system audiences and people looked forward to hearing a rhythm solo in recordings.[1] Duke Reid, the producer, saw this becoming popular and released two records by Lynn Tait and the Comets and Alton Ellis ('Girl, I've Got a Date'). The record was also enhanced by the guitar 'playing a low line like the bass'.[2] This additional ingredient helped to make the music even more popular. This was the beginning of the phenomenon known as Dub. It was created purely by accident and eventually became an acceptable art form.

Dub's beginnings, then, were without the frills of later innovation. It was simply a music devoid of solos. The sound systems, which have always played an important role in developing new trends, attempted to expand this simple concept of the music by emphasizing the drums and bass. In the late 1960s, along with the development of the DJ as an identifiable artist, Dub was developed as an equally identifiable art form. Osborne Ruddock (King Tubby), who was an electronics engineer by training, through contact with the people whose amplifiers he repaired, developed an enthusiasm for both the music and the refinement involved in the reproduction of sound within the context of the sound system. By 1968 he was operating his own sound and

Alton Ellis, one of the early singers during the R&B era of the late 1950's who nearly dominated the Rock Steady era. Today he lives in London and has been releasing some fine material in the Lovers Rock style. (*Photo: Vernon St. Hilaire.*)

The Dub master, Osborne Ruddock (King Tubby), outside his studio in Kingston. (*Photo: D. Morris.*)

gathering a good following. The process of 'dubbing' was beginning to connote more meaningfully than before, and by 1971 Ruddock had already successfully experimented with drums and bass combinations specifically for his own sound. In that same year he engineered the first recorded drums and bass record, 'Psalm of Dub', which was produced by Carl Patterson (of the Studio One act, Carlton and the Shoes), and featured Lloyd Parks on bass. The record sold an incredible 30,000 on release.[3] The record did not feature any of the studio techniques that would later define the Dub movement.

Ruddock stated that when the sound systems began to produce effects on their sounds in playing records and they later attempted to reproduce these effects in the recording studio, proprietors complained that their machines would be affected. Ruddock was fortunate in that he controlled his own four-track recording studio (the mixing board itself being purchased from Byron Lee), but encountered difficulties with cutting-rooms (where the master tapes are transferred on to acetates). The cutters insisted that their equipment would be affected. According to Ruddock, this was encountered in all the studios that had cutting facilities. It was not until Bunny Lee, the producer, threatened the use of force that the resistance of the studios was broken down. The Dub movement was then underway, but still resisted by the media.

As the sound systems became more sophisticated, an attempt was made to induce greater enjoyment in audiences. As the DJ helped to create a more enjoyable atmosphere, so Dub evolved as an attempt to infuse more excitement into the audience. The drums and bass combination was the first attempt. This was superseded by the attempt to create effects over the instruments played on record by varied mixing techniques. Ruddock, who had only recently built his own studio, was initially encouraged by Bunny Lee and Lee 'Scratch' Perry. Perry in particular used Ruddock's studio to mix 'dubs' to promote his records through the sound systems, and backed Ruddock's move to open his own recording studio. Having a foundation in electronics, Ruddock was respected by people in the music business who all urged him to experiment and develop new techniques in reproduction.[4] The Dub movement, therefore, began with the sound system itself. The 'live' techniques employed to keep audiences excited were characterized by the absence of the singer's voice during the playing of a record. Ruddock said he used eight-track tapes to produce the initial dub effects, but because of its lack of professional precision, he soon gave it up. Echo units and reverb were subsequently used – these would add echo to a singer's voice, for example. Certain words uttered by the singer would reverberate as though he were speaking in a hollow cave. Audiences were initially amazed by such electronic gadgetry, and this would increase their enjoyment. So the Dub movement then became recognized as an art form.

From the middle 1960s to the beginning of the 1970s certain producers began to couple a vocal or instrumental side with a 'version' as the B side. The appearance of the 'ridim solo' was responsible for this trend. Others followed, because it was cheaper to record one song and use that same song in its instrumental form on the B side. The initial response by producers was to expand and sustain a market that hungered for the 'ridim solo'. This also occurred almost simultaneously in the United States where James Brown, for example, was responsible for popularizing the extended song. Brown would record a vocal side and extend the instrumentation by keeping the same song on the B side, featuring the instrumental aspects with sparse vocal ad libs. The reason was ostensibly the same: the increased excitement of the audience. So, simultaneous with the development of the 'ridim solo' was the development of technical control of sound effects within the confines of a studio or reproduced on the sound system.

With greater technical sophistication within recording studios, this trend was exploited in the middle 1970s. The engineer, being presented with a song which featured a singer and eight instruments, for example, would begin to emphasize certain instruments from the original song. 'Satta Massagana', for example, the song that was initially made popular by the Abyssinians, had at least six 'versions' played through sound systems, each one featuring a different instrument as its lead voice.[5] If the engineer wanted to emphasize the guitar, he would play its own phrases and then 'dub' it. The 'dub' would entail adding tape echo fed into the mixing board by a revox two-track machine at a speed (usually) of three and three-quarter i.p.s. The engineer would then move the dub button from its upward position downwards, and this sudden cutting of the guitar from the tape would create a spiralling, reverberating effect. The engineer could also feed the tape echo into a phaser, which was then fed into the mixing board to create other effects. The phaser could be tuned to a desired effect and the snare drum, for example, could produce an eerie or weird – but highly danceable – effect. There are other ways of creating a variety of effects, but these are the two most popular. It was the sound man, then, in the first instance who in his efforts to create new sound awareness and excitement for his audience attempted to modernize his set, and the recording engineer who masterminded the recorded innovations into a popular and acceptable dance and music form. This was the first form of music that did not depend solely on the singer, producer, or musician for its creation, but on the engineer and sound man.

Jamaican society does not respect the sound man. Bob Marley, for example, was held in contempt by middle Jamaica, but when the international (the modern) world proclaimed him a star, they quickly accepted him as contributing greatly to the status of Jamaica. But generally the sound man cannot hope to achieve this kind of fame. More than the actual music of Jamaica, the sound man carries his impoverished community with him. It is they he sustains, and they sustain and support him. The music that he plays appeals to the sensibility and sensuality of the urban impoverished settler and, once he has achieved distinction for his sound (is noted for particular taste and style in music and is ahead of the pack), his followers would travel the length and breadth of Jamaica in search of the enjoyment of his music. It is not the responsibility of the sound man to decide who listens to and appreciates his music. He has no control over what type of crowd is attracted to him. But by and large the sound man's audience consists of the inhabitants of an impoverished urban community like Waterhouse (where King Tubby comes from). In this community is a multiplicity of personalities. The hard-working man may be a follower, as well as the 'gun man', the ex-political rebel-rouser turned criminal. It is the latter element, sometimes dressed like modern gun-slingers from mobster movies, with long overcoats, broad-brimmed hats and dark glasses, who carry a .45

pistol, sawn-off shotgun or automatic rifle under their coats and are prepared to terrorize anybody for the silliest of reasons, who are almost totally responsible for the notoriety of the sound man.[6]

King Tubby has experienced all the victimization that plagues the lives of the sound man. Committed to the development of Reggae music as a modern world music, he (along with a number of others) disregards the bitterness of the sound man who is committed, like Jamaican radio and its middle-class adherents, to promoting foreign music (such as Afro-American music), as an example of modern culture. Most of the few sound men who are committed to this type of music also own clubs (Merritone and Psychedelic Disco for example) and cater for middle Jamaica – the people who have financial stability. Because of King Tubby's preoccupation with Jamaican music and its inherent expression of violence, the police have been active in their destruction of his sound. The sound is to be regarded as the cultural conveyor of modern Jamaican culture, and its adherents are distinct in their manifestations from the cultural preoccupations of middle Jamaica. Perhaps the police have been so brutal in the destruction of Tubby's (and the other sound men's) equipment because they directly threaten the foreign-orientated discos.

At a 1976 dance in Morant Bay, King Tubby was warned by the police that he would not be permitted to play there because of the notoriety of the followers he attracted. In spite of their warnings, he proceeded to the venue only to have his sound violently attacked by the police: seven bullets were fired into his hi-fi equipment, pick-axes and big sticks were wielded and released against his speakers, and other equipment was smashed – and the truck that carried his equipment was also attacked. He subsequently sued and won the case, and was still awaiting financial compensation a year after the incident.[7] At other places he was physically prevented from playing by the police.

Ruddock says the sound is often described as 'abominable' or a 'nuisance'. But he also insists that since the sound man pays taxes on the equipment he buys, the government should accept that the sound system is a taxable commodity, thus securing the respectability of the sound system and the sound man. Ruddock also says that drunkenness aggravates expressions of violence in a frustrated community. The lack of security in a dance hall where the sound plays and police non-responsiveness to calls for protection, also contribute to the low regard in which the sound man is held. He contrasts the security measures that are undertaken for a dance at the Sheraton Hotel (one of the most prestigious in Jamaica), for example, and one held within the impoverished community.

The combination of drums and bass, as previously mentioned, was the basis for the further development of the Dub movement. Pat Griffith's attempts to chronicle the role of drums/bass in the evolution of Jamaican music has led him to believe that it was only during the Reggae era that the drummer experienced freedom. Even though, like R&B, Jamaican popular music is usually stated in straight 4/4 time, the rhythmic emphasis has always created another dimension to project variation. The drummer not only kept time, but improvised on off beats. This led, during the Rock Steady era, to the bass player creating 'rests', as Griffith calls it, 'by omitting a bar or half-bar while the drummer combined snare beats with bass drum work'.[8] Eric 'Fish' Clarke, speaking about the role of the drummer in contemporary Reggae, said: 'You still have the straight Rockers time, as the one-drop is with it the same way. It's the straight fours that keep the rhythmic motion . . . one-two-three-four, bok . . .'[9] The combination of drums and bass in contemporary Reggae is equal to the interplay of rhythmic responses in ensemble drumming except that the time-signature is different. The rhythmic responses between drums and bass are open to long and exciting conversations, the bassist playing the barest melody lines between (the bass drum) rests, the drummer, on the other hand, improvising between the rests of the bass and accenting the bass drum on the beat. This foundation continues to create excitement in either live or recorded Dub music. The melody and rhythm of a tune is continued, but in a highly masked and abbreviated form. This goes right back to Ska when the producer was not demanding that the musicians record in a certain (popular) manner. When the opportunity arose, the drummer/bassist would destroy convention by sheer improvisation and experimentation. The leading drums/bass combination during the whole of Ska was Lloyd Knibbs/Lloyd Brevette. Brevette in particular was the innovator of the rests between bars and he has influenced bassists Jackie Jackson and Aston 'Family Man' Barrett into extending his ideas into today's music.

Augustus Pablo has the unusual distinction of being the sole artist in Jamaica to work exclusively as a Dub artist. He started his career in 1969 with a record called 'Java', which was recorded for Randy's Records. It was a straight instrumental on which he played melodica. That same year he recorded 'East of the River Nile' for Herman Chin-Loy's Aquarius Records, and it was voted the top instrumental of that year. His first album, *This Is Augustus Pablo*, was recorded as early as 1970, but did not achieve international recognition until 1974 when it was released in England. This album is a seminal work in that it consists entirely of instrumentals in the now familiar tradition of Dub. The melodies are simple and the instrumentation sparse, while the rhythm is emphasized throughout. This album became the anthem for Dub music lovers and Pablo the archetype. Pablo is unique because he set out to express emotion through the melodica as a lead instrument. Pablo's records sold mainly to roots audiences, but when Dub was recently discovered by white audiences in Britain, he became the main identifying link. Because of Pablo's disinterest in the bright lights of stardom that would come from touring Europe, several imitators have emerged, such as Dr Pablo (an Englishman playing melodica) and Pablo Dove. Pablo's records have also been imitated and released under his own name. And in 1975 Herman Chin-Loy sold Pablo's biggest and most popular record, 'King Tubby Meets the Rockers Uptown', to Island Records. It was acclaimed by a section of the British Rock Press and was No. 1 in *Time Out*'s critics' choice Top Ten list. To the black community it was an expression of roots culture. The record itself was originally recorded as the B side to the Pablo-produced 'Baby, I Love You So' with Jacob Miller (of the Inner Circle) as lead singer. 'King Tubby . . .' was the dub side of 'Baby, I Love You So' but because of its popularity Island placed it on the A side. It sold well and enhanced Pablo's reputation in certain circles.

Born in 1953, Pablo had shown an interest in music since high school days, and would play the church organ with Wailers' keyboards man, Tyrone Downey. He started his own sound system, 'Rockers', while still in high school and attracted a great following among young people, but felt

Jamaican audiences were not readily appreciative of his type of music – Dub/Rockers. He felt that if his local audience had responded appreciably better to what he was doing in the late 1960s, he would have evolved further. Rockers sound was eventually abandoned, but was transferred into his record company which releases all his own records and productions on other artists: the Heptones on a version of 'Love Won't Come Easy', Big Youth on 'Cassava Rock', Tetrack on 'Let's Get Started', Hugh Mundell on the single and the album, 'Afrika Must be Free by 1983', the Immortals on 'You Can't Keep a Good Man Down', and others, including DJ Dillinger. He has recorded two albums for producers Lee 'Scratch' Perry and Tommy Cowan. Neither has been released.[10] Pablo is an independent artist/musician and his involvement in the Dub form has extended its range and scope, and he has been a cultural model in a strictly roots expression that is understood and revered by audiences.

Pablo's early recordings, before 1974, were not characterized by the dubbing techniques that the engineer became famous for. Dub was launched with the highly innovative album, *Pick a Dub*, which was produced by the controversial Keith Hudson, and consisted largely of huge and important hits he had in Jamaica with other artists. Two of the most important were Big Youth's 'S.90 Shank' on which Hudson brought a motor-bike into the studio and recorded it as the engine accelerated, and Horace Andy's 'I'm All Right' ('Before you check me, check yourself . . .'). Hudson's work as a producer was mainly successful and he has given back reputations to those artists who were failing. On 'Pick a Dub' the imagination he brought to bear on the drums/bass combination was incredible, and the album's mixing by Osborne Ruddock expressed all Hudson's ideas and feelings. This was the first Dub album, using sophisticated controlled studio techniques, that made an impact on audiences in England. It became the archetype for other British-released Dub albums which soon followed.

In Jamaica most recording studios have their own labels. Because of the ownership of the studio it facilitates the time involved in mixing the recorded music properly, while the average producer is unable to afford a reasonable amount of time to achieve the effect he may have in his mind. Thus Channel One Studios (with Ernest Hookim as engineer, supported by the youthful Stanley 'Ranking Barnabas' Bright, who is also a prominent percussionist), Joe Gibbs Recording Studio (with Errol T (Thompson) as engineer and producer) and Black Ark Studios (with the infamous Lee 'Scratch' Perry as sole engineer and wizardly producer) all have their own labels titled after their studios. These three studios at any given time dominate the Roots recording scene, or are responsible for distinctive 'sounds' or new musical styles.

Channel One was formed four years ago and quickly became prominent for its distinctive drums sound. Its reputation has been strengthened by the presence of the Revolutionaries (which at one time or another included Noel 'Sly' Dunbar, the innovative drummer, Robby Shakespeare, revolutionary bassist, Ansell Collins, the keyboardist responsible for dropping Jazz/Funk riffs on Reggae, and others). These musicians have given depth and significance to recordings produced exclusively for Channel One, so that other producers have insisted on using the same musicians. Thus particular 'feels' in music are achieved at particular studios. On the other hand, Joe Gibbs Recording Studio would normally use the drums and bass abilities of Sly Dunbar or Carlton 'Santa' Davis, and Lloyd Parks respectively. Under Errol Thompson's producership and engineering prowess, the sound would be thicker, and Thompson would bring his imagination to bear on the finished product by adding sound effects. The most successful Dub album ever produced, both in terms of sales and aesthetic/artistic qualities, was *African Dub, Chapter Three*, the third in a series of four that have so far appeared. The album is well conceived as it uses a number of already popular songs with a Dub interpretation, and beyond that, the pace and tempo of the tracks are consistent. At times Thompson includes the growling of an imagined attacking dog or the chimes of a bell. This has added both colour and surprise to the music. When these albums are released, because they are not recorded with a particular artist in mind, they are usually released under the title of the proprietor, Joe Gibbs and the Professionals. This has led to the belief that the proprietor is himself a musician or at least a producer. However, in the Jamaican context, the proprietor is usually credited with producership only because of the financial contribution he makes. To achieve the distinction in sound that is necessary to draw clientele, the proprietor usually hires the best available engineer, who then acts both as producer and engineer without getting the credit. Within the confines of the recording studio, innovations in the music are achieved by a combination of the engineer and the musicians, with one notable exception.

At Black Ark Studios (sometimes called Black Art Studios), one of the most highly respected producers/engineers in Jamaica is the proprietor, Lee Perry. His background includes working with the Coxsone sound system and in the recording studios with Clement Dodd, and he has one of the most well-equipped four-track studios in the whole Caribbean. Perry originally established himself as the producer and sometimes co-writer of the early Wailers, and produced two albums on them, *Rasta Revolution* and *African Herbsman*, and has subsequently produced some of the finest one-off recordings with a variety of artists. His dubs are particularly sought-after and respected because he had introduced the idea of phasers into Jamaican music. Even on a straightforward vocal recording – for example, George Faith's (otherwise known as Earl George) 'To Be a Lover', Perry has brought a variety of effects, gleaned primarily from his battery of echo units and phasers (he sometimes phases the organ, bass, guitar, horns, and percussion – any instrument, nothing is sacred) to create a startling aural or mental environment through which the singer imparts his emotion. The effect is achieved through a combination of Dub music and vocal prowess, with Perry constantly altering levels, alternating instruments and vocals, and being in total control of the created studio environment. One of his most effective mixes was achieved with Zap Pow, a habitually experimental group, on their 'River' single. The music itself is eerie and mysterious, the arrangements and production spectacular, and Perry brings his imagination to bear on the mix by indulging in all the gadgetry and tricks he can muster.

Dub has now reached a peak of saturation and it seems likely that another Roots music sound will appear in the near future to supplement it.

7 The British Scene

Migration to Britain was in the main activated by the demand for labour, cheap labour, in Britain's war-torn economy. Advertisements were placed in various Caribbean territories, then colonial vassals of the Empire, for vacancies to be filled that the British worker had himself refused. In 1948, for example, the S.S. *Empire Windrush* 'brought 492 passengers (mostly Jamaicans); the majority were skilled or semi-skilled and quickly found work. They were followed in September by another 108 and the movement steadily continued.'[1] The movement continued only because the British government continued to advertise vacancies in those territories. By and large the impetus for emigration was not activated by the internal material conditions of the dependent Caribbean territories, but by the external demand for labour – even though the material conditions of life in the Caribbean were akin to slavery, as the Moyne Report of the 1930s confirmed. During this period, wages were fixed at a shilling and a half per day for agricultural workers in almost all areas of the Caribbean. Although there were strikes and violent upheavals, emigration was still almost negligible. Neither can emigration be explained by population explosion. 'Trinidad and British Guiana, which had the highest rates of population increase, had the lowest rates of emigration.'[2] Thus the primary motivating factor for emigration to Britain was the role that Britain itself played in activating that migration.

Between 1955 and 1962 there were 301,540 migrants from the entire Caribbean area, of whom 178,270 came from Jamaica alone.[3] The numerical superiority from Jamaica points to the area whence cultural influence would emerge.

By 1961 Lord Butler (formerly R.A. Butler, the Home Secretary) pronounced in the House of Commons the need to restrict and control immigration, and by 1962 the Immigration Act was instituted. This limited immigration to three categories: 1. those who had obtained definite job offers; 2. those with skills that were needed in this country; and 3. those who did not qualify in the above categories. Further restrictions were imposed in 1964, 1965, and 1968. In 1964 category 3 was abolished, in 1965 the Labour government imposed a limit of 8,500 to categories 1 and 2, and in 1968 the Asians of Afrika who held British passports (categorizing them as Citizens of United Kingdom and Colonies) had to establish birthplace of parents and grandparents in order to qualify for entry.[4]

Placed within a new and prosperous environment, these Caribbean immigrants expected their economic and educational situation to change dramatically. Those who settled in London consisted of the budding student population based primarily in Earl's Court, Bayswater and Edgware Road; and the working people who settled in Notting Hill and Brixton, with merchant seamen basing themselves in Cable Street, in the East End.[5] The principal form of artistic expression from these early settlers was in the form of music, confined primarily (if it were to receive respectability and acceptance) to Jazz and Latin musical styles. Calypso also received widespread popularity and acceptance – mainly through Lord Kitchener (a Trinidadian Calypsonian) who inspired Harry Belafonte to disseminate the form – in a much emasculated and cocktailish style – internationally. There was, additionally, night-life in places like the 59 Club, the Flamingo, the 77 Club, the Sunset and the Contemporaen. The latter was owned by Esteban, from Santo Domingo, who became famous for his fusion of Latin and Afro-Caribbean music. This club was situated in Mayfair, and the other clubs were in the Soho area of the West End.[6] It is said that Soho was under the control of Caribbeans, and continental Europeans were its primary white audience. Caribbean and Afrikan music received spasmodic acceptance.

The pioneer record label in the United Kingdom for black music was Melodisc, which was founded in 1946 by Emile Shalet who later involved Siggy Jackson (both Eastern European Jews) in a partnership. Because of the war, black music from America, which had already gained widespread popularity in the 1920s and 1930s, was becoming increasingly difficult to obtain. Melodisc, recognizing the need to fill this vacuum, imported and then released Jazz in this country. They had the licence for the Savoy catalogue as well as released products on other labels, among which was Nat King Cole. During this period, the company claims that they were among the only three independent record companies in the United Kingdom.[7] In 1951 Melodisc ventured into promoting and releasing Calypso. Lord Kitchener was residing in England and popularized Calypso on the club circuit, before being signed by Melodisc. In that same year they also released 'Cricket, Lovely Cricket' by Lord Beginner. Melodisc sold these records in the United Kingdom, and exported them to Afrika and the Caribbean which were responsible for 30 per cent of over-all sales.[8] The company then got involved in Afrikan music which sold well both in the United Kingdom and Afrika. In the late 1950s Melodisc began to get involved with Jamaican versions of the Afro-American R&B. Two of their earliest releases were Keith and Enid's 'Worried Over You', and Byron Lee's versions of the music.

Jackson states that sales of a big seller for Calypso, Afrikan High Life and later, Jamaican music, would amount to 300,000 to half a million units of singles. Their most successful hit, however, came in the middle 1960s with Prince Buster's 'Madness'. The music, first Jamaican R&B and then Ska, was played exclusively in discotheques, because BBC radio simply ignored the music. Yet the Mods, a stylish group of English kids who claimed Blue Beat (as the early music came to be known in the United Kingdom from the specialist label that Melodisc issued) identified with it. 'In the early 1960s it became the big thing, and then you had Blue Beat hats, skirts, and so on . . . . Wherever I went, all our records were played (in the discos), but we had a hell of a battle to get them played on the BBC. They didn't want to know. Our records sold more than other hits in the charts, and yet we couldn't get into the charts. Nor could we get the plug. There was this terrific prejudice against black music. It was a hell of a battle.'[9]

Melodisc had their music distributed by a variety of independent distributors, among whom were Selecta, Clyde Factor, Lugtons and H.R. Taylor, of whom Jackson claims:

'We put them into business. They started off selling our gear. And they were the first distributors to come in really big on black music. We had a difficult time convincing people to stock black music. There was animosity and that sort of thing.'[10] H.R. Taylor is now one of the biggest regional distributors of all musics. The stores manager at Lugtons was David Betteridge (now managing director of C.B.S. Records U.K.). Melodisc had no independent distribution of its own. But as pioneers in black music they popularized the music and sold huge quantities. Jackson, confronting the situation of the BBC with no radio plays, resorted to a cartoon detailing sales volume of records in the charts and those that Melodisc had sold that outstripped them. As a result, the BBC commenced playing Blue Beat. But Jackson has also stated that the Press gave his company a fair proportion of coverage.

It is also due to the sound system that the new music began to be disseminated throughout Britain. Jamaicans were importing the records from Jamaica and playing them on their sounds at private and public dances. It was also due to the sounds that the British DJ adopted the practice of scratching out the information on a record. The early sound man, then, was not only responsible for launching mobile discos in this country, but also for developing the discothèque. The Caribbeans' thirst for social entertainment, after working on the factory floor or on public transport, logically led them to recreate the atmosphere and environment of their home. Thus night clubs were opened wherever a number of Caribbeans lived. The night clubs invariably took the form of *shebeens*, illegal gambling houses where liquor was sold without a licence, where prostitutes (mainly of British nationality) hung out, and where pimps, thieves and other hustlers abounded. It was under these circumstances, in a primarily Caribbean male environment (females, as indicated, coming from the home environment because of the absence of Caribbean females, and probably because of other factors), that the music had meaning and relevance.

Other than Melodisc/Blue Beat, a label that came into existence in the early 1960s was owned by Sonny Roberts, Lloyd Harley, and others. They were all Jamaicans and their label was called Planitone Records. Roberts was a carpenter by trade and arrived in the United Kingdom in 1953 to follow his trade, but always harboured the idea of running a record company. This he finally did, using his own limited financial resources, and he was then joined by friends. Planitone was an extremely small label that functioned from an address in Edgware Road. Roberts bought some cutting equipment (from which the tape is transferred to acetate) and a one-track tape recorder and other materials. He then transformed the room into a recording studio and there recorded all his records. He used musicians who earned a living from other sources, and thus they were lacking in a more professional approach that could ensure quality musicianship. Also, the limited studio facilities could not compete with Melodisc. There was no van to distribute their records and no independent distribution. They thus relied solely on parties, dances and personal friends. Among the people they recorded were Dandy Livingstone, Tito Simon, and Mike Elliot (a saxophonist who played on Roberts's sessions).[11]

In 1962 Chris Blackwell, the son of a wealthy plantation owner (of Crosse & Blackwell, as mentioned before), and himself a former Aide-de-Camp to the then Governor General of Jamaica, came to London to study the market for Jamaican music. Blackwell is a white Jamaican of Jewish descent. He had already established Island Records in Jamaica with other Jamaicans and had previously worked with Owen Grey, Jackie Edwards, and other pioneer Jamaican singers. He made two important stops, one at Melodisc and the other at Planitone. In the process of setting up Island (U.K.), he visited Lugtons where he met David Betteridge. Betteridge, with his knowledge of distribution and sales, became a limited shareholder in Island. Blackwell, wishing to familiarize himself with the local Jamaican recording scene, talked with Roberts and offered to help distribute and promote his records. Roberts has said that Blackwell's help, though limited, was needed, and he worked extremely hard. When Roberts moved from the Edgware Road to Cambridge Road in Kilburn, he approached Lee Goptal, an East Indian Jamaican accountant (working in the West End), for the premises. The building had previously been owned by Goptal's father. Roberts says that Goptal was reluctant to rent him the premises as he was suspicious of his motives. Goptal was fascinated by the whole process of recording, disc cutting, hearing the finished product, and distribution.

So he asked Roberts to allow him to distribute some records for him. Goptal then bought a van and sold the records to the shops. Roberts was surprised by Goptal's request to sell the records, but Goptal reportedly said: 'If you give me shit to sell, I can sell it.'[12] When Goptal knew enough about distribution, he approached Melodisc to distribute their records, and subsequently did two jobs: accountancy and record distribution.

When Blackwell asked Roberts about office space, Roberts introduced him to Goptal who rented out to him a floor above Roberts's basement premises. Finally, Roberts encountered competition from Blackwell who was licensing finished masters from Jamaica. The musicianship and the recording quality were better. Before, the sound men would call in at Planitone for records to play on their sets, but once Blackwell established Island, they ceased visiting Planitone and went upstairs instead. Planitone quickly got into financial difficulties and went out of business. Blackwell founded Island and Black Swan Records, and later formed Sue exclusively for R&B, with artists like Inezz Fox and Ike and Tina Turner who put the label in the charts. Blackwell had national distribution from the moment he started Island (through independent companies) and did support distribution himself from a van. His early releases consisted of Kentrick Patrick, Owen Grey, Laurel Aitken, and others. He also went into independent record production with acts like Millie Small who had her first international hit with 'My Boy Lollipop' (for which guitarist Ernie Ranglin did the arrangements) on Fontana Records in May 1964. Previously, the earliest and biggest hit for Island was 'Housewife Choice' by Derrick and Patsy, which sold an amazing 18,000 units in the first five days of issue.[13] It failed to be recorded in the charts. Millie Small's follow-up only barely managed to reach the Top Thirty and thereafter she faded from the scene.

Goptal was beginning to have more involvement in the record business and abandoned his job in 1968 to form Trojan Records with Blackwell. Goptal had already established the Beat & Commercial Company (B&C) primarily for distribution, and instead of competing with Blackwell, they combined forces. Blackwell, who saw the resistance to Jamaican music from the media, expanded his field of operations by investing in the new market of Rock. 'It's important to remember,' said Richard Williams, 'that without the "limited" success of artists like Derrick and Patsy, Jimmy Cliff, Jackie Edwards, Kentrick Patrick, and the Blues Busters, Blackwell would in all probability never have been able to record the groups which now sell millions of records for Island in Britain and America.'[14] Blackwell became the manager of the Spencer Davis Group, a white R&B group (which would now be characterized as Rock), and achieved international success with them on Fontana Records with 'Keep on Running' (composed by Jackie Edwards) and 'Gimme Some Loving'. There is a story about the origins of the latter record. Blackwell had heard Homer Banks, the Afro-American Soul singer's version of 'Lot of Love' and got an idea that a song by the Spencer Davis Group using the same bass line could be a hit, and Stevie Winwood subsequently wrote the song from that concept. Three years later Stax, the company that Banks was signed to, used the bass line from a Trojan hit, 'The Liquidator' by Harry J and the All Stars (a studio band consisting of Aston 'Family Man' Barrett and brother Charlie on bass and drums), to write an international smash, 'I'll Take You There' by the Staples.[15] Because Blackwell was earning money from production and international licensing, Island was able to break more significantly into the British and European market. By 1970 Island had four albums in the album charts simultaneously. They were Rock acts like Jethro Tull, Traffic (with Stevie Winwood as founder), Free, and a Various Artists compilation. By 1970 Island's involvement with Jamaican music was peripheral. The Trojan partnership supplied almost all the Reggae that Blackwell was involved in, while Island only released occasional one-off records, with no major signings except that of Jimmy Cliff in 1965. Cliff ceased to release material on Island after 1967 and was confined to the Trojan label where he received several Top Ten hits between 1969 and 1972.

On the other hand, with Goptal firmly in the chairman's seat, Trojan was going from strength to strength, but with what has been characterized as commercial Reggae: music with a beat, a soft melody and strings behind it. Between 1970 and 1975 the company had already obtained twenty-two Top Thirty chart entries. These hits were obtained through artists like Desmond Dekker (who did not conform to the strings stereotype, but a more genuine reflection of the vocal style, phrasing and musical culture from which the music naturally issued), John Holt, Tito Simon, Horace Faith, Bob and Marcia, Ken Boothe, Greyhound (who later moved to Island after the Trojan/Island split in late 1972), the Pioneers (who were also in the Desmond Dekker mould as regards style and approach), Nicky Thomas (whose manager and 'producer' then was the now well-known Jamaican record magnate, Joe Gibbs), Dandy Livingstone, the Upsetters (a Lee Perry studio band, again consisting of the Barrett brothers), the Melodians, Freddie Notes and the Rudies, and Dave and Ansel Collins (the latter now a famous session musician). Trojan also had a variety of subsidiary labels that were specifically set up to cater for products from certain Jamaican producers, e.g. *Attack* had the material for Bunny Lee (whose biggest hit came from the young Johnny Clarke in 1975), *Upsetter* for Lee Perry, and so on. Trojan also had under licence the Clement Dodd label, Coxsone, while Island had Studio One in the 1960s.

Clement Dodd had formed a partnership with Junior Lincoln (now the London representative of the Jamaican entrepreneur, Tommy Cowan) to form United Kingdom identity for his labels. Lincoln was a director of both and was personally responsible for the administration of the two labels. The relationship between Dodd and Lincoln started in 1966 when Dodd stayed at Lincoln's home and took him to various companies while conducting his business. He subsequently asked Lincoln to supervise his United Kingdom business affairs, which Lincoln did. Sales from both labels could number 20,000 to 40,000 units of a good selling single, but Lincoln was unhappy with the attitude that the two companies were taking in relation to the promotion and publicity of both artists and product, and finally terminated the relationship in 1969 when he started Bamboo Records exclusively to release all of Dodd's material previously released on Coxsone and Studio One. The sales were similar to what Island and Trojan had achieved, but the label seemed to have taken on a new and exciting identity. Although Bamboo was quite small, it competed with Trojan and Pama Records (which was controlled by the Pama Brothers, Harry and Carl) who dominated the Reggae scene here until Bamboo came into existence. Lincoln, in his attempt to popularize the music in Britain, collaborated with

Dodd in bringing over the Soul Vendours, along with Alton Ellis and Ken Boothe, to England in 1967. When he approached Island and Trojan to support the tour financially (as it would help them to promote the acts that they were releasing on their licensed labels), both Blackwell and Goptal refused. Blackwell is reported to have said to Lincoln that it *was mad to do so and* it would be a financial loss. There were eight musicians and two singers. The tour was not well publicized and both Lincoln and Dodd who financed and promoted the tour lost money, and ill-feelings were harboured by the artists who thought they had been ripped off.[16] Bamboo, after its departure from Island/Trojan, found a distributor in CBS, but they failed to sell the music. Bamboo had two vans on the road, distributing the records to black record shops that started springing up in the late 1960s. Bamboo's primary sales were obtained from this source, while CBS was used only as a back-up or support service.

A rift developed between Dodd and Lincoln over the administration of Bamboo Records and they split up in the middle 1970s. Lincoln subsequently formed Ashanti Records which he gave to B&C for marketing and distribution. The most prestigious album project that Lincoln secured was the triple album from Count Ossie and the Mystic Revelation of Rastafari entitled *Grounation*, which consisted of Rasta drumming, poetry recitation, and Jazz fusions. Another prestigious undertaking by Lincoln was the Sharon Forrester album of 1973 on which hitherto unknown musicians in the Reggae genre were employed not only to lay down the rhythm tracks of the album in London, but also to arrange and produce it, and contribute some songs. The album cost Lincoln an unheard-of £12,000 to produce. For Reggae, this was phenomenal. The strings section alone numbered over thirty pieces, and bass guitar was played by Phillip Chin (a Chinese Jamaican now working with Rod Stewart), keyboards by Robert Bailey (formerly with Osibisa) and Geoffrey Chung (who acted as arranger and co-producer; he also played guitar), his brother Mikey Chung (now with the Peter Tosh band, on guitar), and Richard Bailey (Robert's brother, formerly with Johnny Nash and he later made two albums with Jeff Beck), an impressive list of musicians who had little connection with Reggae, with the exception of the Chung brothers. Though the album received good reviews and some radio coverage (it was produced for that specific purpose), it sold dismally. The Mystics' album, likewise, though a solid aesthetic and artistic achievement, sold badly. Thus Lincoln, having been described as 'adventurous' (with which he does not disagree) fell into further financial trouble and eventually wound up Ashanti when Trojan went into receivership in 1975. Lincoln was also responsible for organizing the first meaningful charity show among black artists in this country in 1973. He solicited and received support from Madeleine Bell, Doris Troy (both Afro-American artists), Bob Marley and the Wailers, Nicky Thomas, Marsha Hunte (the black American who sued Mick Jagger for child support and who had previously sung in the musical *Hair*), Shades of Black (who still function from the West Indian Student Centre in Earl's Court as a group of dancers), Ijahman (who was due to appear, but served an eighteen-month period in gaol during the time of the show, and who was later signed by Island) and many others, in aid of the famine victims of Ethiopia. Participating artists also walked around with hats to solicit funds from the audience.[17]

In the middle 1960s Tony Cousins and Bruce White, two British nationals, were involved in a booking agency which they owned called Creole. Seeing the extent to which Reggae was catching on in the charts, they decided to break into the Reggae market. The first act they brought over was the Ethiopians in 1967. In that same year the Ethiopians had a smash in the charts with 'Train To Skaville' on the Pyramid label (controlled by the Pama Brothers). That year also saw Desmond Dekker in the charts with '007/Shanty Town' which reached No. 16 in the charts, as well as Prince Buster with his 'Al Capone' hit which reached No. 20, but remained for some time in the lower reaches of the charts. Creole then brought over Desmond Dekker and later signed him to their own label under the name of the agency. Dekker subsequently had six Top Twenty hits on the Creole label, which had several other hits including Rupie Edwards's 'Irie Feelings' (a toasting, dub-type song that the BBC originally refused to play on radio). It was Desmond Dekker, like Prince Buster before him, who had set a trend among the white kids. 'When we brought Desmond over we gave him a suit, but he insisted that the bottom six inches of the trousers should be cut off. Then the kids began to follow him, they rolled their trousers up and had their hair cut short.'[18] Dekker had always worn his hair very short, like the American crew cut, and wore short jackets and short trousers. The skinheads, white kids affecting the attire and cultural style of Desmond Dekker, then came into being. Like the Mods in imitation of Prince Buster with his zany sartorial splendour, violence was always associated with the skinheads and Reggae.

The exodus from Jamaica since the beginning of the early 1960s included singers and musicians. Bad conditions for artists and victimization by the police in Jamaica, plus the prospect of better opportunities in Britain, were all reasons for the exodus. Thus in the early 1960s the three most important singers had already left Jamaica: Owen Grey, Laurel Aitken, and Jackie Edwards, the early pioneers of the music, from R&B to Ska. Owen Grey continued his association with Island sporadically. His first record for Island was 'Gonna Work Out Fine', a tune made popular by Ike and Tina Turner, and released in early 1963. Grey worked mainly in the North of England and the Midlands, but also in Scotland and Wales. This was because country folk never had the opportunity of being exposed regularly to artists, and responded enthusiastically when they did see them. Promoters also paid well and gave no aggravation. Blackwell was responsible for booking the gigs or getting an agent to do so. Grey toured all over Europe, Germany, Sweden, France, Belgium, Holland, etc., throughout the Sixties. Aitken, on the other hand, did not find life that easy. He had recorded for Melodisc and moved to the Doctor Bird label which was owned by Graham Goodhal. Doctor Bird received its first product through Sonia Pottinger's Tip Top Records, and recorded a variety of tunes with Aitken. But Goodhal encountered a number of problems. The pressing plants had refused to press the records because of their political philosophy, so Goodhal had to manufacture the records in Holland and have them shipped back to England. Among them were 'Haile Selassie', 'Deliverance Will Come', and 'Suffering Still'.[19] Since 1970, when Aitken appeared at the second Reggae Festival at Wembley, he has failed to make public appearances. Jackie Edwards worked as a free-lance artist, mainly playing live and writing songs. He made only one album during the 1960s for Island, which, like Jimmy Cliff's first Island album, consisted of Soul ballads.

Island had a very successful Reggae artist in Jimmy Cliff who scored several Top Twenty hits, but felt his work was being unjustifiably attacked by the white Rock Press. So in 1971 Cliff, accompanied by Guilly Bright (the Panamanian songwriter whom he had met in Argentina during an international song contest where he was voted winner), went to Muscle Shoals Studios in Miami to record a pop album, *Another Cycle,* which emphasized his need to create a new image for himself. The Rock Press thought it was his best album, perhaps only because they understood pop. The album was a collaboration between Cliff and Bright, the latter doing the arrangements and writing the chords, structure, and sequences to fit the lyrics. Bright would also change or extend Cliff's lyric ideas. It sold badly. 'I felt that I wanted to show that I could do other than Reggae, because at the time everybody was putting Reggae down.'[20] Cliff also got into conflict with Bright over the publishing of the songs. For fourteen songs Bright was paid $2,000 (U.S.) advance, as against the agreed $5,000, Bright claimed. The following year, 1972, after Cliff's starring role in the film, *The Harder They Come*, the single was released, but never made the charts. It was claimed that Island ignored the shops' demands for supplies for over three weeks to prevent the record from going into the charts. The motivation being that Cliff was reluctant to sign the option with Island for a further year. Cliff claimed the songwriting of *The Harder They Come* which Bright claimed he co-wrote. Bright has stated that he has never received any money for the royalties from *The Harder They Come.*[21]

In 1970 Chips Richards, who now has a joint business venture with Sonia Pottinger – the label Sky Note (a play on Pottinger's High Note Jamaican label) – joined Trojan Records as a promotions man. He had previously worked with the Pioneers, co-ordinating their engagement schedule and ensuring the smooth operation of their programme. Coming from Kingston 14, a dilapidated Kingston ghetto, he was familiar with a number of popular Jamaican artists. This helped him in his new position at Trojan. One of the first duties he was given was to be introduced to the producers at BBC Radio by Trojan's white radio pluggers.

On his first visit he was introduced to Roger Pusey and Michael Haux who were respectively producing Tony Blackburn and Noel Edmonds on various shows. He was also introduced to Derrick Chilley, head of BBC Radio, to Brian Davis, an executive producer, to Tim Blackmore, a producer who is now head of the regularly financially beleaguered Capital Radio, and to Dave Price who then produced the Emperor Rosko Show (he has since returned to the United States). On this occasion, as on their weekly rounds to the BBC, the pluggers would take six records with them, three pop/Rock and three Reggae. Richards claims that the Reggae product would invariably not reach the producers, because they were conveniently dropped in a box in the reception room, while the pop records were taken direct to the producers. Lee Goptal was the head of B&C and Trojan Records, and also had a stake in all the labels that he owned, licensed or distributed. He had one man as financial controller of all these companies, Brian Gibbon, who had a special interest in the pop company, Charisma. It would seem, then, that Charisma, though under the aegis of B&C, was beholden to a certain powerful influence beyond Goptal that magnetized it to its own survival. In all probability, then, the action by the pluggers, working under the umbrella set-up of B&C, can be seen as deliberate policy. 'Mr Goptal never came to the BBC to see how they (the pluggers) worked, but I did. They were too well paid. They drove company cars and wore three-piece suits. So I think an obscure music, in their opinion, got second-rate treatment. Unless Mr Goptal thumped his desk and insisted and emphasized that "Young, Gifted and Black" by Bob and Marcia should be pushed, nothing would be done.'[22]

It would seem that the lack of commitment to Reggae on the part of Trojan's pluggers contributed to the limited airplay that the music received. It is not like the small company which functioned on a very limited staff and mailed records off to the BBC, and would, therefore, have no control over what finally became of the records. The BBC, as all early Reggae companies have testified, were hostile to the music, but when Trojan hired Robbie Day, an English plugger, who demonstrated his absolute commitment to the music by refusing to accept defeat, the situation was entirely different. Robbie Day visited the BBC on one occasion and attempted to enter the office of one of its producers, Paul Williams (who produced the David Hamilton broadcast). The door was slammed in his face. Day left the office literally crying and could not comprehend the highly prejudiced and discriminatory behaviour of the BBC staff.[23]

Richards remembers an incident that changed his entire attitude to the BBC.

> I was pushing a record called 'Everything I Own' by Ken Boothe, which finally became No. 1, and I was in the BBC offices when it was being played over the radio by Tony Blackburn. Then half-way through playing the record, he stopped it and said something like: 'Oh, utter rubbish! How can anyone in his right mind go out and buy something like this, after listening to the David Gates *real* version?' That got me absolutely mad. I no longer respected anybody. I stopped knocking on doors. I pushed doors and I entered. And I reminded them that they were public servants representing the public, and I was a member of the public. I no longer used the soft smiling attitude. I began to demand. I used to compile scrap-books showing them the demand for Reggae. I wrote letters to them telling them that our records were in the breakers in the British Market Research Board (BMRB), and that our records used to outsell a lot of pop records, and it was because of lack of radio support that we could not have progressed further. Many times they would push our records over to Radio London, saying that because they were Reggae, they could not be pushed on their own programmes. The Radio London thing was, of course, just a one-hour slot show, and was very limited. It could only broadcast to just outside Reading. I reminded them that I was not plugging Reggae records, but music. If slotting Reggae was the norm, then they should not play Rock, Country and Western, Soul, Jazz/Rock, etc., but slot them into programmes just as they had done to Reggae.[24]

Richards then became head of Marketing, Sales and Promotion, and would visit record shops to inform them of Trojan's product. The record shops were always keen to hear of new records and would actually stock them. Trojan had a distribution deal with B&C which had eighteen salesmen on the streets. B&C also had a distribution deal with EMI Records, Enterprise and Lugtons, so they were quite secure in support distribution. However, the majority of salesmen concentrated mainly on pop records coming from Charisma and Mooncrest (another of B&C's companies), along with licensed, owned or distributed labels like People (Soul music), Sussex (Soul – Bill Withers was on the label with whom they received chart action), as well as a number of Reggae labels. But when Webster Shrowder became managing director of Trojan he insisted on some changes which were reflected in the attitude of the sales force.

In 1974 Richards was promoting John Holt's 'Help Me Make It Through the Night' which eventually reached the Top Ten, and had taken him to an interview during the intervals of a *Top of the Pops* taping.

> 'There was someone from the *Sun* newspaper,' said Richards, 'who wrote an article the following day, saying something like: "When I see John Holt destroying Kris Kristofferson's version of 'Help Me Make It Through the Night' my heart bleeds." I took it upon myself to phone this gentleman, to ask him of his musical qualifications for making the statement he made. He had also said that "John Holt was Top of the Flops!" I asked him for his definition of a flop, but he could not give a good answer. So I said: "I put it to you that the publishers of the song commented on what a good job we did. Johnny Pearson, the musical conductor of *Top of the Pops* commented on what a good work it was, and yet you, a little unscrupulous person who just sits behind a typewriter and lets loose with a pen, makes a definition of a flop . . . . Now our record made it to the top, while Kristofferson's version didn't, so that our record was even more a success in the U.K., and we sold more copies." But that is the type of prejudice and deranged mind that we were dealing with.'[25]

Trojan, as well as the entire B&C empire, came to a sudden and unpredictable crash in 1975, at a time when the company was just beginning to extend its limited formulaic musical range to include other areas of expression. The demise of the company, which has to be understood as the most successful black record company to have existed in the United Kingdom, is still the subject of speculation. Creditors suddenly came down on B&C, the parent company, and it was unable to pay. The company was insolvent, but to a limited degree, because Saga Records (a classical company under Marcel Rod, a Jew, which made its millions from cut-price classics) bought it for £32,000. But Richards seems to have a series of possible explanations for the financial downfall of the company. It posed a threat to the white record industry, and Brian Gibbon was the sole financial controller of all B&C's labels, as well as of Goptal's chain of a reputed twenty-four record shops.

> To me Trojan became successful too suddenly. The reason for making that statement is that while you're small, nobody takes much notice of you. But Mr Goptal had a page and a half article in the *Sun* newspaper boasting that a 36-year-old accountant, Jamaican, ruled an empire called Trojan from his office, sat behind the biggest desk with his Caribbean-flavoured music, and said that the popularity of Reggae was unbelievable, and that the mere fact that he owned a chain of stores proved that Reggae was definitely on the move, and that his new artist, Ken Boothe, had caused such a trend in the music industry that he forced creditors to demand money too suddenly. Mr Goptal also stated in the same article that some records sold over 60,000 copies without a single radio play and without chart placing. We had sold a million copies of 'Everything I Own'. It is my opinion, and I'm not stating a fact, I'm entitled to my own opinion: B&C group used to market Charisma. Now Charisma was offered a better deal from Phonogram. Let's say, for argument's sake, that Phonogram had offered Charisma £2 million. Obviously it would have been in the interest of the directors to go with Phonogram. You must remember that Brian Gibbon was financial controller of B&C Marketing and Sales – Trojan, as well as Charisma. And it was he who okayed the deal for Charisma to leave B&C and go to Phonogram. By losing the Charisma catalogue . . . they had big offices in Soho Square, and empty cars running around, and they had also taken over the K-Tel building in Sunbeam Road, Acton, for offices, and there was, of course, the old Trojan building with some beaten down old desks in Harlesden. So to keep three offices going with the limited catalogue they now had as a result of Charisma going to Phonogram, was difficult. Also, I think, it was dangerous for Reggae to grow bigger at that particular time, unless it was controlled by the EMIs, and CBS's, the Pyes, etc. At that time I had five records going up and down the charts, but three were definite hits. I also had a number in the breakers: 'Move Out a Babylon' by Johnny Clarke, 'In the Pocket', a Soul record on the People label, 'No Jestering', 'Natty Bongo' by Owen Grey and 'The Hostage' by Donna Summer. So if you could assume that I could put two of those breakers in the charts, that would make five records in the charts. Now Trojan is a small concern, what would happen to the British pop industry? Think of the damage the British pop industry would have suffered. So it was a glorious day when B&C went bust, they loved it. Just imagine: the same financial director over all the companies. All went bust,

> but Charisma was saved. One might be a coincidence, two might have been, but all? Being financial director, he alone would know the economic state of the companies, and if certain moves were made, the imminent collapse of B&C would have followed. If he didn't know what was going on, God himself would not have known. And incidentally, the same Brian Gibbon is the managing director of Charisma Records, which is now a big independent concern in America.[26]

By the early 1970s a number of independent black Reggae labels were already springing up. Most of them evolved in the same way as Sonny Roberts's Planitone Records. They were financed by ordinary black working people who had no inherited money, no contacts, but only the love of the music and a strength of character and determination. Ethnic-Fight Records was started by Larry Lawrence, himself a Jamaican singer who once recorded for Clement Dodd in Jamaica. The very name of the company indicated Lawrence's philosophical perspective. Count Shelley (real name Ephraim Barrett) was a sound system operator in London and also worked as a builder. He saved up, bought houses, and started Shelley Records which, after going out of business, resurfaced as Third World Records. Third World has now become the largest black Reggae company in the United Kingdom. Its catalogue boasts over sixty album releases in four years, but it does not have the frontal assault that Trojan had on the English market. It remains small, profitable and independent, with no major distribution except Lugtons and its own van sales or the use of other small Reggae distributors, and does well on exports. Atra Records was founded by Brent Clarke in early 1974, functioned reasonably well as a small Reggae company, but ceased to function after 1975 when it was distributed for a very short time by Virgin Records. It would seem that the relationship with Virgin helped the latter company to explore the sales force of Reggae through a distributed label without committing its own financial resources. When the sales were seen to be profitable, a conflict with Atra arose and a working relationship was deemed impossible. Virgin subsequently rivalled Island Records, directly after Atra was dropped, as the biggest distributor of the music. In fact, in 1978, Virgin almost trebled the number of records that Island released. After the fall of Trojan, a number of other labels were formed:

Hawkeye Records, D-Roy, Cha Cha Music, Grove Music, Vital Records, Manic Records, Klik, Sound Tracks, Tropical, Vulcan/Grounation Records, Different, Burning Sounds, Rite Sound, and Ballistic Records (formerly known as Magnum). The two main exceptions were Dip Records, which established itself in the early 1970s and had a string of Lee Perry produced hits (but never made the charts, except the Susan Cadogan 'Hurt So Good' which they had licensed to Magnet Records), and Sonny Roberts made a come-back in 1970 with two new labels, Orbitone and Tackle Records, specializing not in Reggae, but in Soul ballads, R&B, Calypso and Afrikan music. Nationwide and Ital Records (owned by the same person) came into existence around 1973. Recent additions have been Jamaica Sounds/Cancer/Hulk, High Note, Bushay (which is owned by producer Clement Bushay), and Arawak Records (who are also distributors).

Of the early labels, Pama Records, went out of business, so did Bamboo and Ashanti, as well as the hastily put together labels, Vulcan/Grounation, after the collapse of B&C/Trojan. Sound Tracks, Tropical, and Klick also went out of business. Some of the senior staff and directors of Trojan Records reassembled and quickly formed a label to fill the vacuum left by the death of their recent company. Their directors were Junior Lincoln, Webster Shrowder, Chips Richards, and Bob Gilbert. Richards states that when he learned that Phonogram had offered them a distribution deal, he gave the company a year to prove his notion that nothing would come of the relationship to Phonogram in which Charisma was involved as a much more prestigious and powerful company. His suspicions were verified, he states, when he approached the BBC with records to plug and was told by a producer, in front of Vulcan's English secretary, that Vulcan's 'big boss' had instructed him not to play any of their records. When Richards returned to the office and informed his partners of what took place, they refused to believe him.[27] There were also rumours that directors of Vulcan were stealing their own records and selling them at great discount to any buyers. It was also said that Phonogram was alarmed by this behaviour and called in specially trained security men to investigate the matter. Vulcan, who had rented large office space on the Harrow

Road, had an expensive Mercedes van on the road distributing records, and a staff of twenty-two, with future plans of building a recording studio on its premises, soon collapsed. The company's policies were simultaneously adventurous and dull. On the one hand they had released an imaginative album by Ras Michael and the Sons of Negus, *Rastafari*, and on the other, they were engaged in releasing poor singles. The company was also overstaffed for the kind of market which that type of Reggae catered for. So its collapse was no surprise, coupled with the assertions of Richards.

Of all the small companies that went out of business, Klick seemed to have been the most imaginative. They had released a very important album by Big Youth, *Dread Locks Dread*, which was promoted by John Maxwell, a Trinidadian Public Relations man who brought results – publicity – to the artists he handled. That Big Youth album sold over 25,000 copies, an incredible achievement for an album distributed under the circumstances without a major, and especially being a DJ/Toasting record. They had also released an album of remarkable musical achievement, *Negril*, which featured a number of Jamaican session men (including Cedric 'Im' Brooks on tenor, and Leslie Butler on organ and synthesizer) under the direction, compositions and playing of the American-born guitarist (but of immediate Caribbean descent), Eric Gale. The facts leading to Klick's fall are not known, but it seemed that when the company achieved national distribution through Island Records, they were spending vast sums of money on giving the sales reps incentives to sell their records. Their sales could not support the expenditure, and, in addition, they had moved out of their one-room office in Harlesden and into a two-floor building in Portobello Road, which they renovated and refurbished. The demise of Sound Tracks/Tropical was not caused by lack of business acumen. They had received a distribution deal through President Records/Enterprise Distributors, and had obtained a Top Ten hit with 'Midnight Rider' by Paul Davidson. It is claimed that Kassner, a German Jew, had staked his reputation on never having lost a court case for anything, e.g. breach of contract, improper accounting procedures, inaccurate sales figures, false statements, etc. while he was chairman of the board. Having been awarded a silver disc for the sales of 'Midnight Rider', which the BMRB

Delroy Washington, the London-based Reggae artist. (*Photo: D. Morris.*)

Dennis Bovell, Matumbi's leader and independent producer, does the final mix at a recording studio.
(Photo: Vernon St. Hilaire.)

Below: Aswad, based in Ladbroke Grove, London.
(Photo: Vernon St. Hilaire.)

declared for sales of £150,000, it is reported that Sound Tracks accepted a cheque of £80,000 in settlement. Having accepted the cheque, the company ceased trading, ostensibly because that amount of money was thought safe profit, and should not be risked supporting a catalogue that was not selling in sufficient quantities.

The fortunes, or lack of them, of small independents, did not stagnate the local development of British-based artists and productions. The impetus for the growth of locally produced Reggae was obviously a result of the rise of Bob Marley and the Wailers to international status. In West London, where the most important artists seemed to be concentrated, there were Delroy Washington, Aswad, the Cimmarons and Brimstone – three artists who received their inspiration directly from Bob Marley's recording of his first album for Island, *Catch a Fire*. Aswad, signed by a former *Melody Maker* staffer, Richard Williams, was hired by Island Records in the latter part of 1972 (soon after a number of articles on Bob Marley appeared in *Melody Maker* (by Williams), and in *New Musical Express* (by Danny Holloway, who was also hired by Island in that same year as a press officer). Aswad were signed by Island in 1975, recorded an uneven and inexperienced album, and finally left in disgust in early 1978. Delroy Washington, a multi-instrumentalist (but of limited ability, instrumentally) was signed by Virgin Records in 1976 and debuted with an interesting, if ill-produced album, but was later dropped by them. The Cimmarons, on the other hand, were fine instrumentalists, but often recorded versions of other people's compositions. They were eventually signed by Polydor for a reputed £40,000 in late 1977, but were later dropped, ostensibly through poor sales.

The Battersea-based London band, Matumbi, showed enormous potential with their first significant release, 'After Tonight', which officially sold 17,000 copies, though the Mechanical Copyright Protection Society (MCPS) has reportedly confirmed that 81,000 copies were pressed. When Matumbi signed with the reactivated Trojan, they refused to record for the company and remained officially unrecorded until they signed with EMI in 1978. Matumbi assured themselves a place in the public's eye by recording various instrumental albums for Dip Records under pseudonyms, e.g.

4th Street Orchestra, as well as issuing some excellent recordings under the Matumbi Recording Corporation label without the band's name.[28]

It is impossible to assess the contribution of the small black independent labels to the development of Reggae in the United Kingdom and the world. But I have here at least given some idea of the vital and significant role they played.

8 Step Forward/Backward: The Changing Future

Rock Steady, as a musical style and expression, did not take hold of Jamaica, for it did not last very long. From early 1966 to the end of 1967 the music reigned. It changed the format of Ska to include a more specifically Jamaican experience, and simultaneously absorbed the vocal and instrumental influences of Afro-America. By late 1967 the rhythm was changing from the slow, meditative beat of Rock Steady to a faster beat, somewhere between Ska and Rock Steady, with the bass even more prominent. Like all transitions in music, it is difficult to point to a single record as the one that was responsible for the new music. Certainly, Toots and the Maytals' 'Do the Reggay' was the first record to use the name in a recording, but it cannot be said that it was responsible for the change. The word 'Reggae' itself seems to have metamorphosed from the word 'streggae', which defined a sexual activity. Both Bob Marley and Keith Hudson have said that it had a 'low' meaning, and Hudson added that it was shouted out to girls as they passed in the street. So the word presumably translates a social activity into musical terms.

The early Reggae possessed a liveliness and energy that activated the nerve-centres of the person to physical expression – dance! Initially, the music was released on a number of labels, but because of the exploitation by a few producers, many musicians and singers formed their own labels to have more control over the sales of their product. Many such labels folded; it demanded finance, dedication and extreme frugality with money. One hundred records could be sold in one day, and if the money was not put away, it could be spent entertaining friends or on fulfilling personal demanding needs. Yet a few of these labels managed to continue functioning. Augustus Pablo, for example, started his label as early as 1969, and it still survives today, releasing its product in the United Kingdom on Hawkeye Records and other labels. Another, the indefatigable Dennis Brown, formed his own label in the United Kingdom initially in support of his determined cousin, Castro Brown, and it has grown, primarily under the latter's direction, into an important independent company – sufficiently so to pay one of its artists £5,000 on royalties. It has also attracted the attention of a major, EMI, which has agreed to distribute the label.

Thus the impetus for the music's development, in both musical and financial terms, stems from the determination and commitment of some of its artists to transcend the conditions under which they themselves worked. Musicians in Jamaica have not always been well paid. For example, a session musician would receive £5 per recording between 1959 and 1969. In the latter year the fee went up to £7.50 and there was a 25 per cent increase a year later. The Musicians Union in Jamaica helped to bring about these improved fees. But the accessibility of guns and ammunition in the Kingston area also played a significant part in bargaining with producers. Previously, the producer alone carried a gun or guns, the classic example being the late Duke Reid. He dressed like a Mexican bandit at times, wearing a gun in a holster around his shoulders, a belt with bullets, a rifle in his arm, and was the epitome of fear itself. Both Clement Dodd and Harry Johnson occasionally carried pistols. But the musician/sufferer and potential villain could now equally demand what he wanted with aids that were as dangerous as the producers'.

Paul Simon recorded his 'Mother and Child Reunion' in Jamaica, requesting the same musicians that Jimmy Cliff used, and paid them exactly what they asked for: £10 per recording. Chris Blackwell, who is extremely well acquainted with the musical environment in Kingston, was not satisfied with this situation, not from the point of view of exploitation but from that of aesthetic satisfaction. The musicians would only cut a tune of a maximum length of three minutes, and professional producers found this inadequate, because it did not allow sufficient time to play with overdubbing ideas. So Blackwell paid the musicians to lengthen the time of the tune.

Over the last two years, even though the session fee has now increased to £15 or $30.00 J, some musicians had the power, based entirely upon their reputations, to demand from foreign producers as much as £25.00 per recording.[1] Musicians like Sly Dunbar and Robbie Shakespeare can demand literally anything they want, and get it. If the producer does not want to pay them, he will have to look elsewhere.

It can safely be said that the top Jamaican recording artists earn considerably more money than their counterpart Reggae musician in London. In the Jamaican context there are almost no rehearsals prior to entering the studio. The singer sings his lines, or in the case of an instrumentalist, plays his lines, and the musicians fit the backing to suit. The producer merely finances the project. The rhythm track can be laid in one hour, and another session ensues. I have never heard of musicians conducting more than ten recordings on a particular day, but an article in the *Melody Maker* states that both Dunbar and Shakespeare have performed on up to twenty recordings a day.[2] This sounds like extreme exaggeration. Both the musicians and the producer and/or engineer are extremely concerned with what they term a 'good rhythm'. The only time when the producer and/or engineer would complain was if they felt that the musicians were tiring and playing lackadaisically. A more average performance would be ten recordings per day, with a break for lunch as well as the sharing of several joints of marijuana.

When the early Reggae was exported to and subsequently released in the United Kingdom, a similar pattern of alleged rip-offs of the artist or the producer would be levelled against the record company. This may be explained by the historical role of the record company as manipulator of the artists' rightful claim to an income. Blackwell himself commented that a system of exploitation existed whereby the record manufacturer (invariably linked to a particular label) would press a record for his own distribution for every record he legitimately manufactured for the artist or producer.[3] When the artist had a hit, whether a national hit or a record that became popular through reasonable sales and exposure through the sound systems in the United Kingdom, the artist would invariably be brought over for a tour, with a local backing band, not a Jamaican one, and accompanied by his manager (invariably the owner of the label responsible for its licensing to the United Kingdom label). There would also be a middle man awaiting the arrival of the artist to fix dates and arrange a schedule. The artist would initially be impressed, and would welcome any small amount of money he might earn from this avenue. The promoter and/or agent invariably made all the profits, invested his money, and later monopolized this particular income-source, until the artists became wise and threatened violence. It was then that the agent/promoter ceased this form of money-earning and resorted to other forms of earning, either in the record business itself, or in a business directly related to records, e.g. a recording studio, record company, music publishing, etc.

The United Kingdom became a lucrative market for the Jamaican artist, even if it meant a tour of twenty-two dates and a net earning of £2,000, as in the case of Delroy Wilson. Depending on who arranged the tour, it could be a success or failure. The black promoter/agent usually thought black, i.e. for the audience within his own community, whether in Birmingham, Reading, Manchester, or London. But the white promoter understood the needs of the white youth community, in larger and more lucrative places, who were willing to pay to see their heroes. Thus the Jamaican artist who initially achieves a minor hit (or a major one for that matter) would be tempted to remain in the United Kingdom. Prince Jazzbo and Desmond Dekker both had hits, the former a minor hit that propelled trends in both black and white communities, the latter attaining national and international success. But when they decided to remain, their music either changed, degenerated, or was never heard of again (as in the case of Jazzbo). London seems to thwart the development of the Jamaican artist who had already matured by the time of his first hit. Yet they won't go back to Jamaica because they will always remember the exploitation they suffered at the hands of their Jamaican brothers. Thus Alton Ellis, a formidable talent responsible for many trends in the music, feels incapable of returning to Jamaica. For him it is full of bad memories and experiences.

In the United Kingdom the importance of the Blues Dance for the preservation of the music cannot be overestimated. Because of the low skill level of many Jamaicans who came to take up jobs that the Englishman himself did not want, their standard of living was not good. Thus they resorted to the Blues Dance, the turning of a single, two-roomed, or an entire house (abandoned or owned) into a simulated night club where the sound system would be hired to provide the music, and drinks and food (as well as ganja), sold at inflated prices. This was their primary source of revenue: to purchase a house, or domestic utility, or to send home money to dependants. Beyond its financial returns, in a sense, the Blues Dance replaced the role of the preacher and the church for many Caribbeans. The new church was the Blues Dance itself and the preacher was the sound man. Favourites would be Lloydie Coxsone, Moa Ambessa, Fat Man Hi-Fi, Sufferer Sound, Jesus Sound, and others. In the early days Fanso was the ruler of North London. It provides a social outlet mainly in the form of dance. In the Blues Dance almost everything was done silently – out-stretched hands or touching a woman would communicate the need to dance, and this invariably led to 'grinding up' against a wall. The black worker sought comfort and expression through dance, physical, silent, and Jamaican music became the expression of that need.

Other places that catered for these needs were the early clubs like the Roaring 20s in the West End, 007 in East London, and Club Rock Steady and the Four Aces in North London.[4] The last three clubs were the main places where visiting Jamaican artists would play. The West End clubs, primarily the Flamingo, only occasionally had Jamaican acts, and usually through the aegis of a white agent. The latter clubs entertained the black musician/artist as a creative sponge from whom to collect ideas to use on white acts; they were then finally dropped or 'waited in the wings to be discovered'.[5] The young white raver, hip to the black scene, emerged through the efforts of black musicians, whether playing Jamaican, Trinidadian, or Afro-American music. Georgie Fame recorded Calypso, High Life, Ska, and R&B, while his band contained Caribbean and Afrikan musicians. The young white DJs who played Soul or Jamaican music in these clubs eventually became BBC announcers or became involved in other aspects of the recording business.

But how was the transformation of Afro-American music affecting the growth and development of Jamaican music? In every trend (with the exception of Dub and the DJ style) that evolved, Jamaican music made use of the Afro-American experience either vocally or instrumentally. The most noticeable transformation in Jamaican music has been the introduction of instrumental solos in both vocal and instrumental music. As early as 1973, the main form of instrumental solos was the picking guitar or an electric piano or organ playing the melody line in the middle of the tune. In 1973, after Bob Marley and Chris Blackwell had remixed the entire *Catch a Fire* album, the Wailers refused to release the 'foreign' version at home. They released only the rhythm tracks. This was perhaps motivated by two things: 1. the need not to alienate their fans; 2. the need to retain their roots. What eventually precipitated the change in direction were financial rewards. The recordings sold more widely internationally when they included or exhibited instrumental prowess.

In the United Kingdom the Caribbean musician playing Afro-American music, whether Soul or Jazz, had developed a different, perhaps more sophisticated, musical standard. But the Caribbean musician playing Jamaican music was tied to the placenta of the Jamaican womb. Trends activated in Jamaica were imitated or reproduced in Britain. Thus the Cimmarons, initially requested to perform some instrumental chores on the Wailers' first Island album, were personally able to witness the transformation that was beginning to take place in the music, and assimilate this transformation. Thus, also, the paradigm for the United Kingdom (as well as Jamaican) musician was the success of the Wailers playing the new music that they played. This was also due to the *image as rebels* that the group has held for years in the Jamaican musical scene. Once the trend was set by the Wailers, tied to a successful white-owned company (admittedly Jamaican, if only by birth), the stage was set for the encroachment of the white record company as possible manipulator of Jamaican music. In one sense the involvement of the white record company has liberated the sufferer/artist from the hands of the local entrepreneur/producer. His earning power has increased tremendously, but simultaneously he is unaware of the legitimate exploitation he suffers at their hands. One of the two most well-known companies involved in Reggae in the United Kingdom has been transferring money to the United States where it is changed into American dollars, and subsequently arrives in Jamaica in American currency – not cheques or by bank transfer, but in cash. This is then converted on the bad market through business magnates and bought at the rate of $1.00 (U.S.) for $3.00 (J). Thus £1,000 directly transferred to Jamaica from London amounts to $2,610.00 (J), legitimately. That same £1,000 going the former route ends up as over $5,000 (J), the American exchange rate for the pound fluctuating between $1.96 and $2.00. Thus the Jamaican artist, receiving $10,000 advance in Jamaican currency, seems to be making an astounding amount of money, but in actual fact is being paid less than £2,000. Thus it is in the interests of certain record companies to sign Jamaican acts because they are cheaper. An equivalent act, say, to Culture in London would almost certainly demand a minimum of £5,000 advance, if not £10,000. In addition, the white record company would have to subsidize their frequent tours of the United Kingdom and of Europe if they are to emerge as a money-making entity. The only way the Jamaican artist escapes this form of exploitation is by employing a white manager (as in the case of Steel Pulse).

The attitude of white record companies to black artists by and large is illustrated by an incident that occurred in the offices of Sky Note Records, a black label. A representative from Hansa Records (primarily a production company which also shares label identity with Ariola Records, and are quite successful in most of Europe) visited Chips Richards at his office.

> He looked at that nice, big, beautiful poster of Marcia Griffiths, and said: 'She's a good singer.' I said I know. We release Marcia's records in this country. I then asked him, simply out of speculation, how much his company would be willing to pay, by way of advance, for Marcia Griffiths. He said: '£15,000, if you're lucky.' I asked him to take a seat and explained to him that every disco forty-five I release on Marcia Griffiths sold a minimum of 10,000 units, and that an album consists of ten tracks, and that if I wanted to go that way I could release all the tracks as discos, then put them on an album and release that too. When I was finished with that, I could remix the entire album as a Dub, then, in addition, get a DJ to toast over the rhythms. I could then sell possibly 10,000 albums by Marcia, an additional 7,000 as a Dub, and 3,000 as a DJ album. I wholesale my discos for £1.20 to the distributor and £2.40 for an album. If you add all those sales together, you are talking about £150,000. Now, what can a major do for me by offering me £15,000 for an artist

as talented as Marcia Griffiths, when they themselves could well maximize their sales? I could have gotten a licensing deal as well, but why should I give up my label to receive 10 per cent royalties and the major makes 90 per cent? That same Hansa representative looked at Louisa Mark and said his company would be willing to advance £3,000 for her, when Clement Bushay, her producer, released two discos by her with both selling 12,000 units. They come flashing £15,000 or even £50,000 in your face for your label and your artists, and think they can impress you. We don't have national distribution, and that's the only thing I am willing to accept from a major, not a licensing deal.[6]

A similar story was related by Sonny Roberts.

When I recorded the first album by Tim Chandell I took it to Creole Records who listened to it and liked it. I then said I wanted £17,000 advance for it, but he laughed. I also in the past have approached other major companies for distribution deals. They listen to the records and then tell me they cannot sell 2,000 copies. I have been trying for four years to get a distribution deal from Lugtons, but have never succeeded. Anyway, I released the Tim Chandell album and sold 55,000 copies in ten months. His new album has already sold 11,000 copies in two months. Now, if a small company like me can sell that amount of records, what do you think that they can sell? I used to approach Creole with my Afrikan albums, Nkengas and Peter King, but they were never interested. Now I see they are releasing Fela Kuti's albums. They are following my trends. We even get problems with the newspapers. I advertise in *Black Echoes* and I telephoned them to complain that they have put Tim Chandell's album in the Reggae charts. I was telling them that it belonged to the Soul charts, but they said no, it belongs in the Reggae charts. Now, that album is a Soul album and it has some R&B in there, but they put Boney M's 'Rivers of Babylon' which is Reggae, in the Soul charts. The only reason they did that is because Boney M's company is a big white concern. If I had put out Boney M, that would never reach nowhere.[7]

In fact Tim Chandell's album has been the biggest seller among the small independents, black or white, for 1978. If it is considered that a great number of Rock acts who enter the national charts sell no more than 30,000 albums, the whole system of chart entries becomes ridiculous and irrelevant. Island Records, for example, sold 25,000 albums of Third World's *Journey to Addis* which went straight into the national charts. Bob Marley's *Rastaman Vibrations* had sold

Culture, one of the most prominent groups reflective of the deep roots vocal approach. (*Photo: D. Morris.*)

U-Roy, one of Jamaica's most popular DJs/Toasters. (*Photo: D. Morris.*)

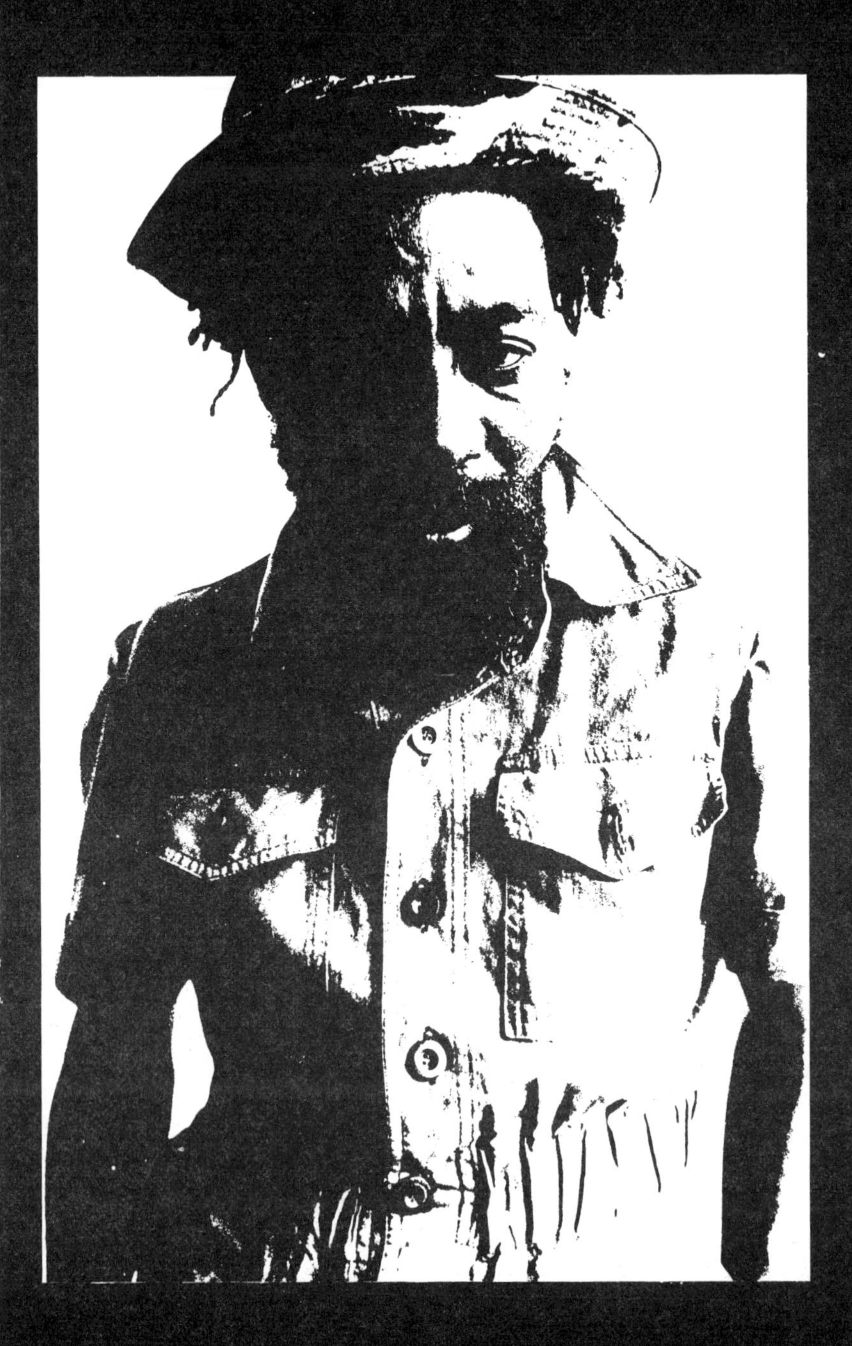

50,000 units and had also entered the charts when it was released in 1976. Why, then, does there exist an anomaly between the white record company and the black one? The British Market Research Board, which is responsible for tabulating sales through certain high road shops, have a list of shops that are considered chart return shops and from which they devise their national charts. This list is available to all the majors that supply these shops with records, and which, based simply upon the advance orders they receive, can put a record into the charts. This system operates for the benefit of the majors, for when they are charted, the BBC immediately begins to give the records air play, which obviously boosts sales even more. Take for example two artists, Elton John and Peter Tosh. Both had singles released simultaneously in late 1978; John's charted at No. 60, while Tosh charted at No. 53. Tosh's single did not make the BBC play list, but John's did.[8]

Some of the white record companies' motivation for entering the Reggae music business is the large market for Reggae in Afrika. I have already pointed out that since the early 1950s Calypso, and later all forms of Jamaican music, sold massively on that continent, so it does not come as a surprise that this market absorbs a greater proportion of sales than that of Europe or America. In fact Jimmy Cliff is reputed to have sold over half a million units of his single, 'A Hard Road to Travel'. Jumbo Vanrenen, an executive of Virgin Records, has stated that U-Roy sells as well as any of their top Rock acts.[9] But if it is seen that U-Roy's records never enter the charts in Europe, and are not being exported to the Caribbean because they have already been released there by the local producer, then one must conclude that they are selling in Afrika. This was verified by a statement made in *Music Week* in 1975 by one of Virgin's export executives who stated that they had sold £150,000-worth of Reggae in 1975, a year in which Virgin was not directly involved in releasing Reggae, but was exporting other companies' products. Thus Sonny Roberts believes that the involvement by some white companies in Reggae is not sincere, and that since Nigeria has now closed its doors to imports and has made it difficult to export money out of the country, there may be repercussions over the next few years.

> Now, all this heavy Reggae music sells a lot in Afrika, but who gets the money? Virgin, Lightning . . . . There are millions of pounds that come out of Afrika, but whose pocket does it go into? The same white man that these Reggae artists sing about, that they are gonna cut his head off, down with colonialism, and up with Rastafari. Those white companies enjoy that, man, because they are using those same words to sell you and me (i.e. black people)![10]

The present music scene in Britain has exploded out of the original success of Bob Marley. That is to say, as a result of his success, there is now a general market in the United Kingdom. The black independents are generally behind this move. One of the pioneers of locally recorded Reggae was Dip Records (before they ceased trading). They stopped as a result of the aggression the company experienced from Jamaican artists abroad, i.e. living in Jamaica. It then developed a policy of producing Reggae primarily from local acts. This has meant a greater investment for them because they pay for the hiring of the recording studio, pay session musicians, disc cutting, sleeves and manufacture, while in the licensing context, they simply buy the master and pay a flat royalty rate. It has also meant that they are attempting to break new acts or new records and this has been an added difficulty. In addition, until 1977, both black and white audiences have been prejudiced against locally recorded Reggae. As a result the small independents initiated a strategy to outwit the buying public. They released records, locally recorded, on a special label that contained no information, or on a white blank. This could then sell as any normal pre-release or imported Reggae from Jamaica. In many instances the public could not tell the difference. Both Island and Virgin also signed local artists and promoted them in the same way that they would approach any Jamaica-based artists. This also contributed to the eventual acceptance of locally based artists.

One of the most important musicians to emerge on the local scene is Dennis Bovell (also known as Dennis Matumbi), the leader of Matumbi. He worked for Dip Records for a long time, producing and recording records under a variety of pseudonyms for the company. He also later became one of the resident engineers at Gooseberry Studios, an important centre for locally recorded Reggae.

Bovell was then sought after by other small black independents, both as session musician and as engineer/producer. He produced a number of local artists including the successful Janet Kay (who was first discovered by Alton Ellis), whose Lover's Rock style, along with Louisa Mark's, has been responsible for the widespread popularity of the form. His one-man involvement in the Reggae scene has caused some small independents to rely on his creative services. Recently, the majors have also been after his services as producer – Radar Records for the Pop Group (a white punk band with indirect links to Reggae, i.e. they utilize the Dub format in their compositions), and Island Records for the Slits.

The majors' interest stems from the connection of the punk movement with Reggae. As at every stage of the black man's colonial history, there emerges a new generation of whites who feel an emotional identification with a particular music–cultural expression of black people. The mods in the early 1960s identified with Ska, and the punks today identify with Reggae, both as a political expression of environment and as a cultural force. This has created new entrepreneurs emanating from this so-called anti-establishment, anarchistic movement. The threat they pose to the music is that because of the canonization of a particular musical style, e.g. the roots style, that created the initial vehicle for their identification, they become the medium of taste and thus hold the adventurous creator in a position of frustration. But today, the white concept of the authentic is linked with the raw and unembroidered musical expression of the stark poverty and social decay that characterize a certain aspect of Kingston life. Thus like the *bald-head* capitalist who rejects the music in one way, they also reject the new social status that the black creator reflects through his improved social condition.

White clubs have now opened their doors to Reggae as a result of the punks' involvement with the music. Rock Against Racism, which Linton Johnson recognizes as the new white left who believe themselves to be the spokesmen and articulators of the black struggle, is an organization of young whites principally concerned with the anti-fascist, anti-racist movement, and have been promoting a number of concerts that feature the combined forces of punk and Reggae acts. This has created reputations for local acts (Aswad, Merger, Misty, Steel Pulse) who have since been accepted by white promoters as a commercial proposition. Clubs such as the 100 Club, Music Machine, Dingwalls, the Electric Ballroom, the Rock Garden and the Nashville have now all opened their doors to Reggae; they would have been firmly closed prior to 1977. This has also led to the development of new styles of performances characterized by improvisation and solos which would not have been presented to black audiences. The inclusion of Caribbeans previously involved with Soul or Jazz and of young blacks born or brought up in this country has added further musical dimensions.

Eddy Grant, the former lead singer with the Equals, a local pop group that became popular in the middle to late 1960s, has, since the group's departure from their former record company, Kassner/President Records, become more involved in the business aspects of the record industry. He now owns the Coach House Studios, which developed from a sixteen-track studio (formerly owned by Manfred Mann) to a twenty-four track. His record label, Ice, has achieved gold disc status in Nigeria while only recently breaking into the charts in this country under the support of the Ensign label (a subsidiary of Phonogram) with his own composition, 'Living on the Front Line'. Grant has also bought out his former boss of President Records who owned a pressing plant in South London. By achieving these goals, Grant has become the only black entrepreneur to control an important aspect of business life in this country. The only serious area he still needs to control is the offer of a distribution deal by one of the majors. In spite of Grant's verbal resolution about the preference for a distribution – rather than a licensing deal – he has finally signed his label over to Virgin Records after an abortive negotiation with Warner Brothers Records. Grant has also managed not to confine himself to Reggae by getting involved with different black artists performing a variety of music.

Aswad can be seen as a local group emerging entirely out of the London scene, with hardly any historical connection with Jamaica other than through the music and the involvement with Rastafari. There are five members in the group and four were born in London, the fifth was born in Jamaica. They all speak with Jamaican accents even though they have descended from a variety of islands: Guyana and Grenada, as well as Jamaica. Their current style is that of a fusion of

Jazz/Funk ideas over a *heavy* Reggae rhythm. I emphasize the word heavy for a specific reason. Many previously involved musicians out of the Soul or Rock school, themselves black, believe that Reggae is a simple music (perhaps like Byron Lee in relation to Ska), and neglect to emphasize that the drums and bass combination express the *form* and *style*, the *foundation of expressing Reggae*. An example of this would be the early aggregation of Merger, the very name spelling out fusion music, but certainly not Reggae as understood by this writer. Aswad's experiments have been fruitful and highly successful.

> 'Speaking for the band,' said George Oban, 'everyone wanted to get that heavy sound in JA Reggae, not exactly with yard kinda feel, because we have to accept the fact that we are a British band, and it is on here the experiences come from. When you play in front of black audiences and you do them musical things, they just stand there and cold you up. Then we started doing some Rock Against Racism gigs, playing some white venues, the crossover scene, and we felt we coulda free up ourselves more musically. You must remember that the Jamaican is himself taken from his roots, Afrika, but look how far we are taken from that. We are even further away, because most of us have been born here. It's a whole new generation born here, so we have to draw our roots from yard (i.e. Jamaica). As a musician, I won't like to think that in thirty years time I would be playing the same kind of thing. We want to progress, man.'[11]

There are other groups with different approaches to style and form. Misty, for example, have an entirely new expression and style. They emphasize the rhythmic aspects of the music through which they express a variety of themes preoccupied with oppression and liberty, death and salvation. It is a fresh and new approach that is markedly different from the Jamaican model, yet as embedded in *roots* as any authentic expression emerging from Jamaica. The concept of roots has changed. It once denoted expression in a drums and bass category, exclusively, with the other instruments simply re-emphasizing the rhythm. Now the concept has evolved to include drums and bass authenticity, with the other instruments playing melody lines or riffs, and containing articulate solos. This is achieved in both Jamaica and the United Kingdom. In Jamaica, Ansell Collins has been the greatest and most articulate expressor of the absorption of Jazz/Funk ideas, with his inclusion of repeated riffs and improvisatory forays.

Both Jamaican Reggae and its British-based counterpart have evolved new styles of expression. This is a response to the new white audiences, as well as a liberation from the restricting confines of the producer who has been a reproducer of certain styles that he believed audiences wanted to hear. While being a good stimulus, this has also had terrible effects on extremely capable artists. Virgin Records, for example, were reputed to have invested £30,000 in the production of the Diamonds by Allen Toussaint, the Afro-American producer who has been responsible for work with Labelle and the Meters. The result was an album that sold neither to the white market nor the black, for different reasons. Jo Jo Hookim, the group's former producer, said he was approached by Virgin to produce the group in a more commercial manner that transcended 'ethnic' categories. He refused to do so. The Diamonds, who were previously a model in vocal ability, is now a group without an identity. The company, noting lack of sales and identity, has returned the group to Hookim in order to generate sales through a roots image.

The concept of fusion music has become the dominant theme in the marketing of commercial Reggae. This has been due largely to the success of Third World who scored internationally with 'Now that We Found Love', a Gamble and Huff composition originally recorded by their protégés, the O'Jays. Island Records have been in the forefront of this movement and have achieved some success with Inner Circle's 'Everything Is Great', the worst example of Reggae/Rock fusion. Third World epitomizes the ideal of fusion music because it seems to be an outgrowth of authentic experimentation with Latin and Afro-American musical forms. Undoubtedly, it would be enormously difficult to propose that authentic roots music could possibly create the international impact that fusion music has. Given the circumstances of our civilization – the upward mobility thrust of the moderns – it is difficult to imagine any real absorption or understanding of roots music. But it seems highly unlikely that roots music will not continue to influence the new directions and forms that Reggae will accommodate in order to become popular and acceptable.

References

Chapter 1

History and Roots

1. Ivan Van Sertima, *They Came Before Columbus: The African Presence in Ancient America*, New York, Random House, 1976, p.13.
2. Clinton Black, *The Story of Jamaica*, revised ed., London, Collins, 1965, p.32.
3. Clinton Black, *Port Royal*, Kingston, Bolivar, 1970, p.12.
4. Carey Robinson, *The Fighting Maroons of Jamaica*, London, Collins/Sangster,1969, p.16.
5. Black, *Port Royal*, op. cit., p.13.
6. Edward Long, quoted in Robinson, op. cit., p.20.
7. ibid., p.24.
8. ibid., p.29.
9. Leonard Barrett, *Soul Force*, New York, Doubleday, 1974, p.77.
10. ibid., p.78.
11. Black, *Port Royal*, op. cit.
12. Orlando Patterson, *The Sociology of Slavery*, London, MacGibbon and Kee, 1967, p.267.
13. ibid., p.268.
14. ibid.; and Robinson, op. cit., pp.31–2.
15. Patterson, op. cit., p.20; and Black, *The Story of Jamaica*, op. cit., pp.33–7.
16. Patterson, op. cit.
17. ibid., p.21; and Black, *The Story of Jamaica*, op. cit., pp.39–40.
18. Robinson, op, cit., Chapter 12.
19. James M. Phillippo, *Jamaica: Its Past and Present*, London, Dawsons, reprinted 1969, p.158.
20. Richard Hart, 'Jamaica and Self-Determination: 1660–1970', *Race*, vol. 13, London, The Institute of Race Relations.
21. Phillippo, op, cit., p.126.
22. Cited in Patterson, op, cit., p.54.
23. Quoted in Lord Oliver, *Jamaica: The Blessed Island*, London, Faber & Faber, 1936, p.85.
24. ibid., p.87.

25. ibid., p.88.
26. Edward Long, *History of Jamaica*, vol. 11, London, Cass, reprinted 1970, p.239.
27. Lord Oliver, op. cit., p.90.
28. Long, op. cit., pp.238–9.
29. Quoted in Lord Oliver, op. cit., p.89.
30. Patterson, op. cit., p.208.
31. Lord Oliver, op. cit., p.99.
32. Paul Edwards (ed.), *Equiano's Travels*, abridged ed., London, Heinemann, 1967, p.57.
33. John S. Mbiti, *African Religions and Philosophy*, London, Heinemann, 1969, p.64.
34. Phillippo, op. cit., pp. .64–7.
35. Lady Nugent's *Journal*, London, West India Committee, 1839, p.66.
36. Phillippo, op. cit., pp.242–3.
37. Judith Bettelheim, 'The Jonkunnu Festival', *Jamaica Journal*, Kingston.
38. ibid.
39. Phillippo, op. cit., pp. 2 5–6.
40. Margaret A. Murray, T *Splendour that was Egypt*, revised ed., London, Book Club Asso n, 1973, p.136.
41. Veronica Ions, *Egypt ythology*, London, Paul Hamlyn, 1965, p.136.
42. Mbiti, op. cit., p.15
43. Susan Feldman, *Afri n Myths and Tales*, London, Dell, 1963, pp. 125–8.
44. Asley Clerk, *Music and Musical Instruments of Jamaica*, Kingston, 1916, p.17.
45. Long, op. cit., p.423.
46. Francis Bebey, *African Music: A People's Art*, London, Harrap & Co., 1975, p.3.
47. Phillippo, op. cit., p.275.
48. Walter Jekyl, *Jamaica Song and Story*, New York, Dover, 1966, p.55.
49. Francis Bebey, op. cit., pp. 26–7.
50. Quoted in Edward Brathwaite, *The Development of Creole Society in Jamaica: 1770–1820*, London, Oxford University Press, 1971, pp. 221–2.
51. Phillippo, op. cit., pp. 241–2.
52. Ortiz M. Walton, *Music: Black, White and Blue*, New York, William Morrow, 1972, pp. 16–17.
53. Frederick C. Cassidy, *Jamaica Talk*, London, Macmillan, 1971, p.274.
54. ibid., pp.274–5.
55. Phillippo, op. cit., p.189.
56. ibid., p.190.
57. Laz E.N. Ekwene, 'African Sources in New World Black Music', *Black Images*, vol. 1, nos. 3 and 4, Toronto, 1972.
58. ibid.
59. ibid.
60. Walton, op. cit., p.10.
61. Jekyl, op. cit., p.10.
61. Jekyl, op. cit., pp. 192–3.
62. Anonymous, *Some Drums and Drum Rhythms of Jamaica* (place unknown; photostat copy found in the Institute of Jamaica).

63. Bebey, op. cit., p.40.
64. ibid., p.120.
65. Lord Oliver, op. cit., p.68.
66. This account of the Morant Bay Rebellion is based upon *The Morant Bay Rebellion*, Kingston, Face of Jamaica, no. 6, n.d.
67. Cassidy, op. cit., p.235.
68. Phillippo, op. cit., p.249.
69. ibid., p.248.
70. Barrett, op. cit., pp.115–16.
71. ibid., p.120.
72. Phillippo, op. cit., p.271.
73. Long, op. cit., pp.248–9.
74. Neville Dawes, 'The Jamaican Cultural Identity', *Jamaica Journal*, vol. 9, no. 1, Kingston.
75. Hart, op. cit.
76. Harold Cruse, *The Crisis of the Negro Intellectual*, part two: *1920s–1930s: The West Indian Influence*, New York, William Morrow, 1967.
77. Sylvia Wynter, 'Richards, Manley, and the BITU', *Jamaican Weekly Gleaner*, London, 12 April 1978, p.15.
78. Alan Kuper, *Changing Jamaica*, London, Routledge & Kegan Paul, 1976, p.28.
79. ibid., p.10.
80. ibid., p.17.

Chapter 2

Rastafari: The Concept of the Black Redeemer

1. Immanuel Geiss, *The Pan-African Movement*, London, Methuen & Co., 1974, p.133.
2. Cheike Anta Diop, *The African Origin of Civilization: Myth or Reality*, New York, Lawrence Hill & Co., 1974, p.168.
3. ibid., p.146.
4. Geiss, op. cit., p.135.
5. ibid.
6. ibid., pp.144 and p.149.
7. Richard Hart, 'The Life and Resurrection of Marcus Garvey', *Race*, vol. 9, London, 1967–8.
8. Roy Augier, Rex Nettleford, and M.G. Smith, *The Rastafari Movement in Kingston, Jamaica*, republished by the Jamaican High Commission, London; originally published by the University of the West Indies, Kingston, 1960, p.2.
9. R.H. Kofi Darkwah, *Menelik of Ethiopia*, London, Heinemann Educational Books, 1972, p.38; also Jean Doresse, *Ethiopia*, London, Elek Books, 1959, p.204.
10. Quoted in Hart, op. cit.
11. Ken Post, 'Ethiopianism in Jamaica: 1930–38', *African Perspectives*, ed. by Christopher Allen and R.W. Johnson, London, Cambridge University Press, 1970.
12. ibid.

13. Doresse, op. cit., p.21.
14. Edward Ullendorff, *Ethiopia and the Bible*, London, Oxford University Press, 1968, p.6.
15. Diop, op. cit., pp.123–5.
16. ibid., p.125.
17. Doresse, op. cit., p.21.
18. ibid., p.23.
19. Diop, op. cit., pp.107–8.
20. Herodotus, *The Histories*, Book V, London, Penguin Books, 1954, p.361.
21. Ullendorff, op. cit., p.15.
22. Yosef Ben Yochannan, E. Walker, D.L. Cobb, and C. Birdsong, *Understanding the African Philosophical Concept Behind the Diagram of the Law of Opposites*, New York, cyclostyled pamphlet copyrighted by Yochannan, 1975, p.11.
23. Ullendorff, op. cit., p.113.
24. Doresse, op. cit., p.62.
25. ibid., p.91.
26. ibid., p.114.
27. ibid., pp.116–17.
28. Darkwah, op. cit., pp.8–14.
29. Augier, Nettleford, and Smith, op. cit., p.3.
30. Leonard Barrett, *The Rastafarians*, London, Sangster/Heinemann, 1977, pp.85–6.
31. Augier, Nettleford, and Smith, op. cit., p.6.
32. ibid., p.8; also *The Ethiopian Orthodox Church, St Mary of Zion*, London, published by the Ethiopian World Federation, Local 33, January 1975, p.43.
33. The Ethiopian Orthodox Church, op. cit., p.43.
34. Augier, Nettleford, and Smith, op. cit., p.8.
35. The Ethiopian Orthodox Church, op. cit., p.44.
36. Augier, Nettleford, and Smith, op. cit., p.10.
37. Barrett, op. cit., p.90.
38. ibid., p.93.
39. Augier, Nettleford, and Smith, op. cit., p.14.
40. Barrett, op. cit., p.95.
41. ibid., pp.96–7.
42. ibid., p.97.
43. Abbot L. Mandefro, *The Ethiopian Orthodox Tewahedo Church and Its Activities in the West*, Kingston, no publisher given, 1971, p.31.
44. Joseph Owens, *Dread*, Kingston, Sangster's Books, 1976, p.110 and p.121.
45. Rex Nettleford, *Mirror Mirror*, London, Collins/Sangster, 1974, pp.68–71.
46. ibid., pp.74–5.
47. E.A. Wallis Budge, *The Mummy*, second ed., New York, Collier Books, 1972, p.27.
48. Diop, op. cit., p.62.
49. Budge, op. cit., p.28.
50. Verena Reckord, 'Rastafarian Music – An Introductory Study', *Jamaica*

Journal, vol. 11, nos. 1 and 2, Kingston, 1977, p.7.
51. Shirley Magnier Burke, Interview with Cedric Brooks, *Jamaica Journal*, vol. 11, nos. 1 and 2, Kingston, 1977, p.14.
52. ibid.
53. Augier, Nettleford, and Smith, op. cit., p.12.
54. Reckord, op. cit., p.7.
55. ibid., p.8.
56. Augier, Nettleford, and Smith, op. cit., p.12.
57. Reckord, op. cit., p.6.
58. ibid., p.9.
59. ibid.
60. ibid.

Chapter 3

The Birth and Development of Jamaican Music

1. Interview with Alton Ellis, London, February 1978.
2. Trevour Fearon, 'The Sound Systems', *Sunday News*, Kingston, 13 March 1977, p.2.
3. ibid.
4. ibid.
5. Interview with Prince Buster, Kingston, September 1977.
6. Mike Head, liner notes to *The Best of Louis Jourdan*, London, 1977, MCA Records, MCFM 2715.
7. Martin Hawkins, liner notes to *The Legenday Sun Performers – Rosco Gordon*, London, 1977, Charly Records, CR 30133.
8. Trevour Fearon, 'Those Were The Days . . .', quoting Byron Lee, *Sunday News*, Kingston, 3 April 1977.
9. ibid.
10. Interview with Byron Lee, Kingston, September 1977.
11. Interview with Theophilius Beckford, Kingston, September 1977.
12. Prince Buster, op. cit.
13. Trevour Fearon, 'Jamaica Pop Music and the Radio Stations', *Daily Times*, Kingston, 20 March 1977.
14. Fearon, 'Those Were The Days . . .', op. cit., quoting Graham Dowling.
15. Lee, op. cit.
16. Fearon, 'Those Were The Days'.
17. Interview with Sonia Pottinger, Kingston, August 1977.
18. Lee, op. cit.
19. Interview with Clement S. Dodd, Kingston, July 1971.
20. Ellis, op. cit.
21. Fearon, 'Those Were the Days', op. cit.
22. ibid.
23. ibid.
24. Interview with Jackie Mittoo, London, July 1977.
25. ibid.
26. ibid.
27. Interview with Tommy Cowan, Kingston, September 1977.

28. Lee, op. cit.
29. Dodd, op. cit.
30. Trevour Fearon, 'The Sound Systems', op. cit.
31. ibid.
32. ibid.
33. ibid.
34. ibid.
35. Cowan, op. cit.
36. ibid.
37. Lee, op. cit.
38. James Carnegie, 'Notes on the History of Jazz and Its Role in Jamaica' *Jamaica Journal*, Kingston.
39. Lee, op. cit.
40. Trevour Fearon, 'The Sound Systems', op. cit.
41. ibid.
42. ibid.
43. Interview with Jackie Mittoo, London, July 1978.
44. Ellis, op. cit.
45. Terry Lacey, *Violence and Politics in Jamaica*, Manchester, Mancheste University Press, 1977, p.46.
46. ibid.
47. ibid.
48. Interview with John Roberts, Kingston, September 1977.
49. ibid.
50. Lacey, op. cit., p.124.
51. Roberts, op. cit.
52. Lacey, op. cit., p.124.
53. ibid.
54. ibid.
55. ibid., p.135.
56. ibid.
57. Roberts, op. cit.
58. Lacey, op. cit., p.138.
59. ibid., p.141.
60. ibid., p.95.
61. Roberts, op. cit.
62. Garth White, 'Rudie Oh Rudie', *Caribbean Quarterly*, published by University of the West Indies, Extra Mural Department, Kingston, 1967.
63. Lacey, op. cit., p.86.
64. Roberts, op. cit.
65. Scotty Bennett, 'Big Youth', *Black Echoes*, London, 26 June 1976.
66. Carl Gayle, 'The Everything Man', *Black Music*, London, March 1975.
67. Trevour Fearon, 'Protest and Pop Music', *Daily Times*, Kingston, 27 March 1977.
68. ibid.
69. Shirley Magnier Burke, Interview with Cedric Brooks, *Jamaica Journal*, vol. 11, nos. 1 and 2, Kingston, 1977.
70. Trevour Fearon, 'Protest and Pop Music', op. cit.

Chapter 4

Bob Marley, Peter Tosh, Bunny Wailer – Three Modernists

1. 'The Magic of Marley', *Daily Gleaner*, Kingston, 30 September 1977.
2. Interview with Brent Clarke, London, October 1978.
3. 'The Magic of Marley', op. cit.
4. Cathy McKnight and John Tobler, *Bob Marley*, London, Star Books, 1977, p.61.
5. ibid., p.63.
6. Interview with Sid Bucknor, London, August 1977.
7. Interview with Bunny Wailer, London, July 1972.
8. Ray Coleman, 'Bunny Livingstone', *Roots News*, vol. 1, Kingston, 1975.
9. Henderson Dalrymple, *Bob Marley: Music, Myth and the Rastas*, London, Carib-Arawak, 1976, p.17.
10. ibid.
11. Interview with Bunny Wailer, Kingston, October 1977.
12. Interview with Peter Tosh, Kingston, October 1977.
13. ibid.
14. Interview with Bob Marley, London, August 1972.
15. The whole section on the Wailers' stay in London in 1972, and the subsequent development of and conflicts with the band, was supplied by Brent Clarke, op. cit.
16. Wailer, op. cit.
17. 'The Devil is like a Vampire always Seeking Souls', *Roots News*, vol. 2, Kingston, n.d.
18. Tosh, op. cit.
19. Chris Brazier, 'Bob Marley', *Melody Maker*, London, 11 February 1978.
20. ibid.
21. Richard Williams (a now defunct weekly column in *Melody Maker*, London, 23 April 1977).
22. Neil Spencer, 'Days Of Hope', *New Musical Express*, London, 6 May 1978.
23. Tape of Peter Tosh's speech recorded by Karl Pitterson and transcribed by Carl Gayle, *Jah Ugliman*, vol. 1, Kingston, October 1978.
24. Clarke, op. cit.
25. ibid.

Chapter 5

The Power of the Spoken Word

1. Scotty Bennett, 'The Right Time', *Black Echoes*, London, August 1976.
2. ibid.
3. ibid.
4. Interview with Osbourne Ruddock, Kingston, September 1977.
5. Interview with Pat Kelly, London, August 1978.
6. Bennett, op. cit., quoting U-Roy.

7. Interview with Errol Dunkley, London, November 1975.
8. Bennett, op. cit.
9. Winston Blake, 'Check That Barrage of Monotonous Religious Music', *Jamaican Daily News*, Kingston, 31 July 1977.
10. Pat Griffith, 'Skanker With Action', *Black Echoes*, London, August 1976.

Chapter 6

The Dub Masters

1. Interview with Jackie Mittoo, London, July 1978.
2. ibid.
3. Interview with Osbourne Ruddock, Kingston, September 1977.
4. Interview with Augustus Pablo, Kingston, September 1977.
5. Interview with the Abyssinians, London, July 1978.
6. ibid.
7. Ruddock, op. cit.
8. Pat Griffith, 'The Drum in Reggae', *Black Echoes*, London, 7 January 1978.
9. ibid.
10. Pablo, op. cit.

Chapter 7

The British Scene

1. Frank Field and Patricia Haikin (eds), *Black Britons*, London, Oxford University Press, 1971, p.4.
2. ibid., p.6.
3. R.B. Davidson, *Black British*, London, Institute of Race Relations, Oxford University Press, 1966, p.3.
4. Field and Haikin, op. cit., p.11.
5. Sebastian Clarke, *Black Arts in Britain: 1920–1976*, unpublished paper presented at the second World Black and Afrikan Festival of Arts and Culture, Lagos, Nigeria, February 1977.
6. ibid.
7. Interview with Siggy Jackson, London, November 1978.
8. ibid.
9. ibid.
10. ibid.
11. Interview with Sonny Roberts, London, November 1978.
12. ibid.
13. Mark Plumber, 'Reggae', *Melody Maker*, London, 26 July 1971.
14. Richard Williams, 'The Facts Of Reggae', *Melody Maker*, London, 19 February 1972.
15. Richard Williams, 'Black Gold Of Jamaica', *Melody Maker*, London, 30 September 1972.

16. Interview with Junior Lincoln, London, November 1978.
17. ibid.
18. Royston Eldridge, *Melody Maker*, London, 25 November 1969.
19. Interview with Graham Goodhal, London, April 1970.
20. Quoted in Sebastian Clarke, 'Jimmy Cliff: A Hard Road To Travel', *Rock*, New York, 27 August 1973.
21. Interview with Guilly Bright-Plumber, Paris, June 1978.
22. Interview with Chips Richards, London, November 1978.
23. ibid.
24. ibid.
25. ibid.
26. ibid.
27. ibid.
28. Conversations with John Kpiaye and Dennis Bovell, London, November 1978.

Chapter 8

Step Forward/Backward: The Changing Future

1. Interview with Robbie Shakespeare, Kingston, September 1977.
2. Vivien Goldman, 'The Reggae Heartbeat: Freedom Into Form', *Melody Maker*, 23 December 1978.
3. Richard Williams, 'Black Gold Of Jamaica', *Melody Maker*, 30 September 1972.
4. Sebastian Clarke, 'The Burning Reggae Years', *Black Echoes*, 14 February 1976.
5. ibid.
6. Interview with Chips Richards, London, November 1978.
7. Interview with Sonny Roberts, London, November 1978.
8. Conversations with Roger Aimes (head of EMI's A&R department for black product, London, November 1978).
9. Quoted in *Black Music and Jazz Review*, vol. 1, no. 2, London, May 1976.
10. Roberts, op. cit.
11. Interview with Aswad, London, December 1978.

Selected Discography

THE ABYSSINIANS

RECORD LABEL	RECORD NO.	ALBUM TITLE
Different	GET 1100, 1977	*Forward to Mount Zion*
Front line	FL 1019, 1978	*Arise*

BOB ANDY

Sky Note	SKLP 15, 1978	*Lots of Love*

ASWAD

Grove Music	GMLP 6, 1979	*Hulet*

BLACK UHURU

Third World	TWS 925, 1978	*Love Crisis*

DENNIS BROWN

Laser	LASL 1, 1979	*Words of Wisdom*
Lightning	LIP 7, 1978	*Visions of . . .*
Third World	TWS 934, 1977	*West Bound Train*

BURNING SPEAR

One Stop	STOP 1001, 1978	*Social Living*
Island	ILPS 9431, 1977	*Dry and Heavy*
Island	ILPS 9412, 1976	*Man in the Hills*
Island	ILPS 9377, 1975	*Marcus Garvey*

PRINCE BUSTER

Melodisc	MS 6	*Tutti Fruitti*

JIMMY CLIFF

Warner Bros.	K 56558, 1978	*Give Thanx*
Island	SW 9343, 1974	*Struggling Man*
EMI	MS 2141, 1973	*Unlimited*
Trojan	TRLS 16, 1969	*Jimmy Cliff*

CULTURE

Front Line	FL 1040, 1979	*Cumbolo*
Front Line	FL 1016, 1978	*Harder than the Rest*
Lightning	LIP 1, 1977	*Two 7s Clash*

GEORGE FAITH

Island	ILPS 9504, 1977	*To Be a Lover*

THE GLADIATORS

Front Line	FL 1035, 1979	*Naturality*
Front Line	FL 1002, 1978	*Proverbial Reggae*

MARCIA GRIFFITHS

Sky Note	SKYLP 9, 1978	*Naturally*

THE HEPTONES

Greensleeves	GREL 6, 1979	*Good Life*
Third World	TDWD 1, 1978	*Better Days*
Island	ILPS 9381, 1976	*Night Food*

JOE HIGGS

Grounation	GROL 508, 1975	*Life of Contradiction*

JOHN HOLT

Creole	CTLP 109, 1974	*Time Is the Master*
Trojan	TRLS 75, 1973	*One Thousand Volts of Holt*

KEITH HUDSON

Joint	JT 003, 1978	*Rasta Communication*
Atra	ATRALP 1001, 1975	*Torch of Freedom*
Mamba	001, 1974	*Flesh of My Skin*

ISRAEL VIBRATION

Harvest	SHSP 4099, 1979	*The Same Song*

GREGORY ISSACS

Front Line	FL 1020, 1978	*Cool Ruler*
Deb	DEBLP 04, 1978	*Mr Issacs*
Conflict	COLP 2002, 1978	*Extra Classic*

BOB MARLEY AND THE WAILERS

Island	ILPS 9517, 1978	*Kaya*
Island	ILPS 9498, 1977	*Exodus*
Island	ILPS 9383, 1976	*Rastaman Vibration*
Island	ILPS 9281, 1974	*Natty Dread*
Island	ILPS 9241, 1973	*Catch a Fire*
Trojan	TRLS 89, c.1970	*Rasta Revolution*
Calla	EPC 82066/CBS, 31584, c.1962–5	*The Birth of a Legend*

MATUMBI

Harvest	SHSP 4090, 1978	*Seven Seals*

RAS MICHAEL AND THE SONS OF NEGUS

Grounation	GROL 505, 1976	*Rastafari*
Trojan	TRLS 132, 1976	*Tribute to the Emperor*
Trojan	TRLS 103, 1975	*Dadawah*

MIGHTY DIAMONDS

Front Line	FL 8001, 1979	*Deeper Roots – Back to the Channel*
Channel One	1978	*Stand up to Your Judgement*

COUNT OSSIE AND THE MYSTIC REVELATION OF RASTAFARI

Dynamic	DNYLS 1001, 1975	*Tales of Mozambique*
Ashanti	NTI 301, 1973	*Grounation*

AUGUSTUS PABLO

Trojan	TRLS 115, 1976	*Ital Dub*
Tropical	TROPS 101, 1974	*This Is Augustus Pablo*

RICO

Island	ILPS 9485, 1977	*Man from Wareika*

THE ROYALS

Ballistic	UAG 30206, 1978	*Israel Be Wise*

STEEL PULSE

Island	ILPS 9568, 1979	*Tribute to the Martyrs*
Island	ILPS 9502, 1978	*Handsworth Revolution*

THIRD WORLD

Island	ILPS 9569, 1979	*The Story's Been Told*
Island	ILPS 9554, 1978	*Journey to Addis*
Island	ILPS 9443, 1977	*96° in the Shade*

PETER TOSH

Rolling Stones	CUN 39109, 1978	*Bush Doctor*
Virgin	V2081, 1977	*Equal Rights*
Virgin	V2061, 1976	*Legalise It*

WAYNE WADE

Grove Music	GMCP 3, 1979	*Dancing Time*

BUNNY WAILER

Island	ILPS 9512, 1978	*Protest*
Island	ILPS 9415, 1976	*Blackheart Man*

DELROY WASHINGTON

Virgin	V 2088, 1977	*Rasta*
Virgin	V 2060, 1976	*I-SUS*

	DELROY WILSON	
Eji	EJI 1001, 1977	*Mr Cool Operator*

	YABBY YOU VIBRATION	
Grove	GMLP 001, 1978	*Deliver Me from My Enemies*

The DJ/Toaster

	DR ALIMANTADO	
Ital Sounds	ISDA 5000, 1979	*King's Bread*
Greensleeves	GREL 1, 1978	*Best Dressed Chicken in Town*

	BIG YOUTH	
Trojan	TRLS 123, 1976	*Natty Cultural Dread*
Klik	KLP 9001, 1975	*Dread Locks Dread*

	DILLINGER	
Black Swan	ILPS 9455, 1976	*Bionic Dread*
Mango	ILPS 9385, 1976	*CB 200*

	I–ROY	
Grounation	GROL 54, 1976	*Truths & Rights*

	JAH LION	
Island	ILPS 9386, 1976	*Colombia Colly*

	JAH WHOOSH	
Trojan	TRLS 157, 1978	*Religious Dread*

	LINTON KWESI JOHNSON/POET AND THE ROOTS	
Island	ILPS 9566, 1979	*Forces of Victory*
Front Line	FL 1017, 1978	*Dread Beat & Blood*

	PRINCE FAR I	
Front Line	FL 1013, 1978	*Message from the King*

	PRINCE MOHAMMED	
Burning Sounds	BR 1005 LP, 1979	*African Roots*

	TAPPER ZUKIE	
Front Line	FL 1032, 1978	*Tapper Roots*
Front Line	FL 1006, reissued 1978	*MPLA*

	U–ROY	
Virgin	V2092, 1977	*Rasta Ambassador*
Virgin	V2048, 1975	*Dread Inna Babylon*

Dub

Grove	GMLP 4, 1978	*Beware*
Tempus	TEMPLP 001, 1978	*Black Beard, Strictly Dub Wise*
Hit Run	APLP 9001, 1978	*Creation Rebel*
Lightning	LIP 11, 1979	*Joe Gibbs and the Professionals: African Dub, Chapter 2*
Lightning	LIP 12, 1979	*African Dub, Chapter 3*
Fay	FMLP 304, 1975	*King Tubby Meets the Upsetter*
Cha Cha	CHALP 005, 1978	*The Revolutionaries, Jonkanoo Dub*
Atra	ATRALP 1002, 1975	*Second Street Dreads, Pick a Dub*
Ballistic	UAS 30229, 1979	*Liberated Dub*
Trojan	TRLS 153, 1979	*Negrea Love Dub*
Front Line	FLX 4002, 1979	*Cry Tuff Dub Encounter, Part Two*

Various Artists

Bamboo	BDLP 203, 1969	*The History of Ska*
Trojan	TALL 1, 1971	*The Trojan Story*

Selected Artists and Musicians Directory

ABYSSINIANS, THE

Founded in 1968 by Donald Manning and Bernard Collins who were later joined by Linford Manning (formerly with Carlton and the Shoes). Their first composition *Satta Massa Gana* has been recorded at least fifty times by different artists, mainly in Dub interpretations. Their next big hit was *Declaration of Rights*. They have recorded two albums, 'Forward to Mount Zion' and 'Arise'. Since 'Arise' Bernard Collins has left the group and the brothers have been joined by their elder brother, Carlton Manning.

ALCAPONE, DENNIS

Born in Clarendon in 1946 and attended Tarrant school. He started his DJ career working with the El Paso disco in 1965. His first real hit was with producer Keith Hudson in 1969 with *El Paso*, followed by a number of others including *Spanish Omega* and *It Must Come*. He has recorded albums for the Third World and Trojan labels. Lately he has been silent.

ALIMANTADO, DOCTOR

Born in Kingston circa 1950, given name Winston James Thompson. He has been known variously as Winston Cool, Youth Winston, etc. He first recorded for producer Lee Perry, but the record wasn't released. His first released record was *Judgement*, produced by Dave Allen in 1968. *A Place Called Africa* was produced by Lee Perry and released in 1971. His first international hit was *The Best Dressed Chicken* which was available on import in 1974, and re-recorded on an album of the same name in 1978. Apart from being a DJ he also sings and his most important single was *Reason for Living*, recorded after a near tragic accident.

ANDERSON, ALBERT

Generally known as Al. Born in New York in 1950. He started playing trombone at Mt Clairide High School and was later expelled. He turned to electric bass, then guitar with the Centurians and Red Bread respectively. He came to London in 1969 and played High Life with Remi Kabaka. He joined Bob Marley for sessions in 1972 and later toured with the band.

After leaving he worked with Peter Tosh. He is currently recording his first solo album.

ANDY, BOB

Born Kingston, 1944. He started his professional career with the Paragons in the early 1960s. *Love at Last* was one among many hits for Clement Dodd's Coxsone label. He left the group to go solo in 1967 and recorded his first hit, *I've Got to Go Back Home* for Dodd. In 1969 he teamed up with Marcia Griffiths and recorded *Young, Gifted and Black* which became a chart hit in Britain. His albums include 'Bob Andy Song Book' (Coxsone), 'The Music Inside Me' (Sound Tracks), and 'Lots of Love and I' (Sky Note).

ANDY, HORACE

Born Horace Hinds, Kingston, 1951. Began his professional career in 1970 with *Something on My Mind* (Coxsone). First big hit, *Skylarking* (Coxsone, 1972); *Problems* was first recorded for Leonard Chin's Santic label. His album, 'The Best of Horace Andy', a collection of rejected singles, was released in 1974 (Coxsone). His first album, 'In the Light', was recorded for Everton Da Silva's Hungry Town label (1977). He now lives in Harford, Connecticut.

ASHER, CLIMAX

Born Max Edwards, Savannah La Mar, 1952, and grew up in Kingston. He first learnt trumpet at Alpha Catholic School, then turned to alto sax and trombone, and simultaneously picked up the drums. He played in both Alpha's junior and senior bands and left in 1968. He went straight into Jazz, playing with Ernest Ranglin and Aubrey Adams behind singer Buster Brown. He has been a member of Generation Gap and Tomorrow's Children, and played experimentally with Zap Pow for a number of years. He has also worked on sessions as part of the Soul Syndicate and has recorded his first single, *Rocker's Arena*, for Bronze Records in Britain.

BECKFORD, THEOPHILIUS

Born Kingston, 1935. He bought a piano in 1955 and taught himself to play it. He listened mainly to R&B and began to sing and play professionally in 1957. His biggest hit was *Easy Snappin'* achieved in the late 1950s. He has been a seminal session musician since the 1950s, appearing with Prince Buster, Higgs and Wilson, Alton and Eddie, Jimmy Cliff, Keith and Enid, Owen Grey, Desmond Dekker, and many others. He still plays sessions, but has not toured overseas.

BIGGS, BARRY

Born Kingston, 1946. Started professionally in 1968 as a singer and recorded a version of Stevie Wonder's *My Cheri Amour* for producer Harry Johnson. His first big local hit was *One Bad Apple* for Dynamic Sounds where he now works as producer and engineer. His first British hit was *Work All Day* (1976) which was recorded and shelved in 1972.

BLACK SLATE

The group consists of George Brightley (London, 1960, keyboards), Desmond Mahoney (St Thomas, JA, 1955, drums), Keith Drummond (Mandeville, JA, 1955, lead vocals), Chris Hanson (Kingston, JA, 1956, lead guitar), Cledwyn Rogers (Anguilla, 1955, rhythm guitar), and Elroy Bailey (Ras Elroy, London, 1958, bass and vocals) and was formed in 1974. They worked primarily as a backing band for such acts as Delroy Wilson, Leroy Smart, Dennis Brown, Owen Grey, Johnny Clarke, Ken Boothe, and Alton Ellis before having their own big hit, *Sticks Man*, in 1976. Since then they have released a single, *Live up to Love*.

BLUES BUSTERS, THE

Consists of Lloyd Osborne Campbell, born Kingston, 1946 and moved to Montego Bay at the age of 3, and Phillip James, born Montego Bay, 1941. They both knew each other in junior school and later drifted apart, Lloyd singing with the junior Baptist Church Choir, while Phillip appeared in a show, *The Show Boat Follies*, with his father. They got back together while at secondary school. Their first record was *Little Vilma* which was a No. 1 hit in Jamaica. Their biggest international hit was *Behold* which made both the British and American charts in the early 1960s. They have recorded mainly in the R&B format.

BOOTHE, KEN

Born Kingston, 1948. He has lived in Trench Town for most of his youth and began his career with *World's Fair* in 1964. He also recorded *You're No Good* for Sonia Pottinger's Tip Top label in 1965. He came to fame via Clement Dodd's Coxsone/Studio One labels during the Rock Steady era (mid-1960s) and toured Britain in 1967 with Alton Ellis and the Soul Vendours. He topped the British charts with *Everything I Own*, produced by Lloyd Charmers for the Trojan label.

BRIGHT, STANLEY

Born Kingston, 1950, and known as Ranking Barnabas for his DJ ability. After leaving primary school he hung around Channel One studios where he is now one of the two resident sound engineers. He also runs the Channel One sound system with Ernest Hookim, and is well known as a percussionist and drummer.

BRIMSTONE

The group consists of Sam Jones (Sierra Leone, 1957, vocals and keyboards), Gus Phillips (Dominica, 1945, rhythm guitar), Leo Charles (Dominica, 1959, drums), Peter Harris (May Pen, Jamaica, 1955, lead guitar), John Thomas (Trinidad, 1948, percussion), Vivienne Clarke (England, 1958, vocals and percussion), and Wayne Griffith (Trinidad, 1951, bass). Formed in 1977 by Sam Jones and Gus Phillips, the band has so far recorded a single, *Final Judgement* (Grove, 1978) and another, *Release Me* (Karnak, 1979), and are currently recording their first album.

BROOKS, CEDRIC

Born Kingston, 1943. Started his musical career at Alpha at the age of 11 and was taught the clarinet by Ruben Delgado. He also played a little piano and started on alto sax in 1962 when he began playing with the Vagabonds. During this early period he supported artists like Alton Ellis, Jimmy James, Higgs and Wilson, Laurel Aitken. He then became a member of Kes Chin and the Souveneirs (combo unit), as well as playing with the Cavaliers, Granville Williams (big band) with whom he played baritone sax, and Lesley Butler. He also toured with Carlos Malcolm in the Bahamas and pianist Cecil Lloyd. He made a number of excellent singles under the name 'Im and David' (the latter, David Madden of Zap Pow) for Studio One in the 1960s. He formed the Mystic Revelation of Rastafari in 1974 and their first recording, an album, was financed by the Institute of Jamaica. He later formed the Light of Saba and recorded two albums for Total Sounds. He appeared on the highly acclaimed 'Negril' album with Eric Gale and recorded an album, 'United Africa', for Aquarius Records. He still works as a session musician.

BROOKS, MIKE

Born Edmund Brooks, Westmoreland, 1953. Formed first group, the Tots, in 1972 and recorded *Earth Is the Fullness* for co-operative label, Harvest; hit with *Guiding Star* for G.G. label in 1977 and a number of singles for various other labels: Total Sounds and Federal.

BROWN, AL

Born Kingston, 1947. Recorded his first song, *Dying Love*, for the Coxsone label in 1969 and also recorded an album of the same name. He also worked with the Volcanoes and Skin, Flesh and Bones, of which he was an original member. He has had his first big hit in Britain with a version of Al Green's *Here I Am Baby* for Trojan Records. He has been working with the Seventh Extension band and also pursuing his solo career.

BROWN, DENNIS

Born Kingston, 1957. He attended Mrs Brown Infant School and Central Branch Primary. His first important engagement was with the Falcons. Later, he recorded his first song, *Love Grows*, for the Coxsone label and his first major hit, *No Man Is an Island*, and an album of the same title was released in 1972. He has worked with producers Winston Holness (Niney, the Observer) and Joe Gibbs/Errol Thompson with whom he had his first British hit, *Money in My Pocket*. His most recent album was 'Words of Wisdom' (Laser/Warner Brothers).

BRUMMER, WADE (TRINITY)

Born Kingston, 1954. Dillinger took him to Channel One in 1975 and recorded his first song, *Set up Yourself*, produced by Jo Jo Hookim. Before that he worked as a live DJ for Veejay Dub Master, and since then he has recorded prolifically for a number of producers, and is highly regarded as one of the innovative new DJs.

BUNNY, BINGI

Born Eric Lamont, Kingston, 1955. Regular session guitarist and a founding member of Morwell Esquire with Louis Davis and Morris Wellington in 1974. He played rhythm guitar with Bongo Herman from 1969 to 1973. The Morwells debuted with *Swing and Dine* on their own label. Also recorded 'Presenting The Morwells' album in 1975. He has done sessions for Prince Far I, Dennis Brown, Culture, and Cornell Campbell, among others.

BURNING SPEAR

Born Winston Rodney, St Ann, circa 1948. The group was formed in 1968 with two harmony singers, Rupert Hines and Delroy Wilmington, but were later dropped by Rodney. He first recorded two albums for Clement Dodd's Coxsone/Studio One labels: 'Rocking Soul' and 'Burning Spear', before signing to Island in 1975, for whom he recorded five albums, including 'Dry & Heavy', 'Man in the Hills' and 'Marcus Garvey'.

BUSTER, PRINCE

Born Cecil Campbell, Kingston, 1938. He changed his name to Muhammed Yusef Ali in the late 1960s after being converted to the Muslim faith. He began his career as a singer and dancer at the age of 9 with a group of four. At the age of 10 he started his career as a boxer, but still pursued the music business. He worked for Clement Dodd's Coxsone sound system in the 1950s and later formed his own sound, Voice of the People. He was one of the early pioneers of both R&B and Ska for which he became internationally known. His many hits included *Judge Dread, Alcapone Guns Don't Argue* and *Madness*.

CABLES, THE

The group was formed by lead singer Keble Drummond, born St Elizabeth, 1946, and consisted of Bobby Dockerty, Clarendon, 1950, and Vincent Stoddard who left for the States in 1975. Since then he has been replaced by Elbert Steward, Manchester, 1950. Their first known recording was *You Lied* for the Tip Top label in 1966. After a two-year lay-off they returned, recording for Studio One from 1968 with the massive hit, *Baby Why*. They left the company in 1970 and recorded for Harry J in 1970 under various pseudonyms, Herbie Carter, Eric Fatter, etc.

CHUNG, GEOFFREY

Born Manchester, 1951. Attended St George's High School where he picked up the acoustic guitar, learning from his brother, Mike. He sang with his brother at school socials and formed their first band, the Mighty Mystics, in 1965, and also supported Bob Andy, Marcia Griffiths, Chosen Few, Roy Shirley, among others. He then attended the University of the West Indies at Mona, studying biochemistry. He dropped out in the second year to pursue a musical career. He sang with and learnt music theory from Peter Ashburn. He then joined the Now Generation. He has worked with almost every musician in Jamaica and is a producer and sound engineer.

CHUNG, MICHAEL

Born Manchester, 1950. Started playing drums in the early 1960s and by the end of 1968 he was playing drums with Inner Circle. He taught himself to play guitar, base, and keyboards and played with the Mighty Mystics. He also played with Ernest Wilson and was a member of Now Generation. He has played sessions for producers Harry Johnson, Lee Perry, Winston 'Niney' Holness, Derrick Harriot, and Clancy Eccles, among others. He has been a member of Word, Sound and Power (Peter Tosh's backing band) since 1977. He has also recorded an album with his own compositions which is unreleased.

CLARKE, ERIC

Born Kingston, 1951. Generally known as 'Fish'. The brother of singer Johnny Clarke, he commenced playing drums at 13 while at Alpha Catholic School. When he left Alpha he joined a steel-band for a short while and then started singing. The first band he joined was the Ruiners in 1969, then played with the Avengers and Soul Syndicate. As a drummer he has supported such luminaries as the Heptones, Gregory Issacs, Burning Spear and Prince Far I. He has recorded solo ventures featuring his singing.

CLIFF, JIMMY

Born Kingston, 1944, and took up singing before he entered his teens. He made a number of unreleased recordings for various producers before getting a release on *Hurricane Hattie*. One of the early singers of Ska. Travelled to the World Fair, New York, in 1964 as a singer/dancer with Byron Lee's band. He met Chris Blackwell in New York and on his invitation came to London in 1965 where he signed with Island Records. He achieved international popularity in the late 1960s with songs like Cat Stevens's *Wild World, Wonderful World, Beautiful People*, and others. He starred in the film *The Harder They Come* and has been signed to Warner Brothers where he has made several albums, none of which achieved popularity in the West.

CONGOES, THE

The group consists of Roy Del Johnson (Ras Roy), born Hanover, 1943, and Cedric Myton (Jah Cedric), born St Catherine, 1947. The group was formed in 1975, although both singers were involved in different musical projects. Jah Cedric worked with the Tartons, Ras Michael and the Royal Rasses, recording *Humanity* in 1974. Their first album, 'Heart of the Congoes' was produced by Lee Perry, their second album was released in France by CBS.

CULTURE

The group consists of Joseph Hill, lead vocals, Albert Walker and Kenneth Paley, harmony vocals, and they were all raised in St Andrew. Joseph Hill played with the Soul Defenders and other groups before recording his first solo disc for Clement Dodd, *Behold the Land*. The other two were involved in singing, but not professionally. In 1976 under the name African Disciples they were recording for Joe Gibbs, but had their name changed to Culture. Since then they have made three important albums, 'Two 7s Clash', 'Harder than the Rest' and 'Cumbolo'.

DAMBALA

Group consists of Gus Anyia, Nigeria, Horace McKenzie, Guyana, Alvin Christie, Liverpool, James St Louis, St Lucia, Thomas Cadette, St Lucia and Kelvin Lovell, Barbados. They are all part of the new wave in Reggae and have been living in the United Kingdom for a number of years. They appear mainly live and have recorded one single, *Zimbabwe*.

DAN, MICHAEL

Born Michael Dorane, Newmarket, 1948, and left the island as a baby for California. Both his parents belonged to the church and play the piano. At the age of 8 he came to London where he has been living ever since. He plays a variety of instruments: bass, guitar, all keyboards, and a little drums. At 15 he formed his own band, the Soul Funk, and toured Germany. He had his own label which finally went out of business. He works as a sound engineer and produces his own records.

DAWKINS, CARL

Born Spanish Town, 1948. Started singing in primary school and professionally in 1962 performing live stage shows. His first record was *Baby I Love You* for JJ in 1966. In 1969 his *This Land* was banned by radio. His first album was 'Bumpty Road' for the Harry J label, 1976.

DOBSON, DOBBIE

Born Highland Dobson, Kingston, 1942. Started singing at Kingston College in 1960 and formed the Deltas group there. In the early 1960s he sang as a duo with Chuck Joseph. Their first record was *Baby How Can I* for Tip Top in 1961. He also recorded for Duke Reid (1961) and Clement Dodd (1964). Has worked variously as salesman, civil servant, proof-reader for the *Daily Gleaner*, among other jobs. His biggest hits came via Rupie Edwards's Success label in 1971: *Wonderful Song* sold 40,000 in Jamaica and the Caribbean, *Endlessly*, which was released in the United Kingdom by Ashanti. He has produced the Meditations on the album, 'Message from the Meditations', and other acts. His album, 'Sweet Dreams', sold 30,000 in the Caribbean. He also has his own label in Jamaica and the United States.

DREAD, RANKING

Born Winston Brown, Kingston, 1956. While in high school he played a sound system with Tapper Zukie. He has been a protégé of Tapper Zukie and has recorded *This Little Girl Is Mine* with Errol Dunkley and an album, 'Kunta Kinte Roots' for Burning Sounds. He has DJed with the Prince Danny sound (1970–3), Sir George (1973–6) and Ray Symbolic Sound.

DUNBAR, LOWELL

Born Kingston, 1952. Generally known as Sly, he started playing drums professionally at the age of 15 when he recorded *Night Doctor* for Ansell Collins. He was the drummer on Collins's first international hit, *Double Barrell*, 1967. Since then he has been Jamaica's busiest session drummer appearing on almost every recording artist in the country – Dennis Brown, Heptones, Dillinger, Mighty Diamonds, Jimmy Cliff, Culture, etc. He is now the resident drummer with Peter Tosh and has pursued a simultaneous solo career, recording two albums for Virgin's Front Line.

DUNKLEY, ERROL

Born Kingston, 1950. He started singing at the age of 9 and professionally at the age of 11 with Prince Buster as producer. He entered a number of singing competitions and won several. He paid his own school fees from money he earned as a singer. His first No. 1 hit was *You're Gonna Need Me* for Joe Gibbs's Amalgamated label at the age of 14. In the late 1960s he formed a label with Gregory Issacs, but it was short-lived. He has recorded albums for Sonia Pottinger's High Note label, and two for Ephraim Barrett's Third World Records. He has been living in London over the last few years.

EDWARDS, RUPIE

Born St Ann, 1945. He is known primarily as a producer attached to his own label, Success, which he founded in the mid-1960s. He has produced such artists as Errol Dunkley, Dobie Dobson, Gregory Issacs, and many others. He achieved his biggest hit as a solo artist with *Irie Feelings* which made the Top Ten in Britain.

EDWARDS, WILFRED JACKIE

Born Kingston (date not known) and grew up on Maxfield Avenue where Channel One Studios are currently located. He is one of the vocal pioneers of Jamaican music, beginning in the mid-1950s when he sang in the Nat King Cole style. In those years he recorded songs like *Tell Me Darling* and *Heaven Just Knows*. He came to Britain in the early 1960s and recorded an album for Island, 'The Most of Wilfred Jackie Edwards' that contained mainly ballads. His most popular composition was *Keep on Running* for the Spencer Davis Group in the mid-1960s. He did very little recording in the 1960s, and with producer Bunny Lee he has made several albums in the 1970s.

ELLIS, ALTON

Born Kingston (date not known) and was brought up in the Maxfield Avenue area. He was influenced by the style of singing that emerged from the free black churches, Baptist and Pukkimina. He was originally a dancer, but turned a singer and recorded. In early 1960 he entered the Opportunity Hour singing contest with a Cole Porter tune, *Begin the Begin*, and won. Worked as a duo with Eddy Perkins, but came to fame with Duke Reid and Clement Dodd respectively. His best album has been 'Sunday Coming', produced by Dodd for the Studio One label.

ELLIS, BOBBY

Born Kingston, 1932. He learnt trumpet at the age of 12 at Alpha under Raymond Harper and played in the school band under clarinetist Ruben Delgado. He first recorded with Coxsone/Studio One in 1964 with the Mighty Vikings. He has worked as a resident session musician with Studio One since the mid-1960s and with Sound Dimension, the studio band that replaced Soul Brothers/Soul Vendours. He has supported such artists as Burning Spear (for whom he is musical director), Bob Marley, Delroy Wilson, Ken Boothe, and Gregory Issacs.

ETHIOPIANS, THE

Originally consisted of Stephen Taylor (1944–75), St Mary, and Leonard 'Sparrow' Dillon, Portland (date not known). They first recorded for Coxsone/Studio One in 1965, *Lay It On*, with harmony vocals by Bunny Wailer and Peter Tosh. As part of the rude boy era, they recorded *I'm Gonna Take Over Now*; also, *Everything Crash*. Their most popular tune has been *Train to Skaville*, as well as *Hong Kong Flu*. Their most recent album has been 'Slave Call' released on Third World in the United Kingdom.

FAR I, PRINCE

Born Michael James Williams, Spanish Town, 1945. He served his DJ apprenticeship with Sir Mike (1962–4), El Toro Sound (1964–7), and others. His first recording was *The Great Bugga Wugga*, issued under the name of King Cry Cry, and produced by Bunny Lee, 1967. One of his early popular hits was *Heavy Manners* for Joe Gibbs, 1976, and recorded an album of the same name for the label. His most popular and innovative album was 'Message from the King', produced by himself and issued in the United Kingdom in 1978.

GARDENER, BORIS

Born Kingston, 1943. Started his career in 1961 with the Rhythm Aces and recorded *One Thousand Teardrops* for R&B Records. He left to work with Kes Chen and the Souvenirs. He also left to play with Carlos Malcolm's Afro-Jamaican Rhythm (1964–7) and recorded an album for the now de-funct Scepter label of the United States. He formed the Broncos in 1967 and changed the name to Boris Gardener Happening in 1968. Since then he has recorded a number of soft Reggae albums for Federal and Dynamic labels. He has been doing sessions as a bassist and rhythm guitarist since the mid-1960s. Became the resident bassist with Lee Perry at the Black Ark Studios in 1976 and has appeared on albums with the Heptones, Max Romeo, the Congoes, Jah Lion, Junior Murvin, etc.

GLADIATORS, THE

The trio originally consisted of Albert Griffiths (vocals and guitar), Clinton Fearon (vocals and guitar), and David Webber who left and was replaced by Dallimore Sutherland (bass and vocals). In 1967 they recorded for Coxsone, *You Are the Girl*, 1967. They have recorded three albums for

Front Line: 'Trenchtown Mix-Up', 1976, 'Proverbial Reggae', 1978, and 'Naturality', 1979.

GORDON, VIN

Born Kingston, 1947. Nicknamed Don D. Jnr after Don Drummond. Started on bass tuba at the age of 9 at Alpha under the tutorship of Len Hubert. He began his professional career at Studio One supporting a number of the label's artists – Bob Marley, Delroy Wilson, Ken Boothe, etc. He is known as a trombonist and is highly regarded in Jamaica.

GREY, OWEN

Born Kingston (date not known). Started his singing career in the mid-1950s performing R&B ballads. Migrated to Britain in 1960 and recorded for Island in 1963, *Gonna Work Out Fine*. In 1967 he had his first chart success in the United Kingdom: *Shook, Shimmie And Shake*. He has worked throughout Europe and the Middle East. His career before 1976 was preoccupied with the love theme. Since then he has recorded a variety of songs concerned with other themes, *Natty Congo* being his biggest roots hit.

HAMMER, PRINCE

Born Berres Simpson, Kingston, 1953. A DJ whose early apprenticeship was served with Vee Jay Dub Master. He has recorded a number of singles including *Yarmer Rock, Addis Ababa* and the famous *Dreadlocks Thing* for Joe Gibbs.

HAMMOND, BERESFORD

Born Hugh Beresford Hammond, St Mary, 1954. Was a member of the Baptist church when still young and began his career there in the choir. As a teenager he belonged to the vocal group, Total Togetherness. He joined Sonny Bradshaw's band in 1972, then sang with United Stars, an umbrella for highly rated session musicians. He also sang lead with Tuesday's Children for two years before joining Zap Pow in late 1974. His first album was recorded for Aquarius and was produced by guitarist Willie Lindo who also wrote all the tunes. He is Jamaica's most popular Soul artist.

HEPTONES, THE

The group consisted of Leroy Sibbles, Kingston, 1949, Earl Morgan, Kingston, 1945, and Barry Llewelwyn, Kingston, 1947, and was started in 1965. They were coached by the Pioneers and recorded first for Studio One/Coxsone in 1966 with *A Change Has Got to Come*. Their first big hit came in 1966 with *Fatty Fatty* and later scored with *Only Sixteen, Baby*, and others. In the mid-1970s they recorded three albums for Island, the most important being 'Party Time' under Lee Perry's producership. Leroy Sibbles left the group in 1978 to live in Canada and was replaced by Doldhie 'Naggo' Morris, St Mary, 1947. He has worked with the Heptones since 1974 as session vocalist. He has also worked extensively with other vocalists. The Heptones' name was given by Earl Morgan and originally meant the Hept ones, but changed through time.

HIBBERT, OSSIE

Born Kingston, 1954. Started playing piano in 1969, taught by Lloyd Willis. He has worked as a session musician for producers Lee Perry, Bunny Lee, Winston Holness, and Errol Thompson, among others. He also learned sound engineering at Channel One under Ernest Hookim. He controls his own label, Ossie Sound and Earthquake, and among his artists is Earth and Stone.

HIGGS, JOE

Born Kingston, circa 1937. He started singing and playing guitar in 1956 and entered the Vere John's Opportunity Hour talent show and won. He recorded as a duo, Higgs and Wilson, throughout the late 1950s and early 1960s. Their biggest hit was *Manny O* which sold over 30,000 copies in Jamaica. His career has been dogged by bad luck, but he is a prolific and meaningful songwriter. Songs include *Days of Reward, Life of Contradiction*, and *Hard Times Don't Bother Me*. He has been an important influence in the development of Bob Marley as a singer.

HILTON, SHEILA

Born London, 1956, and came to Jamaica at the age of 3. She attended secondary school and later the Jamaica Commercial Institute. Worked at Total Sounds as a secretary, then an air stewardess with Air Jamaica. She also became a well known model in the country in the early 1970s. Her first tune was *Life in the Country* for Harry Johnson with whom she still works. She has also recorded Exuma's *Letter to Miami*. Her most recent hit was *Breakfast in Bed.*

HOLT, JOHN

Born Kingston, 1947. He attended Greenwich Town Primary, Calabar High, and Kingston Technical High School. Won the Vere John contest in 1962 and recorded *Forever I'll Stay* that same year. He joined the Paragons with Bob Andy, Tyrone Evans, and Howard Barrett in 1965 and hits include *Love at Last, Happy Go Lucky Girl* and *On the Beach*. In 1968 he went solo and recorded *Tonight* for Duke Reid. Since then he has scored in Britain with *Help Me Make It Through the Night.*

HUDSON, KEITH

Born Kingston, 1947. After working at a variety of jobs Hudson went into producing. His niche was introducing the new and outrageous into popular acceptance. He has produced DJs like Dennis Alcapone, Big Youth *(S.90 Skank)*, Jah Whoosh, and others. He has also revived the careers of Alton Ellis *(Big Bad Boy)*, Horace Andy *(I'm All Right)*, and many others. He started singing professionally in the mid-1970s, recording mainly albums, the most important of which were 'Flesh of My Skin', a work of tremendous importance, 'Torch of Freedom' and 'Rasta Communication'.

INNER CIRCLE

The group was formed in 1968 and from the inception was confined to the hotel resort circuit. Thus their music achieved cosmopolitan middle-of-the-road flavour. The group consists of Ian Lewis, bass, Roger Lewis, guitar, and Jacob Miller, vocals. They attained international fame by combining Rock and Reggae. Their two albums for Capital were musical failures. They are currently signed to Island and have achieved some success via disco.

ISRAEL VIBRATION

The group consists of Cecil Spence ('Skeleton'), Albert Craig ('Apple'), and Lascelles Bulgrin ('Whiss'), all born in Kingston and victims of poliomyelitis. They were housed at the Mona Rehabilitation Centre until they grew locks; it conflicted with the establishment and they had to leave. They were members of the Twelve Tribes of Israel organization, a member of whom paid for the recording and manufacture of their first hit *Why Worry*. They are currently signed to Harvest and have had their first album released, 'The Same Song'.

ISSACS, GREGORY

Born Kingston, circa 1950. One of his earliest hits that established his career was *Love Overdue* in 1974. He was the co-founder of African Museum, a record label that folded in the early 1970s, but later revived. He has also established his own distribution outlet, Cash & Carry. His albums include 'Soon Forward', 'Cool Ruler' and 'Mr Issacs'. One of his most distinguished singles was *Mr Know It All* (DEB).

JAH, SONS OF

The group was formed by Trevour Bow (Kingston, 1951) in 1976 and currently consists of Derrick Donaldson (Clarendon, 1953) and Howard Haughton (Kingston, 1954). Their first single, *Bankrupt Morality* was released on their own label, Natty Congo, in 1978. They have also released an album of the same name. They all live in London. Their most recent album was 'Burning Black', 1979.

JARRETT, WINSTON

Born St Ann, 1941. Started singing with Alton Ellis in the late 1950s and was a member of the Flames, the vocal group that supported Alton Ellis. The group was disbanded in 1967 and he formed a new group, the Righteous Flames. Their first record was *Born to Be Loved* (Coxsone). In 1969 Lee Perry produced their *Zion I Love You*. He has written *True Born African* and *Sunday Coming* for Alton Ellis. The other members of the Righteous Flames are Junior Green and Egga Gardener.

JOHNSON, LINTON KWESI

Born Clarendon, 1952. He moved to Britain in 1963, settling in Brixton. He attended Tulse Hill School and Goldsmith College, majoring in sociology. He has worked sporadically as a journalist, broadcaster and librarian. His work in poetry was influenced by the traditional

Euro-American source until he began listening to the DJ in Reggae. This influenced his own work and he has since recorded two albums, 'Dread Beat & Blood' (1977) and 'Forces of Victory' (1979).

KAY, JANET

Born London, 1958. Attended Brondesbury High School, Wembley, and later did secretarial work. She was first recorded by Alton Ellis, *Loving You*, 1977. Then she recorded *That's What Friends Are For* and *I Do Love You* for D-Roy. Then she had her biggest hit with *Silly Games* produced by Dennis Bovell and available through Arawak/Scope.

KELLY, PAT

Born Kingston, circa 1949. He attended Kingston Technical High School, studying electronics. In the late 1960s he replaced the late Slim Smith in the Techniques and recorded *You Don't Care* as lead singer for Duke Reid. He is also a sound engineer, working first at Randy's Recording Studio, and later free-lancing. In 1969 he went solo and recorded *How Long*, produced by Bunny Lee. The Beatles, hearing this tune, offered his United Kingdom record company £25,000, but they refused to sell. His albums include *Lonely Man* and *Talk About Love*.

LINDO, EARL 'WIRE'

Born Kingston, 1953, and attended Excelsior High School. In the early 1970s he met and worked with Aston Barrett ('Family Man') and worked extensively on sessions. He became a member of the Wailers in 1973, left after a short time, and worked with Taj Mahal in 1975. He has since worked almost exclusively as a session musician (keyboards) and has recorded tracks for an album of his own compositions.

LINDO, WILLIE

Born Ivor Lindo, Clarendon, 1949. He made his own guitar at 15 and has been self-taught. He began playing with Ron Wilson and the Comets in 1967, then joined the Jamaica Supremes in 1968, then Sonny Bradshaw in 1968, then the Boris Gardener Happening. His first album was 'Far and Distant' and his second 'It's Not Too Late' for Village Records. He works extensively as a session guitarist.

LIVINGSTONE, DANDY

Born Robert Livingstone Thompson, Kingston, circa 1944. He came to England at the age of 15 and attended secondary school then college to pursue engineering. He cut his first record, *What a Life*, for the Carnival label and later teamed up with Sugar Simone to work as a duo. One of his most popular tunes was *Rudy a Message to You*. He became a regular chart entrant and is known for *Suzanne Beware of the Devil*.

LLOYD, JAH

Born Patrick Francis, St Catherine, 1949. Started his singing career with the Meditators in 1965 and recorded *Bus Style* as a solo artist for Rupie

Edwards's Success label. He worked for Lee Perry as a salesman in 1970 and recorded *Zion Rock* for the Team label. He also discovered and recorded the Mighty Diamonds for his own label, Team. He has been known primarily as a DJ and has had his first album, 'Colombia Colly' produced by Lee Perry under the Jah Lion name. He then recorded his second album, 'Jah Lion', produced by himself for Front Line.

LONDON, JIMMY

Born Trevour Shaw, St Catherine, 1949. Started singing in school and formed his first group, the Inspirations, in 1964, and recorded *Tighten Up* for Lee Perry in 1967. Recorded *Reggae Fever* album for Joe Gibbs in 1968. Recorded *Bridge over Troubled Water* album for Randy's in 1971. Recorded a number of singles for Dynamic in 1972–3. Recorded an album for Phil Pratt, 'Jimmy London in England'.

MARK, LOUISA

Born London, 1960. Her first recording, *Caught You in Lie*, produced by Lloydie Coxsone for Safari, 1974, was a massive local hit. She then recorded *All My Loving*, before joining Clem Bushay for *Keep It Like It Is* for Trojan, 1976. She then made two singles for Bushay's own label, *Even Though You're Gone* and *6 Sixth Street*, 1978.

MARLEY, BOB AND THE WAILERS

Born Robert Nesta Marley, St Ann, 1944. Moved to Trench Town in the late 1950s and formed the Wailers in 1963. Then auditioned for and was chosen by Clement Dodd and Sid Bucknor to record their first song, *Simmer Down*. Between 1963 and 1965 they recorded a number of singles and albums for Coxsone/Studio One, most of which are contained on the two album set, 'The Legend of Bob Marley and The Wailers' (CBS/Calla). Between 1968 and 1970 the original Wailers recorded two albums for Lee Perry: 'African Herbsman' and 'Soul Rebel'. In 1972 they signed to Island and recorded two albums, 'Catch a Fire' and 'Burnin' ' before breaking up (1973). The vocal trio consisted of Peter McIntosh and Bunny Livingstone. The new Wailers consisted primarily of a backing band with the foundation of Aston and Carly Barrett with other musicians coming and going. He is also supported by a female vocal trio, the I-Threes (Rita Marley, Judy Mowatt, Marcia Griffiths). He has since recorded a number of albums for Island.

MARQUIS, HERMAN

Born Kingston, 1927. Started at the age of 14 at Alpha playing clarinet, then alto sax, and later took a correspondence course in music from an American school. His first session was with Duke Reid in 1959 playing with the Techniques. Since then he has worked exclusively as a session musician supporting most of the recording acts in Jamaica.

MATUMBI

The group was formed and masterminded by Dennis Bovell (born St Peter,

Barbados, 1953) in 1971. Bovell studied the bass while at secondary school and played in the school orchestra. Prior to that he learned six-string guitar from his uncle when 6 years old. The group consists of Glen 'Bagga' Fagan, vocals, Gladstone Venn, vocals, Webster 'Tasmanian' Johnson, keyboards, Fergus Jones, percussion, Bunny Donaldson (Jah Bunny), drums, Patrick and Henry Tenrew, trumpet and tenor sax respectively. They first recorded *Brother Louie* in 1971 for Trojan. Their first hit was *After Tonight* for Safari. They have been signed to Harvest since 1978 and have recorded an album, 'Seven Seals'. They all live in London. Bovell has also been a prolific producer and sound engineer and has worked with Janet Kay, Errol Dunkley, the Pop Group, the Slits, and Brown Sugar, among others.

MELODIANS, THE

The group was formed in 1962 by Brent Dowe (born St James, 1946). They worked primarily as a stage group until being discovered by Ken Boothe in 1966. They recorded *Later On* and *She's Gone* for Coxsone, then to Duke Reid with *You've Caught Me Baby*. They have received their biggest hits via Sonia Pottinger's Gay Feet label: *Little Nut Tree, Swing And Dine*,etc. In 1970 they recorded *Rivers of Babylon* for Beverley's. After Lesley Kong's death they returned to Duke Reid for a short spell. Dowe then went solo in 1973. A member of the group, Tony Brevette, became mentally ill in 1970.

MICHAEL, RAS AND THE SONS OF NEGUS

The band was formed by Ras Michael and consists of a number of percussionists. For recordings they use session musicians. Michael himself was born in Kingston, circa 1943. He was originally influenced by the church and began propagating the concept of Rastafari through song. He recorded his first tune, *The Lion of Judah,* in order to pay for a regular radio show he had, dealing mainly with Rastafari. His first album was the brilliant 'Dadawah', produced by Lloyd Charmers (1972); others include 'Freedom Sounds' and 'Rastafari'.

MIDAS, RAS

Born Lorenza Nemhard, Kingston, 1950. Started singing in the church choir from the age of 10 and formed his first group, the Shadows, in 1968. Discovered by Richard Collins and recorded *Dread Feelings, Hard Times* and *Cover Me,* all released in London, 1969. Dropped out of music and graduated from Kingston Technical High School and later worked as a welder. In 1976 he recorded *Kuda Abamba* for Harry Johnson which was released by Island in the United Kingdom. His first album for Harry J was 'Rain & Fire', released in 1978.

MIGHTY DIAMONDS

The group consists of three vocalists: Lloyd Ferquson, Fitzroy Simpson, and Donald Shaw who were all born in western Kingston. The group came together in 1969 and was relatively unknown until discovered by DJ/singer

Pat Francis (Jah Lion) who produced their first hit *Shame and Pride* in 1974, followed by an album entitled 'The Right Time' in 1975. They were then signed by Virgin in the United Kingdom and had their roots approach altered by being produced by Afro-American Allen Toussaint. Recently they have again altered their style to express their original direction. Their albums include 'Ice On Fire', 'Planet Earth' and 'Deeper Roots – Back to the Channel'.

MISTY

The group was formed in 1975 and consists of Tony Henry, bass, Vernon Hunte, organ, Antoinette McCalla, vocals, Julian Peters, drums, Delvin Tyson, vocals, Bertie McKay, rhythm guitar, Barry Facey, guitar, and Wolford 'Perky' Tyson, lead vocals. They collectively come from Jamaica, St Kitts, St Vincent, Grenada, and Guyana. They ran a collective organization, People Unite, which was destroyed by the police in Southall, 1979, and members of the band were charged with various offences. They have released their own recordings, *See Them a Come* being the most recent. They are also releasing an album of their own material.

MITTOO, JACKIE

Born Kingston, 1948, and grew up both in St Ann and Kingston. He was taught the piano by his grandmother at the age of 4 and played classical music at an early age. At 13 he was playing with the Rivals and the Sheiks and at 15 was the pianist with the Skatalites. He recorded a number of instrumentals for Coxsone/Studio One where he was the producer/arranger for all the labels' product from 1965–8. One of his most outstanding singles was *Ram Jam*, 1967. A recent album was 'The Original' (Third World), 1978.

MORGAN, DERRICK

Born Kingston, circa 1937. One of the pioneers in Jamaican music, his early records include *Blazing Fire* and *Housewife's Choice*. Others include *Tougher than Tough*, *Rudy in Court*, and his biggest hit, *Moon Hop*, which scored in the British charts. As a singer he has done little in recent years.

MOWATT, JUDY

Born Kingston, circa 1947. Her first group was the Gaylettes, formed in 1964. For Sonia Pottinger's label, she recorded *Silent River*, *I Like Your World*, among others. The group broke up in 1970. She then went solo and recorded *I Shall Sing* and Trevour Rhone's *I'm Alone*. She later joined the Soulettes which became the I-Threes (See Bob Marley). She still pursues a solo career and created a stir with *I'm a Black Woman* in 1978.

MURVIN, JUNIOR

Born Murvin Smith, Port Antonio, 1949. As a singer he toured with the Falcons (Dennis Brown, Cynthia Richards, Noel Brown) in 1969 until 1971. He also successively joined Ray and the Jaguars, the Tornadoes,

Young Experience. 1975 saw him produce his own *Conversation*. He recorded *Miss Cushy* for Sonia Pottinger in 1967 as Junior Soul. He wrote *Tang Tang Festival* for Derrick Harriot in 1968. In 1976 he had his biggest hit, *Police & Thieves*, with Lee Perry, and also recorded an album of the same name for Perry which was released through Island.

MCKAY, FREDDY

Born in St Catherine, 1947. He used to record under the names Little Freddy and, as a duo, Freddy and Lloyd. During the Rock Steady era he recorded *Love Is a Treasure* for Duke Reid, 1966. In 1970 he recorded *Picture on the Wall* with Coxsone/Studio One. In 1974 he recorded *Lonely Man* for Dynamic, and in 1976 won the annual song festival with *Dancer's Festival*. His latest album was 'Creation' (Plant, 1979).

PABLO, AUGUSTUS

Born Horace Swaby, St Andrew, 1953. He taught himself piano from the age of 13, then played with Tyrone Downey while at Kingston College. He started playing melodica while still at school. His first recording was *Java* for Randy's in 1969; he also recorded his first version of *East of the River Nile* in 1969 for Aquarius. His first album was 'This Is Augustus Pablo' for Randy's, 1970. He recorded a number of singles, including *Pablo in Dub*, which were together placed on an album, 'Thriller', but he did not play on all the tracks credited to him. 'Ital Dub' was released by Trojan in 1974. His latest recordings include 'East of the River Nile' and 'Africa Must Be Free by 1983 Dub' (1978 and 1979 respectively).

POPPIN, KEITH

Born Keith Smith, Westmoreland, 1949. Started singing with the Rocking Horse group in 1971 and went solo in 1973 with *Same Thing for Breakfast*. Other tunes include *Envious* (also album of same name, 1976), *Time Slipping Away* for Joe Gibbs, 1975. He toured the United Kingdom in 1976.

RANGLIN, ERNEST

Born Manchester, 1932, and at the age of 4 picked up his uncle's ukulele and began playing. At 14 he took up the guitar seriously while attending Badmin College, Kingston. At 15 he began his professional career with the Val Bennett Band and listened to Jazz extensively. He also played with Eric Deens, Bobo Motto. From 1951 he played periodically in the Bahamas. His first recording engagement was with Lance Haywood in 1959. While in Jamaica he was the A&R man for Island from 1960–2, and arranged for Owen Grey, Jackie Edwards, Keith and Enid, etc. In 1964 he came to Britain where he again worked for Island, arranging Millie Small's hit, *My Boy Lollipop*. That same year he won the *Melody Maker*'s award as top Jazz guitarist. He returned to Jamaica in 1965 and played with Monty Alexander from 1973; also with Randy Weston, and he arranged for Melba Liston. He has made several albums for Federal and Island. He has worked extensively as a session guitarist for all the leading producers and artists in Jamaica. His last album was 'Ranglin Roots' (Aquarius, 1977).

RICHARDS, MICHAEL 'BOO'

Born Kingston, 1947. He started off on piano under Aubrey Adams in 1965. While Adams was absent he picked up the drums. His father was a drummer and also influenced him into playing drums. In the mid-1960s he was a member of Yardbroom, then played with the Mighty Diamonds in 1967, subsequently joined the In Crowd in 1969 and recorded *Mango Walk* with them for Sound Tracks. He has supported such acts as John Holt, Bunny Wailer, Harold Butler, Culture, Dennis Brown, etc. He has also worked with Now Generation in the past.

ROBINSON, MICKEY

Born St Andrew, 1954, and came to Britain while still young. He has been playing rhythm guitar since 1973. He has worked live with Delroy Wilson, Roy Shirley, and is a member of Tapper Zukie's band. He has recorded with Tapper Zukie, Tim Chandell, Junior English, Tito Simon, and others. He is also pursuing a solo career.

RODRIQUEZ, RICO

Born Kingston, 1933. While at Alpha he started on the saxophone at the age of 10, then changed to trombone because of the demand. He played in both the junior and senior Alpha school bands. His first recording session was in 1958, Theophilius Beckford's *Easy Snappin'* for Clement Dodd. He became sought after and worked on acts like Laurel Aitken, Derrick Harriot, Prince Miller, Jackie Edwards, etc. At the beginning of the 1960s he worked with Count Ossie, playing mainly for community entertainment without financial gain. He later worked for producer Moodie who had a label, Blue Beat, and whose product appeared on the London Blue Beat label. The music he played was Rasta music, and he left Jamaica before Ska became popular. In England he played R&B with several musicians. He has recorded several instrumental albums for small labels and appeared on numerous recording sessions. His first album for Island was 'Man from Wareika', 1977.

I-ROY

Born Roy Reid, St Thomas, 1944. Attended Dinthill Technical College on a government scholarship studying accountancy. He has worked as an accountant before turning to DJing. He formed his own disco, Son's Junior, and toured throughout Jamaica until discovered by Harry Moodie. Recorded his first tune, *Musical Pleasure*, in 1970. His albums include 'Presenting I-Roy', 'Truths & Rights', and 'Cancer'.

U-ROY

Born Ewart Beckford, Kingston, circa 1936. He was influenced by Count Machuki, one of the earliest DJs in Jamaica, and started working professionally with Dickie's Dynamic, then Sir George Atomic, then much later King Tubby. He first recorded *Wake the Town* for Duke Reid and has since been one of the most prolific DJs. His albums include 'Dread Inna Babylon', 'Son of Africa', and 'Natty Rebel'.

SCORCHER

Born Errol Archer, St Catherine, 1956. He worked as a DJ with King Teddy in 1970 and recorded his first tune, *Leggo Me in Babylon* for the Suck Finger label. His most important hit was *Ille Rock Dread* for Total Sound in 1977.

SKULLY

Born Noel Simms, Kingston, 1935. He started his professional career as a singer and dancer in the theatre. He also worked in pantomime. He began playing percussion professionally in 1965 and has worked with a number of acts among whom are: Peter Tosh, Max Romeo, Big Youth, Dennis Brown, etc. He recorded *Give Me Another Chance* for Clancy Eccles in 1977.

SLICKERS, THE

The group was formed in 1968 by Derrick Crooks (brother of Sidney Crooks) who was born in Westmoreland, 1937. The other members of the group left and he was joined by Ras Abraham, Portland, 1958. The group's first recording, *Run Fatty*, was released by Beverly's in 1969. Their biggest and most famous hit, *Johnny Too Bad*, was recorded for Dynamic. Their other hit was *Fight against the Law*. They have recorded an album for Dynamic which is unreleased.

SMART, HORACE

Born Horace Grossett, Kingston, 1958. Started his career in 1968 while still at school. He joined the Supernaturals in 1974. Prior to that he was a member of Blue Jeans with Rod Taylor and Barry Brown in 1972. He recorded *Peace & Love* for Lee Perry in 1973, and later *Rough a Rough* in 1977. He has recorded an album for Lee Perry which has not been released.

SPANNER

Born Anthony Price, Portland, 1953. Started his DJ career at the age of 14 playing for Sons Junior, followed by four years as an apprentice jockey. He went back to DJing and worked for Supreme of Love from 1974–6. He first recorded under Winston Riley, *Bandulu Star* on the Mummy label. He also recorded *Uptown Thing* for the Heavy Weight label in 1977.

STEEL PULSE

The band was formed in 1972 in Handsworth, Birmingham, its nucleus consisting of David Hinds (lead vocals, guitar), Basil Gibbidom (lead guitar, vocals) and Ronnie McQueen (bass). Other members now consist of Fonso Martin (vocals, percussion) and Steve Nesbitt (drums). In 1976 they released their first single, *Kibudu, Mansetta and Abuku* on Dip. In 1977, through Tempus Records, they released *Nyah Love* on Anchor. They were then signed by Island and have released two albums 'Handsworth Revolution', and 'Tribute to the Martyrs'.

STEWART, TINGA

Born Neville Stewart, Kingston, 1950. Attended St Aloyius Boys' School and belonged to the church choir. He formed the Wild Cats in 1967 and recorded *She's Gone* for Derrick Harriot's Move & Groove label. He joined the Boris Gardener's Happening in 1971 and later won the Festival Song contest in 1974 with *Play The Music* for Federal. He recorded *Rainy Night in Georgia* for Channel One in 1977.

STITT, KING

Born Kingston, circa 1939. He started his DJ career as an assistant to King Sporty in 1957 for the Coxsone sound which he later took over himself. Though he recorded exclusive acetates for Coxsone they were never released. In 1969 he recorded *Fire Corner* for Clancy Eccles. He also recorded a number of other tunes for Eccles including *Lee Van Cleef, Vigorton 2,* and *Herb Man Shuffle*. He is now largely unrecorded.

STONE, JAH

Born Gladstone Fisher, Kingston, 1956. Began his DJ career with Vee Jay Dub Master in 1974. He recorded several singles for Vee Jay including *Kojak* with Barbara Jones, *Picture on the Wall,* and later *Fat Thing,* produced by Bim Sherman for the Scorpio label.

TAMLINS, THE

The group consists of Carlton Smith (St Andrew, 1948), Junior Moore (St Andrew, 1948), and Winston Morgan (Clarendon, 1946) and has been going since 1968. Among their recordings are *Eighteen with a Bullet, Black Beauty, Hard to Confess,* and *Stars*. They have provided vocal backing for Peter Tosh, Barry Biggs, Byron Lee and the Dragonaires, and Judy Mowatt.

TAYLOR, ROD

Born Kingston, 1957. He began singing at the age of 12 at the Bohemia Club and first recorded in 1974, *Bad Man Comes And Goes* for Channel One, *Garden of Eden* for Bunny Lee's Jackpot label, *Every Little Thing* for Randy's *Jump & Dance* with Clint Eastwood for Ossie Sound, and his biggest hit, *In the Right Way*, 1979.

TAYLOR, VIC

Born Kingston (date not known). Started singing in 1965 and was a commercial artist after having studied at the Jamaica School of Art; he replaced John Holt in the Paragons after he left, and he has worked with Lyn Tait and the Comets, Tommy McCook, and joined Byron Lee and the Dragonaires in 1969 with whom he recorded an album, 'Vic Taylor Does It His Way'.

THIRD WORLD

The group consists of Bunny 'Rugs' Clarke (lead vocals and rhythm guitar), Willie Stewart (drums), Richard Daley (bass), Irvin 'Carrot' Jarrett (percussion), Michael 'Ibo' Cooper (keyboards and vocals), and Stephen 'Cat' Coore. The group came together in 1973 with Cooper and Coore who were members of Inner Circle, and the others joined later. They have recorded several albums, but it was only with *Now that We Found Love*, a disco number, that they hit internationally.

THOMAS, RUDDY

Born Rudolph Thomas, Kingston, 1951. He is also known as Flick Wilson. He started singing at the age of 5 and sang with Bobby Aitken and the Carib Beats at the age of 10. At the age of 13 he recorded *Parents Fault* for Coxsone and worked as harmony vocalist for Dennis Brown, Horace Andy, B.B. Seaton, Alton Ellis, etc. In 1971 he worked as an assistant engineer for Treasure Isle and recorded *Lick & Run* for the label. In 1973 he went to work for Joe Gibbs as an assistant engineer, and recorded as an artist. Records include *Let's Make a Baby* (1975), *Feeling Soul* (1976). He is also the lead vocalist for the We The People band.

TOSH, PETER

Born Peter McIntosh, Westmoreland, 1944, and moved to Kingston at the age of 15. He was a member of the Wailers from 1962 to 1973. After the group left Coxsone in 1965 he did a number of solo recordings for the Wail & Soul label. Since 1975 he has recorded four albums 'Legalise It', 'Equal Rights', 'Bush Doctor', and 'Mystic Man'.

TRADITION

The group consists of Lesley McNeil, Chris Henry, Tony Mathews and Paul Thompson and they have been recording since 1977 with Venture on which they released 'Moving On', their first album, subsequently licensed to RCA. Their second album was 'Alternative Routes' and a third, untitled and produced by Kofi Ayivor, is due for release.

WAILER, BUNNY

Born Bunny O'Riley Livingstone, Kingston, 1946. A member of the Wailers from 1962 to 1973. He made a number of solo recordings after 1965 and after 1973 when the group broke up. His first album, 'Black Heart Man', received critical acceptance and his follow-up, 'Protest', was poorly received.

WALLACE, LEROY 'HORSEMOUTH'

Born Kingston, 1947, where he studied drums and printing at Alpha from the age of 9, the former under Len Hibberts. He played in the school band and left at 18. He worked with the *Jamaican Times*, the Government Printing Office, and with Clement Dodd's printing factory. He has been influenced by Jonkunnu, Pocomania and other natural religions. He started professionally with the Mighty Vikings until 1971. Simultaneously he worked with the Soul Syndicate from the late 1960s. He also supported a number of Studio One's acts: the Heptones, Delroy Wilson, Alton Ellis,

Jackie Mittoo, Marcia Griffiths, etc. He was a member of the Black Disciples, the band that supported Burning Spear on record. He has also worked with Inner Circle for two years, Byron Lee and the Dragonaires, Now Generation, and Generation Gap. He was the leading actor in the film, *Rockers*.

WALTON, JAH

Born Silbert Walton, St Ann, 1957, he began DJing with Sound Tracks from 1973–5 and later joined the police force for one year, then recorded for Joe Gibbs, *Gourmanezan*, 1976. Other records include *Girl I've Got a Date* with Brent Dowe for Sonia Pottinger, *Trod On* with Culture for same, and *Queen Majesty* with the Techniques.

WASHINGTON, DELROY

Born Westmoreland, 1951, and migrated to the United Kingdom in 1960. He started singing in the church choir and cut his first record for Lord Koos in 1971. He has recorded two albums for Virgin, 'I-SUS' (1976), and 'Rasta' (1977). He is currently recording his third album for release.

WILSON, DELROY

Born Kingston, 1948. He started singing at the age of 13 while at school and entered competitions at the Ward Theatre. His first record was *If I Had a Beautiful Body* for Coxsone, but *Spit in the Sky* was his first big hit. He formed the Links label with Ken Boothe, the Gaylads, and the Melodians in 1969, but it quickly went under. His *Put Yourself in My Place* was recorded for Sonia Pottinger, and his monster hit and PNP anthem, *Better Must Come*, was released in 1971.

WRIGHT, WINSTON

Born St Thomas, 1944. Started playing harmonica in high school, then took up the piano, having been taught by the school's music tutor. He played organ for the St Gabriel Church and was a member of the Mercury's of Clarendon at the age of 21. He then became a member of Lyn Tait and the Comets and recorded several albums with them. He was part of the backing group that supported all of West Indies Records and Federal's artists for three years. He was also a member of Tommy McCook and the Supersonics until 1970; later played with the Vikings, the Sheiks, Byron Lee, and subsequently worked as a top session musician, supporting almost all the acts in Jamaica. He also does sessions on guitar and bass.

YOUTH, BIG

Born Manley Augustus Buchanan, Kingston, 1951. Started DJing with the Tippatone sound and recorded his first record, *Movie Man*, for Gregory Issacs and then *Black Cinderella*. He was one of the innovative DJs during the mid-1970s and started a new movement when he recorded 'Dread Locks Dread' in 1975. Other albums include 'Natty Cultural Dread'.

ZAP POW

The group was formed by David Madden and Dwight Pickney in 1970 and consists of Madden, trumpet, Pickney, guitar, Glen Da Costs, tenor sax, Michael Williams, bass, Cornell Marshall (formerly with Third World), drums, and Beres Hammond, vocals. Regarded highly as the most experimental band in Jamaica, they recorded *This Is Reggae Music*, 1972, and *River*, 1977, both experimental and advanced at the time of release. Both received extensive air play in Jamaica, but received poor sales. They recorded an album, 'Revolutionary Zap Pow', 1973, for Harry Johnson.

ZUKIE, TAPPER

Born David Sinclair, Kingston, 1955, and worked with the Viego sound. He arrived in the United Kingdom in 1973 and recorded his first record, *Jump & Twist*, for Larry Lawrence's Ethnic-Fight. He subsequently cut his first album, 'Man Ah Warrior', for Clem Bushay. In 1975 he recorded *Judge I O Lord* for Lloydie Slim. His first important album was 'MPLA' for Klik in 1976. One of his most important singles was *She Want a Phensic*. He also owns his own label and produces Junior Ross and the Spears and other new acts.

Additional List

ASWAD

The band consists of Angus Gaye (London, 1959, drums), Brinsley Forde (Guyana, 1952, rhythm guitar), Donald Griffiths (Jamaica, 1954, lead guitar) and Tony Robinson (London, 1957, bass), and was formed in 1975 by George Oban, the former bassist with the band. Their first album 'Aswad' was released by Island, 1976; their second, 'Hulet', was released by Grove, 1979. They supported Burning Spear at the Rainbow, 1977, and appeared on his Island album, 'Live'. They have worked in the studio with Alton Ellis, Brown Sugar, Bob Marley, Lloyd Charmers, Mighty Diamonds, Delroy Washington, and U-Roy.

BLACK UHURU

The group is led by Michael Rose along with two harmony singers. There is no biographical information available on them. They first became popular with an album produced by Prince Jammy for Third World, simply titled 'Black Uhuru'. They have since recorded a number of singles including *Plastic Smile* for D-Roy and *Abortion*, available on import from Taxi. They are the hottest group to emerge from Jamaica since Culture in 1977.

CHARMERS, LLOYD

Born Lloyd Tyrell, Kingston, 1947. The first group he sang with was the Charmers with Roy Willis. In 1964 he went solo, recording for Coxsone/Studio One, with *Loneliest Boy in Town*. They left the company and joined Prince Buster's outfit and hit with *Time after Time* in 1969. He then formed the Uniques with Slim Smith and Martin Riley and recorded for producer Bunny Lee. Then he turned producer, first producing the Uniques and other artists including Ken Boothe (with whom he had his biggest hits), Ras Michael, B.B. Seaton, Bob Andy, Marcia Griffiths, and a number of others.

CHIN, ALBERT 'TONY'

Born Kingston, 1948, and attended Kingsway College. Since college he has been playing guitar and joined the Soul Syndicate in 1968 as well as the Aggrovators. He has done numerous sessions for Mighty Diamonds, Johnny Clarke, Delroy Wilson, Dennis Brown, Horace Andy, etc. He has also worked with the Revolutionaries.

LEVI, I-JAHMAN

Born Trevour Sutherland, Kingston, 1946. Started singing professionally in 1962 with *Red Eyes People* for Duke Reid. Came to England in 1963 and formed the Vibrations in 1965 playing Soul. Then he formed Youth and Rudi with Carl Simmonds. In 1975 he recorded *Jah Heavy Load* for Dip, followed by *I Am a Levi* and *Chariot of Love*. He worked with Rico Rodriquez on some sessions and followed this up in 1978 with an album for Island, 'Haile I Hymn'.

PARKES, LLOYD

Born Kingston, 1948. Started professionally with the RHT Invincibles. His solo single was *Say You Love Me* for Winston Riley and he later joined the Techniques as the lead singer after Pat Kelly left. He formed Skin, Flesh and Bones in 1968 and they supported most of the Jamaican artists for a long time. His solo albums include 'Officially', 'Girl in the Morning', and 'Loving You'. He now plays with the Revolutionaries and is considered one of the leading bassists in Jamaica.

Index